W9-AEN-969

Teach Yourself
VISUALLY™
iMac®

Visual

by Guy Hart-Davis

WILEY

Wiley Publishing, Inc.

Teach Yourself VISUALLY™ iMac®

Published by
Wiley Publishing, Inc.
10475 Crosspoint Boulevard
Indianapolis, IN 46256
www.wiley.com

Published simultaneously in Canada

Copyright © 2010 by Wiley Publishing, Inc., Indianapolis, Indiana

No part of this publication may be reproduced, stored in a retrieval system or transmitted in any form or by any means, electronic, mechanical, photocopying, recording, scanning or otherwise, except as permitted under Sections 107 or 108 of the 1976 United States Copyright Act, without either the prior written permission of the Publisher, or authorization through payment of the appropriate per-copy fee to the Copyright Clearance Center, 222 Rosewood Drive, Danvers, MA 01923, 978-750-8400, fax 978-646-8600. Requests to the Publisher for permission should be addressed to the Permissions Department, John Wiley & Sons, Inc., 111 River Street, Hoboken, NJ 07030, 201-748-6011, fax 201-748-6008, or online at www.wiley.com/go/permissions.

Library of Congress Control Number: 2009941351

ISBN: 978-0-470-56803-3

Manufactured in the United States of America

10 9 8 7 6 5 4 3 2 1

Trademark Acknowledgments

Contact Us

For general information on our other products and services please contact our Customer Care Department within the U.S. at 877-762-2974, outside the U.S. at 317-572-3993 or fax 317-572-4002.

For technical support please visit www.wiley.com/techsupport.

Wiley Publishing, Inc.

Sales

Contact Wiley
at (877) 762-2974 or
fax (317) 572-4002.

Praise for Visual Books

"Like a lot of other people, I understand things best when I see them visually. Your books really make learning easy and life more fun."

John T. Frey (Cadillac, MI)

"I have quite a few of your Visual books and have been very pleased with all of them. I love the way the lessons are presented!"

Mary Jane Newman (Yorba Linda, CA)

"I just purchased my third Visual book (my first two are dog-eared now!), and, once again, your product has surpassed my expectations.

Tracey Moore (Memphis, TN)

"I am an avid fan of your Visual books. If I need to learn anything, I just buy one of your books and learn the topic in no time. Wonders! I have even trained my friends to give me Visual books as gifts."

Illona Bergstrom (Aventura, FL)

"Thank you for making it so clear. I appreciate it. I will buy many more Visual books."

J.P. Sangdong (North York, Ontario, Canada)

"I have several books from the Visual series and have always found them to be valuable resources."

Stephen P. Miller (Ballston Spa, NY)

"Thank you for the wonderful books you produce. It wasn't until I was an adult that I discovered how I learn — visually. Nothing compares to Visual books. I love the simple layout. I can just grab a book and use it at my computer, lesson by lesson. And I understand the material! You really know the way I think and learn. Thanks so much!"

Stacey Han (Avondale, AZ)

"I absolutely admire your company's work. Your books are terrific. The format is perfect, especially for visual learners like me. Keep them coming!"

Frederick A. Taylor, Jr. (New Port Richey, FL)

"I have several of your Visual books and they are the best I have ever used."

Stanley Clark (Crawfordville, FL)

"I bought my first Teach Yourself VISUALLY book last month. Wow. Now I want to learn everything in this easy format!"

Tom Vial (New York, NY)

"Thank you, thank you, thank you...for making it so easy for me to break into this high-tech world. I now own four of your books. I recommend them to anyone who is a beginner like myself."

Gay O'Donnell (Calgary, Alberta, Canada)

"I write to extend my thanks and appreciation for your books. They are clear, easy to follow, and straight to the point. Keep up the good work! I bought several of your books and they are just right! No regrets! I will always buy your books because they are the best."

Seward Kollie (Dakar, Senegal)

"Compliments to the chef!! Your books are extraordinary! Or, simply put, extra-ordinary, meaning way above the rest! THANK YOU THANK YOU THANK YOU! I buy them for friends, family, and colleagues."

Christine J. Manfrin (Castle Rock, CO)

"What fantastic teaching books you have produced! Congratulations to you and your staff. You deserve the Nobel Prize in Education in the Software category. Thanks for helping me understand computers."

Bruno Tonon (Melbourne, Australia)

"Over time, I have bought a number of your 'Read Less - Learn More' books. For me, they are THE way to learn anything easily. I learn easiest using your method of teaching."

José A. Mazón (Cuba, NY)

"I am an avid purchaser and reader of the Visual series, and they are the greatest computer books I've seen. The Visual books are perfect for people like myself who enjoy the computer, but want to know how to use it more efficiently. Your books have definitely given me a greater understanding of my computer, and have taught me to use it more effectively. Thank you very much for the hard work, effort, and dedication that you put into this series."

Alex Diaz (Las Vegas, NV)

Credits

Executive Editor
Jody Lefevere

Sr. Project Editor
Sarah Hellert

Technical Editor
Dennis R. Cohen

Copy Editor
Scott Tullis

Editorial Director
Robyn Siesky

Editorial Manager
Cricket Krengel

Business Manager
Amy Knies

Sr. Marketing Manager
Sandy Smith

Vice President and Executive Group Publisher
Richard Swadley

Vice President and Executive Publisher
Barry Pruett

Project Coordinator
Patrick Redmond

Graphics and Production Specialists
Andrea Hornberger
Jennifer Mayberry
Heather Pope

Quality Control Technician
John Greenough

Proofreader
Susan Hobbs

Indexer
Potomac Indexing, LLC

Screen Artists
Ana Carrillo
Jill A. Proll

Illustrators
Ronda David-Burroughs
Cheryl Grubbs

About the Author

Guy Hart-Davis is the author of *iMovie '09 Portable Genius, iLife '09 Portable Genius*, and *iWork '09 Portable Genius*.

Author's Acknowledgments

My thanks go to the many people who turned my manuscript into the highly graphical book you are holding. In particular, I thank Jody Lefevere for asking me to write the book; Sarah Hellert for keeping me on track and guiding the editorial process; Scott Tullis for skillfully editing the text; Dennis Cohen for reviewing the book for technical accuracy and contributing helpful sugggestions; and Ana Carrillo, Ronda David-Burroughs, Cheryl Grubbs, and Jill Proll for creating the pictures.

Table of Contents

chapter 1 Getting Started with Your iMac

Set Up Your iMac 4

Start Your iMac and Log In 6

Connect Your iMac to the Internet 8

Connect Your iMac to a Wired Network 10

Connect Your iMac to a Wireless Network 12

Connect a Printer to Your iMac 14

Connect an iPhone or iPod to Your iMac 16

Connect External Drives to Your iMac 18

Give Commands from the Menus and Toolbar 20

Open, Close, Minimize, and Hide Windows 22

Put Your iMac to Sleep and Wake It Up 24

Log Out and Shut Down Your iMac 26

chapter 2 Sharing Your iMac with Other People

Create a User Account for Another User 30

Configure Your iMac So Several People Can Use It 32

Share Your iMac with Fast User Switching 34

Turn On Parental Controls for an Account 36

Choose Which Applications a User Can Run 38

Prevent a User from Seeing Inappropriate Content 40

Control Whom a User Can E-mail and Chat With 42

Set Time Limits for Logging On 44

See What a Controlled User Has Done on the iMac 46

chapter 3   Running Applications and Creating Documents

Open and Close an Application. 50

Install an Application 52

Switch Quickly to Other Applications 54

See All the Windows Open on Your iMac. 56

Create and Save a Document 58

Close and Open a Document 60

Edit a Document. 62

Use Mac OS X's Help System. 64

chapter 4   Managing Your Files and Folders with the Finder

Understanding Where to Store Files on Your iMac 68

Using the Finder's Four Views Effectively 70

Look Through a File without Opening It. 72

Search for a File or Folder 74

Save a Search in a Smart Folder 76

Create and Name a New Folder 78

Copy a File from One Folder to Another 80

Move a File from One Folder to Another 82

Rename a File. 84

View the Information about a File or Folder 86

Compress Files for Easy Transfer 88

Burn Files to a CD or DVD 90

Erase a CD or DVD. 92

Throw a File in the Trash. 94

Table of Contents

chapter 5 Surfing the Web with Safari

Open and Close Safari 98

Open a Web Page 100

Follow a Link to a Web Page 101

Open Several Web Pages at Once 102

Find Your Way from One Page to Another 104

Return to a Recently Visited Page 106

Change the Page Safari Opens at First 108

Keep Bookmarks for Web Pages You Like 110

Find Interesting Web Sites 112

Download a File from the Internet 114

Keep Up to Date with News Feeds 116

Choose Essential Security Settings 118

chapter 6 Sending and Receiving E-mail and Files

Open and Close Apple Mail 122

Set Up Your E-mail Account 124

Send an E-mail Message 126

Get Your Messages and Read Them 128

Reply to a Message 130

Send a Message on to Someone Else 132

Send a File via E-mail 134

Receive a File via E-mail 136

Get Your E-mail on Any Computer 138

Create Notes 140

Create To-Do Items 142

Reduce the Amount of Spam You Receive 144

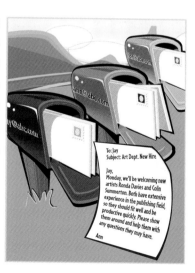

chapter 7 Keeping Yourself Organized with iCal and Address Book

Open and Close iCal 148

Find Your Way around the Calendar 150

Create a New Calendar 152

Create a One-Shot Appointment 154

Create a Repeating Appointment 156

Create a To-Do Item 158

Share Your Calendar with Other People 160

Subscribe to a Calendar Someone Is Sharing 162

Open and Close Address Book 164

Add Someone to Your Address Book 166

Change the Information for a Contact 168

Organize Your Contacts into Groups 170

chapter 8 Chatting with Text, Audio, and Video

Open and Close iChat 174

Add Someone to Your Buddy List 176

Chat with a Buddy Using Text 178

Chat with a Buddy Using Audio and Video 180

Send and Receive Files While You Chat 182

Table of Contents

chapter **9**   Enjoying Music, Video, and DVDs

Open and Close iTunes 186

Add Your CDs to the iTunes Library 188

Buy More Songs Online. 190

Play Songs. 192

Play Videos 194

Create Playlists of Songs You Like. 196

Have iTunes Create Playlists for You 198

Create a Custom CD of Your Songs 200

Listen to Radio Stations over the Internet 202

Enjoy Podcasts 204

Watch a DVD on Your iMac. 206

chapter **10**   Making the Most of Your Photos

Open and Close iPhoto 210

Import Photos from Your Digital Camera. 212

Browse through Your Photos 214

Crop a Photo to the Right Size 216

Rotate or Straighten a Photo 218

Remove Red-Eye from a Photo 220

Improve the Colors in a Photo 222

Add an Effect to a Photo 224

Sort Your Photos into Events. 226

Create Albums of Your Photos 228

Create a Slideshow of Your Photos. 230

Publish Photos to a MobileMe Gallery 232

Send a Photo via E-mail. 234

Take Photos or Videos of Yourself 236

 chapter **11** **Creating Your Own Movies**

Open and Close iMovie 240

Import Video from a Tape Camcorder 242

Import Video from a Digital Camcorder. 244

Import Video from a Digital Camera. 246

Import Video Files from Your iMac. 248

Create a Movie Project. 250

Select the Video Footage You Want to Use 252

Build the Movie Project from Clips 254

Add Transitions between Video Clips 256

Add a Still Photo to the Movie Project 258

Create a Soundtrack for the Movie. 260

Add Titles and Credits 262

Share the Movie on YouTube 264

chapter **12** **Customizing Your iMac to Suit You**

Change Your Desktop Background. 268

Set Up a Screen Saver 270

Make the Dock Show the Icons You Need 272

Create Hot Corners to Run Exposé Easily. 274

Give Yourself More Desktop Space. 276

Add a Second Monitor So You Can See More 278

Make the Keyboard and Mouse Easier to Use. 280

Make the Screen Easier to See 282

Table of Contents

Tell Spotlight Which Folders to Search. 284

Control Your iMac with Your Voice. 286

Save Time by Running Applications Each Time You Log In 288

Save Power by Putting Your iMac to Sleep. 290

Choose When to Check for Software Updates. 292

chapter 13   Using Your iMac on a Network

Connect to a Shared Folder. 296

Share a Folder on the Network. 298

Connect to a Shared Printer 300

Share Your iMac's Printer on the Network. 302

Share Your iMac's Screen with Another Mac. 304

View Your iMac's Screen from Another Mac 306

Connect Remotely to Your iMac via Back to My Mac 308

chapter 14 Keeping Your iMac and Your Data Safe

Understanding Threats to Your iMac and Your Data. 312

Install Antivirus Software. 314

Scan Your iMac for Viruses 316

Turn Off Automatic Login 318

Increase the Security of the Mac OS X Firewall 320

Recognize and Avoid Phishing Attacks 322

chapter 15 Maintaining and Troubleshooting Your iMac

Reclaim Space by Emptying the Trash 326

Keep Your iMac Current with the Latest Updates 328

Back Up Your Files with Time Machine 330

Recover Your Files from a Time Machine Backup 332

Remove Applications You No Longer Need. 334

See Which Application Is Causing Your iMac Problems 336

Force a Crashed Application to Quit. 338

Recover When Mac OS X Crashes. 340

Solve Problems with Corrupt Preference Files. 342

Troubleshoot Disk Permission Errors 344

Repair Your iMac's Hard Disk 346

Reinstall Mac OS X to Solve Severe Problems 347

How to use this book

Do you look at the pictures in a book or newspaper before anything else on a page? Would you rather see an image instead of read about how to do something? Search no further. This book is for you. Opening *Teach Yourself VISUALLY iMac* allows you to read less and learn more about the iMac.

Who Needs This Book

This book is for a reader who has never used the iMac. It is also for more computer literate individuals who want to expand their knowledge of the different features that the iMac has to offer.

Book Organization

Teach Yourself VISUALLY iMac has 15 chapters.

Chapter 1, Getting Started with Your iMac, shows you how to set your iMac up and start using it. You learn how to connect your iMac to a network and the Internet, connect extra devices, and log in and out.

In Chapter 2, Sharing Your iMac with Other People, you set up a user account for each person who will use your iMac and decide which actions each person may take on it. You and the others can then switch quickly from one account to another.

Chapter 3, Running Applications and Creating Documents, gives you information about opening and closing applications and creating documents with them. You also learn to install other applications and switch quickly among open applications.

Chapter 4, Managing Your Files and Folders with the Finder, explains where to store files on your iMac, how to use the Finder's views effectively, and how to look quickly into a file. The chapter also shows you how to move, copy, and rename files and folders, and how to burn CDs and DVDs.

Chapter 5, Surfing the Web with Safari, brings you up to speed on using the Safari browser to view Web pages. You learn how to navigate from page to page, bookmark the pages you like, and download files.

In Chapter 6, Sending and Receiving E-mail and Files, you set up your e-mail account in the Mail application that comes with your iMac. You can then send and receive e-mail messages, transfer files via e-mail, and create notes and to-do items.

Chapter 7, Keeping Yourself Organized with iCal and Address Book, shows you how to manage your appointments and your contacts on your iMac. iCal enables you to track your commitments and share them with others, and Address Book makes it easy to keep contact information organized.

Chapter 8, Chatting with Text, Audio, and Video, explains how to use your iMac's iChat application to chat with buddies using either text or audio and video. You can transfer files to your buddies while you chat.

Chapter 9, Enjoying Music, Video, and DVDs, covers creating a music library in iTunes from your CDs and downloads; enjoying music, videos, and Internet radio; and creating playlists and burning them to CD. You also learn how to watch DVDs on your iMac.

In Chapter 10, Making the Most of Your Photos, you import photos from your digital camera, organize them, and edit them. You can then publish your photos online or send them via e-mail.

Chapter 11, Creating Your Own Movies, explains how to start working with iMovie, the powerful movie-editing application your iMac includes. You learn to import your footage, build a movie project, and post it to the YouTube video-sharing site.

Chapter 12, Customizing Your iMac to Suit You, shows you how to adjust your iMac's hardware and software to match your preferences — for example, putting the applications you need in the Dock, giving yourself more desktop space, and adding a second monitor.

Chapter 13, Using Your iMac on a Network, covers sharing your iMac's folders and printer on a network and connecting to folders and printers others are sharing. You can even control your own iMac from another Mac across the Internet.

Chapter 14, Keeping Your iMac and Your Data Safe, explains how to protect your iMac and your data from both local and Internet threats. You learn to install antivirus software, turn off automatic login, and avoid phishing attacks.

Finally, Chapter 15, Maintaining and Troubleshooting Your iMac, shows you essential maneuvers for keeping your iMac and Mac OS X in good shape and recovering from problems. You learn to reclaim disk space, keep Mac OS X updated, close crashed or misbehaving applications, and recover from system crashes.

Chapter Organization

This book consists of sections, all listed in the book's table of contents. A *section* is a set of steps that show you how to complete a specific computer task.

Each section, usually contained on two facing pages, has an introduction to the task at hand, a set of full-color screen shots and steps that walk you through the task, and a set of tips. This format allows you to quickly look at a topic of interest and learn it instantly.

Chapters group together three or more sections with a common theme. A chapter may also contain pages that give you the background information needed to understand the sections in a chapter.

What You Need to Use This Book

To use this book to the fullest, you need an iMac running Mac OS X. This book shows Mac OS X version 10.6, Snow Leopard, but if your iMac runs Mac OS X version 10.5, Leopard, you will find that almost everything works the same way.

If you have a Mac other than an iMac, you can still use this book, but you will need to make allowances for minor differences caused by the hardware being different.

Using the Mouse

This book uses the following conventions to describe the actions you perform when using the mouse:

Click

Press your left mouse button once. You generally click your mouse on something to select something on the screen.

Double-click

Press your left mouse button twice. Double-clicking something on the computer screen generally opens whatever item you have double-clicked.

Right-click

Press your right mouse button. When you right-click anything on the computer screen, the program displays a shortcut menu containing commands specific to the selected item.

Click and Drag, and Release the Mouse

Move your mouse pointer and hover it over an item on the screen. Press and hold down the left mouse button. Now, move the mouse to where you want to place the item and then release the button. You use this method to move an item from one area of the computer screen to another.

The Conventions in This Book

A number of typographic and layout styles have been used throughout *Teach Yourself VISUALLY iMac* to distinguish different types of information.

Bold

Bold type represents the names of commands and options that you interact with. Bold type also indicates text and numbers that you must type into a dialog box or window.

Italics

Italic words introduce a new term and are followed by a definition.

Numbered Steps

You must perform the instructions in numbered steps in order to successfully complete a section and achieve the final results.

Bulleted Steps

These steps point out various optional features. You do not have to perform these steps; they simply give additional information about a feature.

Indented Text

Indented text tells you what the program does in response to you following a numbered step. For example, if you click a certain menu command, a dialog box may appear, or a window may open. Indented text may also tell you what the final result is when you follow a set of numbered steps.

Notes

Notes give additional information. They may describe special conditions that may occur during an operation. They may warn you of a situation that you want to avoid, for example the loss of data. A note may also cross reference a related area of the book. A cross reference may guide you to another chapter or another section within the current chapter.

Icons and buttons

Icons and buttons are graphical representations within the text. They show you exactly what you need to click to perform a step.

 You can easily identify the tips in any section by looking for the TIPS icon. Tips offer additional information, including tips, hints, and tricks. You can use the TIPS information to go beyond what you have learned in the steps.

Getting Started with Your iMac

The iMac is a beautifully designed computer and comes with the powerful, easy-to-use Mac OS X operating system. In just a few minutes, you can set up your iMac and begin using it. This chapter shows you how to get started with your iMac, use the Mac OS X interface, and connect extra devices to the iMac.

Set Up Your iMac 4

Start Your iMac and Log In 6

Connect Your iMac to the Internet 8

Connect Your iMac to a Wired Network 10

Connect Your iMac to a Wireless
   Network 12

Connect a Printer to Your iMac 14

Connect an iPod or iPhone to Your iMac 16

Connect External Drives to Your iMac 18

Give Commands from the Menus and
   Toolbar 20

Open, Close, Minimize, and Hide
   Windows 22

Put Your iMac to Sleep and Wake It Up 24

Log Out and Shut Down Your iMac 26

Set Up Your iMac

If you have just bought your iMac, you need to connect its hardware and create your user account before you can use it.

Your user account is where you store your files and settings. The first user account you create is the administrator account, which can create other user accounts later for other users.

Set Up Your iMac

Set Up Your iMac's Hardware

① Unpack the iMac from its box.

② Position the main unit on your desk or table.

③ If you have a wireless keyboard, turn it on by pressing the power button on its right side. If you have a wired keyboard, connect its cable to a USB port at the back of the iMac.

④ Connect your speakers to the audio out port.

⑤ Connect your microphone to the audio in port.

⑥ If you have a wireless mouse, turn it on by moving the on/off switch on its underside. If you have a wired mouse, connect its cable to a USB port on the keyboard or at the back of the iMac.

⑦ Connect the power supply to the iMac and plug it into a power source.

⑧ Press the power button to start the iMac.

Note: On most iMacs, the power button is located at the back of the unit, at the lower left corner looking from the front.

Create Your User Account

1 In the Welcome screen, click your country or region and then click the arrow. Follow through the registration information screens to the Create Your Account screen.

2 Type the user's full name.

3 Change the account name that Mac OS X suggests as needed.

Note: *You cannot change the account name afterward. You can change the other items.*

4 Type a password.

5 Click **Continue**.

6 In the Select a Picture for This Account screen, click **Take photo snapshot** to take a photo of yourself using the iMac's camera.

Note: *You can also use a picture from the picture library. Click **Choose from the picture library**, and then click the picture you want.*

7 Click **Continue**, and then finish the installation.

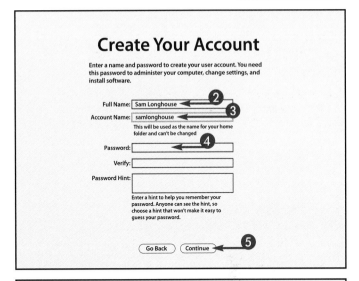

Create Your Account

Enter a name and password to create your user account. You need this password to administer your computer, change settings, and install software.

Full Name: Sam Longhouse

Account Name: samlonghouse

This will be used as the name for your home folder and can't be changed

Password:

Verify:

Password Hint:

Enter a hint to help you remember your password. Anyone can see the hint, so choose a hint that won't make it easy to guess your password.

Go Back   Continue

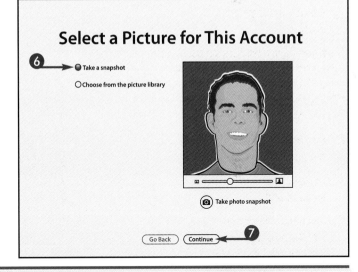

Select a Picture for This Account

Take a snapshot

Choose from the picture library

Take photo snapshot

Go Back   Continue

TIP

Should I create a MobileMe account?

This is entirely up to you. Mac OS X setup encourages you to sign up for an account with MobileMe, Apple's online service. MobileMe gives you an e-mail account, space for storing data online and publishing Web sites and photos, and a way to synchronize data among Macs. After a 60-day free trial, a MobileMe account costs $99 per year, or $149 for a family account. You can find discounted prices at online sites such as Amazon.com.

You need to have an Internet connection to set up a MobileMe account. If you do not yet have an Internet connection, you can set up an account later from the MobileMe pane in the System Preferences window.

Start Your iMac and Log In

When you are ready to start a computing session, start your iMac and log in to Mac OS X.

Start Your iMac and Log In

① Press the power button on the iMac.

Note: *On most iMacs, the power button is located at the back of the unit, at the lower left corner when you are looking from the front.*

A window showing the list of users appears.

Note: *Your iMac may not display the list of users and Log In window. Instead, it may simply log you in automatically or show a different Log In window. Chapter 2 shows you how to change this behavior.*

② Click your user name.

The Log In window appears.

③ Type your password in the Password field.

● If you cannot remember your password, click **Forgot Password**.

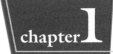

● Mac OS X displays your password hint at the bottom of the Log In window.

④ Click **Log In**.

Note: *Instead of clicking **Log In**, you can press* Return.

The iMac displays your desktop, the menu bar, and the Dock. You can now start using the iMac.

TIPS

Why does my iMac not display the list of user names but goes straight to the desktop?

If you do not see the list of names and then the Log In window, your iMac is set to log in automatically. Logging in automatically is convenient when you are the only user of your iMac, but it means that anyone who can start your iMac can log in. Chapter 2 shows you how to turn off automatic login.

Why does my iMac not show the list of user names?

Instead of the list of user names, you may see a window with a Name field and a Password field. Type your user name and your password, and then click **Log In** (●). Hiding the list of user names gives extra security and is widely used in companies, but it is usually not necessary for iMacs used at home.

Connect Your iMac to the Internet

To browse the Web and use e-mail, you must connect your iMac to the Internet. This section shows general steps for using a DSL router or cable router connected directly to your iMac. The specifics depend on your Internet service provider and the equipment they supply; some providers install the router and make sure it is working, whereas others provide a self-install kit. If you have a network that includes an Internet connection, see the next four pages.

Connect Your iMac to the Internet

① Connect the DSL router or cable router to your iMac with an Ethernet cable as instructed.

② Click .

③ Click **System Preferences**.

④ In the System Preferences window, click **Network**.

⑤ In the Network preferences pane, click **Ethernet**.

⑥ Open the Configure IPv4 pop-up menu and choose **Manually**.

⑦ Type the next IP address after the router's address. For example, if the router uses the IP address **10.0.0.2**, type **10.0.0.3**.

Note: Most DSL routers and cable routers use an address in the 192.168.0.x range, the 192.168.1.x range, the 10.0.0.x range, or the 10.0.1.x range, where x is a number between 1 and 255.

⑧ Type the subnet mask.

Note: Most DSL routers and cable routers use the subnet mask 255.255.255.0.

⑨ Click **Apply**.

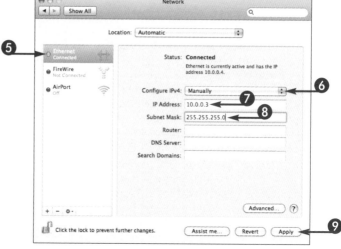

⑩ Click **Safari** () on the Dock.

⑪ In the Safari browser window, type the address for the router and press `Return`.

Note: *If the router prompts you for a password, type the password provided in the documentation.*

⑫ In the router's control screens, choose settings for the router following your ISP's instructions.

⑬ Click **Apple** to display the Apple Web site to test your Internet connection.

⑭ Click the **Minimize** button () to minimize the Safari window to the Dock.

⑮ In Network preferences, open the Configure IPv4 pop-up menu and choose **Using DHCP**.

⑯ Click **Apply**.

⑰ Click the **System Preferences** menu and click **Quit System Preferences** to close System Preferences.

⑱ Click the minimized Safari window on the Dock.

The Safari window reappears, and you can browse the Internet.

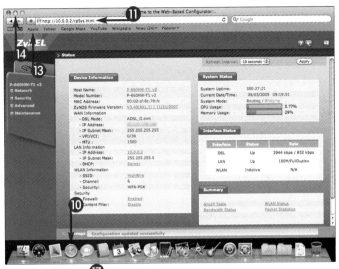

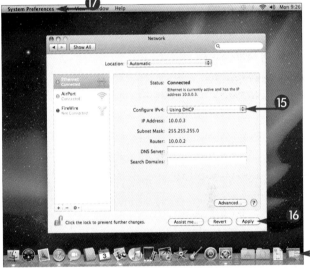

TIP

Which kind of Internet connection is better, DSL or cable?

A digital subscriber line, or DSL, provides a high-speed Internet connection over a phone line. DSL divides the phone line into a data part and a voice part, so you can connect to the Internet even when the phone is in use. Cable Internet provides Internet access through your cable TV cabling. Both cable and DSL speeds depend on your location, so ask the providers what speeds are available and how much service costs. Ask how many other users will share the same network circuit; the more users, the more the speed drops.

If you cannot get either DSL or cable Internet service, look at satellite services, which are available in remote locations where DSL and cable are not. The other alternative is a dial-up connection using a modem and a phone line, but this is very slow compared to the other options.

Connect Your iMac to a Wired Network

If you have a wired network, you can quickly connect your iMac to it so that the iMac can use the network's Internet connection and can share files and printers with other computers on the network.

Connect Your iMac to a Wired Network

① Connect one end of a network cable to the Ethernet port on the back of your iMac.

② Connect the other end of the network cable to an Ethernet port on your network switch or network router.

Your iMac automatically detects the network connection and tries to apply suitable settings.

③ Click .

The Apple menu opens.

④ Click **System Preferences**.

The System Preferences window opens.

⑤ Click **Network**.

The Network preferences pane opens.

6 Click **Ethernet**.

7 Verify that your iMac has an IP address.

8 Click the **System Preferences** menu and click **Quit System Preferences**.

9 Click **Safari** (🧭) on the Dock.

A Safari browser window opens and displays your iMac's home page, the page Safari opens automatically.

You have now connected your iMac to the network and the Internet.

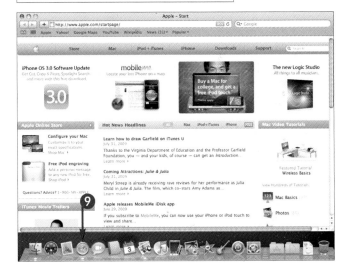

 TIPS

How does a computer network work?

A wired network has a network switch or network router that directs the data around the network. Each computer connects to the switch or router via network cables. You typically connect your Internet router to the switch or router as well to share the Internet connection on the network; some Internet routers have a network router built in. Networked computers can also share files and printers with each other.

What is an IP address and what is DHCP?

An IP address is a number that identifies a computer on a network. An IP address consists of four groups of one, two, or three digits, such as 10.10.0.100 or 192.168.1.10. DHCP stands for Dynamic Host Configuration Protocol and is a way of allocating IP addresses to computers on the network. When a computer joins the network, it requests an IP address and other connection information from the DHCP server. Most cable and DSL routers act as DHCP servers.

Connect Your iMac to a Wireless Network

If you have set up a wireless network, you can connect your iMac to it. Wireless networks are convenient for both homes and businesses because they require no cables and are fast and easy to set up.

Your iMac includes a wireless network card called AirPort. AirPort is the name Apple uses for its wireless networking hardware and software.

1 Click the AirPort status icon ( ) on the menu bar.

The menu opens and displays a list of the wireless networks your iMac can detect.

*Note: If the AirPort menu shows AirPort: Off, click **Turn AirPort On**. Then open the menu again to see the available wireless networks.*

● The networks in the No Network Selected part of the list are networks that connect using wireless access points. These are called *infrastructure wireless networks*.

● The networks in the Devices part of the menu are networks created by individual computers. These are called *ad hoc wireless networks* or *peer-to-peer wireless networks*.

● A lock icon ( ) indicates that the network is secured with a password.

2 Click the network to which you want to connect your iMac.

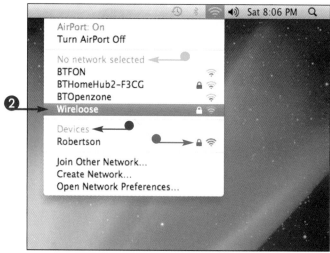

If the wireless network uses a password, your iMac prompts you to enter it.

③ Type the password in the Password field.

● If you want to see the characters of the password to help you type it, click **Show password** (□ changes to ☑).

● If you do not want your iMac to remember this wireless network for future use, click **Remember this network** (☑ changes to □).

④ Click **OK**.

Your iMac connects to the wireless network, and you can start using network resources.

● The AirPort status icon on the menu bar changes from 🛜 to 🛜 when the connection is established. The number of arcs on the AirPort status icon indicates the strength of the connection, from one arc to four arcs.

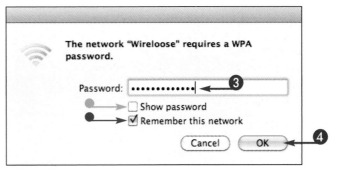

 TIPS

How do I disconnect from a wireless network?

When you have finished using a wireless network, you can disconnect from it by turning AirPort off. Click the AirPort status icon (🛜) on the menu bar and then click **Turn AirPort Off** (●).

What kind of wireless network do I need for my iMac?

Wireless networks use several different standards. The latest standard is 802.11n, also called Wireless-N, and provides the fastest data rates. At this writing, Wireless-N is a draft standard rather than a final standard, and not all Wireless-N equipment works together correctly at full speed. The best choice for a Mac wireless network is one of Apple's wireless access points, such as AirPort Extreme.

Connect a Printer to Your iMac

To print from your iMac, you need to connect a printer and install a *driver*, the software for the printer. Mac OS X includes many printer drivers, so you may be able to connect your printer and simply start printing. But if your printer is a new model, you may need to locate and install the driver for it.

Connect a Printer to Your iMac

① Connect the printer to the iMac with a USB cable.

Note: *If the printer is connected to another Mac, connect to it as explained in Chapter 13.*

② Plug the printer into an electrical socket and switch it on.

③ Click .

The Apple menu opens.

④ Click **System Preferences**.

● The System Preferences window opens.

⑤ Click **Print & Fax**.

The Print & Fax preferences pane opens.

If your printer appears in the list, you have connected it successfully. Go to step **12**.

⑥ If your printer does not appear, click **Add** (⊞).

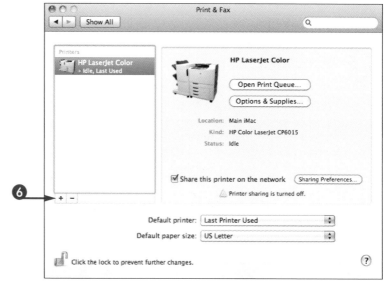

The Add Printer dialog opens.

7 Click **Default**.

The Default pane opens.

8 In the Printer Name list field, click the printer.

9 If you want, change the printer's name.

10 Also optionally, change the description of the printer's location.

11 Click **Add**.

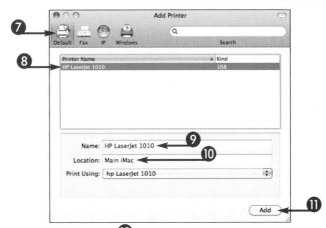

● Mac OS X adds the printer.

12 Click the **System Preferences** menu.

13 Click **Quit System Preferences**.

The System Preferences window closes.

TIPS

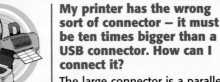

What should I type in the Name field and Location field when adding a printer?

You can type anything you want in the Name field and the Location field. This information is to help you identify the printer. If you have many printers, and some are attached to different computers, making each printer's name and location descriptive helps you keep the printers straight.

My printer has the wrong sort of connector — it must be ten times bigger than a USB connector. How can I connect it?

The large connector is a parallel port, which some older printers have. To connect the printer to your iMac, buy a parallel-to-USB adapter cable. Before you do, make sure that Mac OS X has a printer driver for your printer.

Connect an iPhone or iPod to Your iMac

If you have an iPhone or an iPod, you can connect it to your iMac to synchronize music, videos, and information such as appointments and addresses. To connect the iPod or iPhone, you need the cable that came with the device. The cable has a USB connector at one end and a Dock connector at the other end.

Connect an iPhone or iPod to Your iMac

Connect an iPhone or iPod

① Insert the cable's USB connector in a USB port on your iMac.

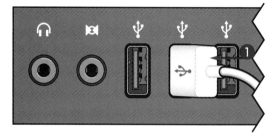

② Insert the cable's Dock connector in the Dock connector port on the bottom of the iPhone or iPod or in the device's dock.

Your iMac detects the iPhone or iPod and launches iTunes for synchronizing it.

If you connect an iPhone that contains photos you have not synchronized with iPhoto, iPhoto opens.

Note: *If you have not used this version of iTunes yet on your iMac, you must agree to its license agreement and choose settings before you can synchronize the iPhone or iPod. See Chapter 9 for information on iTunes.*

Choose Synchronization Settings for the iPhone or iPod

1 Click the **iPhone** or **iPod** in the Devices list.

2 Click each tab of the control screens in turn, and choose settings.

3 Click **Sync**.

Disconnect an iPhone or iPod

1 Click the eject button () for the iPhone or iPod in iTunes.

2 Press in the clips on the Dock Connector end of the cable, and then pull the connector and the iPhone or iPod apart, or remove the device from its dock.

TIPS

How can I tell when it is safe to disconnect my iPhone or iPod?

You can safely disconnect an iPhone unless the screen shows "Sync in Progress." To cancel a sync, drag your finger across the **Slide to Cancel** slider on the screen. Different iPod models use different messages, but see if either the iPod's screen or the iTunes readout displays "Do Not Disconnect" or "Eject Before Disconnecting." Also see if a rotating icon appears next to the iPod's listing in the Devices category of the Source list.

I am running out of USB ports on my iMac. Is there an alternative to unplugging cables and plugging them back in?

Buy a USB hub, a device that plugs into your iMac and provides extra ports. You can position the hub conveniently for your USB devices. You can find USB hubs at any good computer store, online or offline, including the Apple Store. Buy a powered hub for devices that do not have their own power supplies. Buy an unpowered hub for devices that do have power supplies.

Connect External Drives to Your iMac

Your iMac's built-in hard drive contains enough space for many files and applications, but you may need to connect an external drive to provide extra storage, a place for backup using Time Machine, or to transfer large files easily. You can connect an external drive to your iMac by using the USB ports or FireWire ports.

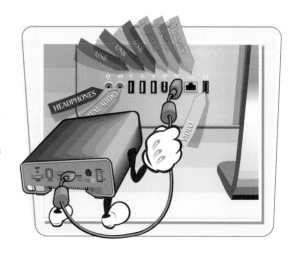

Connect External Drives to Your iMac

Connect an External Drive

❶ On the back of your iMac, identify the port you need for the external drive.

● Use a USB port for a USB-connected external hard drive, a miniature drive, or a memory card reader.

● Use the FireWire 400 port to connect external hard drives that use the FireWire 400 standard.

Note: If your iMac has no FireWire 400 port, use an adapter to connect a FireWire 400 drive to the FireWire 800 port.

● Use the FireWire 800 port to connect external hard drives that use the FireWire 800 standard.

Note: FireWire 800 is twice as fast as FireWire 400. So if your device can use either, choose FireWire 800.

❷ Connect the external drive to the iMac using the right type of cable.

❸ If the external drive needs a power supply, plug it in.

❹ If the external drive has a power switch, turn it on.

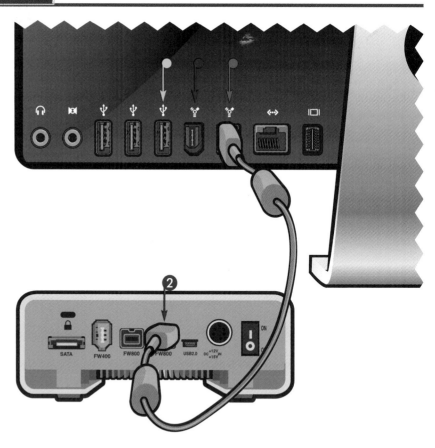

Use an External Drive

① Click **Finder** () on the Dock to open a Finder window.

② Click the drive in the Devices list in the Sidebar.

You can then copy or move files to or from the drive or create new folders on it.

Disconnect an External Drive

① Open a Finder window showing the drive.

② Click the eject button () next to the drive.

Mac OS X dismounts the drive and removes it from the Finder window and from your desktop.

③ Disconnect the drive from the USB port or the FireWire port.

Note: You must always eject a drive using these steps before you disconnect an external drive. Otherwise, you may corrupt or lose files on the drive or on your iMac.

TIP

Should I choose USB or FireWire when I buy an external drive?

FireWire 800 is much faster than USB or FireWire 400, so it is the best choice for high-capacity drives. But if you need to connect the drive to Windows PCs as well as to your iMac, USB is better because all PCs have USB ports but few have FireWire ports.

If you need to carry an external drive with you, a miniature USB drive is usually best. These are also called "thumb drives" or "key drives," are built to withstand life in a pocket, and contain memory chips rather than delicate rotating platters.

Give Commands from the Menus and Toolbar

The easiest ways to give commands in Mac OS X are by using the menus and the toolbar. The menu bar at the top of the window shows the Apple menu (⬛) on the left followed by the menus for the active application. Any open window can have a toolbar, usually across its top but sometimes elsewhere in the window.

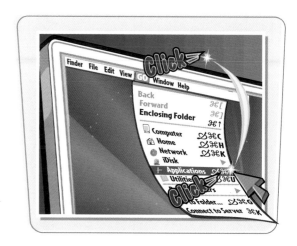

Give Commands from the Menus and Toolbar

Give a Command from a Menu

① On the Dock, click the application you want to activate, the Finder (🖼️) in this example.

Note: *You can also click in the application's window if you can see it.*

② On the menu bar, click the menu you want to open.

The application opens the menu.

③ Click the command you want to give.

The application performs the action associated with the command.

Choose among Groups of Features on a Menu

① On the Dock, click the application you want to activate, the Finder (🖼️) in this example.

② On the menu bar, click the menu you want to open.

The application opens the menu.

③ Click the option you want to choose.

The application activates the feature you chose.

Give a Command from a Toolbar

1 On the Dock, click the application you want to activate, the Finder (🖥) in this example.

2 Click the button on the toolbar.

The application performs the action associated with the command.

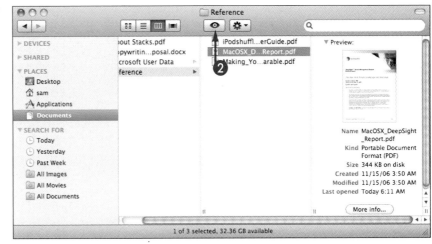

Choose among Groups of Features on a Toolbar

1 On the Dock, click the application you want to activate, the Finder (🖥) in this example.

2 In the group of buttons, click the button you want to choose.

● The application highlights the button you clicked to indicate the feature is turned on.

● The application removes highlighting from the button that was previously selected.

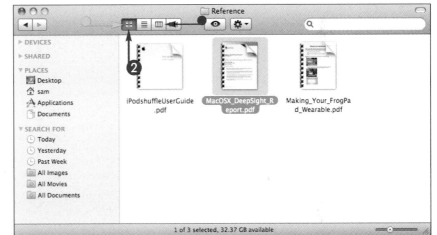

 TIPS

Is it better to use the menus or the toolbar?

If the toolbar contains the command you need, using the toolbar is usually faster and easier than using the menus. You can customize the toolbar in many applications by opening the **View** menu and choosing **Customize Toolbar**. Use this command, or other similar commands, to put the buttons for your most-used commands just a click away.

Can I also give commands using the keyboard?

You can give many of the most widely used commands from the keyboard as well as from the menus or the toolbar. Each menu lists keyboard shortcuts next to their commands. This symbol (●) represents the Command key, (●) represents the Option key, (●) represents the Control key, and ⇧ represents the Shift key.

Open, Close, Minimize, and Hide Windows

Most Mac OS X applications use windows to display information so that you can see it and work with it. You can resize windows to the size you need, position them so that you can see the windows you require, minimize windows to icons on the Dock, or hide an application's windows from view.

Open, Close, Minimize, and Hide Windows

Open a Window

1 Click anywhere on the desktop.

Mac OS X activates the Finder and displays the menu bar for it.

Note: *Clicking anywhere on the desktop activates the Finder because the desktop is a special Finder window. You can also click* **Finder** *(* ![icon] *) on the Dock.*

2 Click **File**.

The File menu opens.

3 Click **New Finder Window**.

A Finder window opens, showing your Home folder.

Move, Resize, and Zoom a Window

1 Click the window's title bar and drag the window to where you want it.

2 Click the lower right corner of the window and drag until the window is the size and shape you want.

3 Click the **Zoom** button (![zoom icon]).

The window zooms to its optimal size.

4 Click the **Zoom** button (![zoom icon]) again.

The window zooms back to its previous size.

Close a Window

① Click the **Close** button ().

The window closes.

Note: You can also close a window by pressing
⌘ + W . *If you need to close all the windows of*
the application, Option *-click the* ***Close*** *button*
( ) *or press* ⌘ + Option + W .

Minimize or Hide a Window

① Click the **Minimize** button ().

Mac OS X minimizes the window
to an icon on the right side of the
Dock.

Note: You can also minimize a window by pressing
⌘ + M .

② Click the icon for the minimized
window.

Mac OS X expands the window to
its original size and position.

Note: Press and hold Shift *while minimizing or*
restoring a window to see the animation in slow
motion.

TIPS

What does zooming a window do?

Clicking the **Zoom** button ()
on a window changes its size to
the size that Mac OS X judges
will best show the window's
contents. If this size does not
show what you want to see,
drag the lower right corner of
the window to change the size.
Clicking again returns the
window to its previous size.

How can I find out where a window is located?

To quickly see what folder
contains a file or folder,
⌘ -click the window's name
in the title bar. The window
displays a pop-up menu
showing the folder *path*, the
sequence of folders to this
folder. You can click a folder
in the path (●) to jump
straight to that folder in the
Finder, or click the title bar to hide the pop-up menu again. This works
in any application, not just in the Finder.

Put Your iMac to Sleep and Wake It Up

When you are ready for a break but you do not want to end your computing session, put the iMac to sleep. Sleep keeps all your applications open and lets you start computing again quickly. When you wake your iMac up, your applications and windows are where you left them, so you can immediately resume what you were doing.

Put Your iMac to Sleep and Wake It Up

Put Your iMac to Sleep

 Click .

The Apple menu opens.

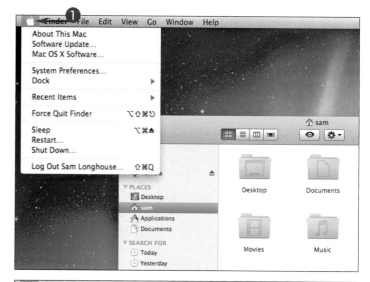

② Click **Sleep**.

The iMac turns its screen off and puts itself to sleep.

Note: *You can also put your iMac to sleep by pressing its power button for a moment.*

Wake Your iMac

1 Click the mouse button or press any key on the keyboard.

The iMac wakes up and turns on the screen. All the applications and windows that you were using are open where you left them.

The iMac reestablishes any network connections that it normally uses and performs regular tasks, such as checking for new e-mail.

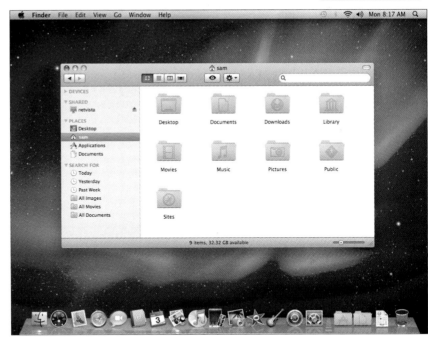

 TIPS

What happens if there is a power outage while my iMac is asleep?

If a power outage occurs while your iMac is asleep, the iMac loses power and crashes, and you lose any unsaved work. For this reason, you should save any unsaved work before putting your iMac to sleep. You may also want to consider buying an uninterruptible power supply, a battery-based device which enables a computer to ride out power outages.

When should I use sleep and when should I shut down my iMac?

Normally, it is better to put your iMac to sleep rather than shut it down. Sleep lets you start using your iMac again much more quickly than starting it from being off, and it uses only a minimal amount of power. Shut down your Mac only when you do not need to use it for several days.

Log Out and
Shut Down Your iMac

When you have finished using your iMac for now, end your computing session by logging out. Mac OS X closes all the applications and documents you were using. From the login screen, you can log back in when you want to start another computing session.

When you have finished using your iMac and plan to leave it several days, shut it down. Shutting down makes Mac OS X close all the applications and documents you were using and then turns off the iMac.

Log Out and Shut Down Your iMac

Log Out from Your iMac

① Click .

The Apple menu opens.

② Click **Log Out**.

The iMac shows a dialog asking if you want to log out.

③ Click **Log Out**.

Note: *Instead of clicking **Log Out**, you can wait for one minute. After this, the iMac closes your applications and logs you out automatically.*

The iMac displays the window showing the list of users. You or another user can click your name to start logging in.

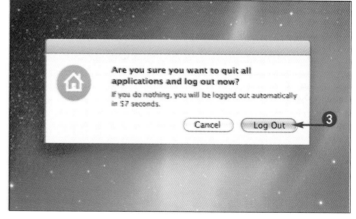

Shut Down Your Mac

1 Click .

The Apple menu opens.

2 Click **Shut Down**.

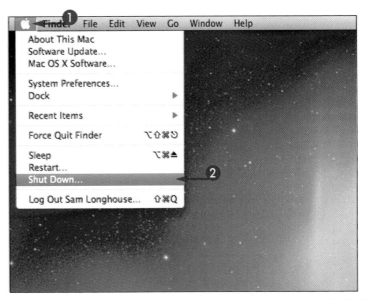

The iMac shows a dialog asking if you want to shut down.

3 Click **Shut Down**.

Note: *Instead of clicking Shut Down, you can wait for one minute. After this, the iMac shuts down automatically.*

The screen goes blank, and the iMac switches itself off.

TIPS

Do I need to save my documents before logging out?

Yes. Before you log out, you should save any unsaved changes that you want to keep. If closing a document will lose unsaved changes, Mac OS X warns you and asks if you want to save the changes ( ). But if you leave your iMac after clicking **Log Out**, unsaved changes can prevent the iMac from completing the logout. So it is better to save changes yourself and quit all applications before logging out.

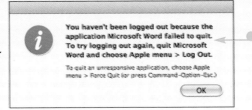

Must I log out, or can I stay logged in?

If you are the only user of your iMac, and you keep the iMac somewhere other people cannot get to it, you can stay logged in if you want. But if your iMac has other users, or other people can reach it, log out to ensure that other people cannot access or delete your files.

Sharing Your iMac with Other People

Mac OS X makes it easy to share your iMac with other people. Each user needs a separate user account, a private space for keeping documents, e-mail, and settings. You can apply restrictions to an account, prevent a user from seeing inappropriate content, and control what the user can do with the iMac.

Create a User Account for Another User 30

Configure Your iMac So Several People Can Use It 32

Share Your iMac with Fast User Switching 34

Turn On Parental Controls for an Account 36

Choose Which Applications a User Can Run..38

Prevent a User from Seeing Inappropriate Content..40

Control Whom a User Can E-mail and Chat With..42

Set Time Limits for Logging On.....................44

See What a Controlled User Has Done on the iMac..46

Create a User Account for Another User

The first time you run your iMac, you set up a user account for yourself with administrator privileges, which means you can configure Mac OS X. You can then create a separate user account for each other person who uses your iMac regularly. This allows users to have their own folders for documents and use the settings they prefer.

① Click the **Apple** icon (■).

② Click **System Preferences**.

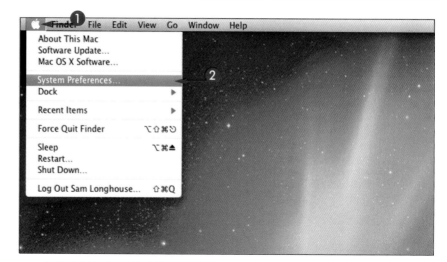

The System Preferences window opens.

③ In the System area, click **Accounts**.

Note: *You must use an Administrator account to create another account. To check whether you are an administrator, see if your account shows Admin in the Accounts window.*

The Accounts pane opens.

④ Click the lock icon (🔒) to unlock System Preferences.

System Preferences displays a dialog asking you to type your password.

⑤ Type your password in the Password field.

⑥ Click **OK**.

The lock opens.

⑦ Click ⊞.

The New Account dialog opens.

⑧ In the New Account pop-up menu, choose **Standard**.

⑨ Type the user name, such as John Brown, and short name, such as john.

⑩ Type the user's initial password in the Password field and the Verify field.

⑪ Click **Create Account**.

The New Account dialog closes, and the new account appears in the Other Accounts list.

How do I choose a good password for a user?

For security, each user should choose his password after logging in. Only the user should know his password. Even you, the administrator, should not know other users' passwords. When you create a new user account, set a password to secure the account against hackers. Tell the user the password, and ask the user to create a new password the first time he or she uses the account. To change the password, the user clicks the **Change Password** button in the Accounts window. The Change Password dialog opens, and the user can type the new password. The user can click 🛟 in the Change Password dialog to open the Password Assistant (⬤), which produces hard-to-break passwords.

Configure Your iMac So Several People Can Use It

When you have created an account for each user, turn on Fast User Switching so that multiple people can use the iMac without logging out. With Fast User Switching, your applications remain open in the background when another user logs in. When you log in again, you can resume where you left off.

Configure Your iMac So Several People Can Use It

① In System Preferences, click **Accounts**.

The Accounts pane opens.

Note: To open the System Preferences window and unlock the settings, see the section "Create a User Account for Another User," earlier in this chapter.

② Click **Login Options**.

The login options pane appears.

③ In the Automatic Login pop-up menu, choose **Off**.

④ Click **Show fast user switching menu as** (☐ changes to ☑).

⑤ Click ⬍.

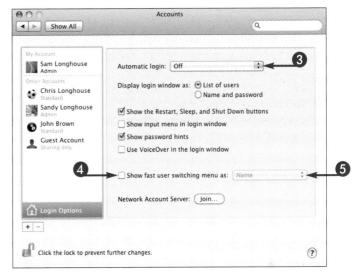

The Show Fast User Switching Menu As pop-up menu opens.

⑥ Click **Name** if you want the Fast User Switching menu to show user names. Click **Short name** to use short names, or click **Icon** to use icons.

Note: Using names for the Fast User Switching menu is clearest but takes most space on the menu bar. Short names are more compact, and icons are most compact.

Fast User Switching is now enabled.

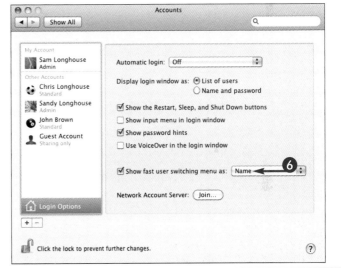

Why should I not use automatic login with Fast User Switching?

Automatic login lets anyone who can turn on your Mac use the account set for automatic login. So when you turn on Fast User Switching, choose **Off** in the Automatic Login pop-up menu to ensure that whoever logs in to the iMac uses his own user account.

Are there any disadvantages to Fast User Switching?

Fast User Switching saves time and effort when several users need to share your iMac, but it can make your iMac run more slowly because applications are open in both the current user's session and any sessions running in the background. If your iMac runs too slowly, try turning Fast User Switching off and see if performance improves. You may also be able to improve performance with Fast User Switching on by adding RAM to your iMac.

Share Your iMac with Fast User Switching

When Fast User Switching is switched on, two or more users can use your iMac without logging out. Only one user can use the keyboard, mouse, and screen at a time, but each other user's computing session keeps running in the background, with all her applications still open.

Share Your iMac with Fast User Switching

Log In to the iMac

① In the login window, click your user name.

Mac OS X prompts you for your password.

② Type your password.

③ Click **Log In**.

Your desktop appears.

Display the Login Window

① When you are ready to stop using the iMac for now, but do not want to log out, click your user name or icon on the menu bar.

② Click **Login Window**.

● The login window appears. Your user name shows a check mark icon (⬤) and the words *Currently logged in.*

Any of the iMac's users can log on by clicking his user name.

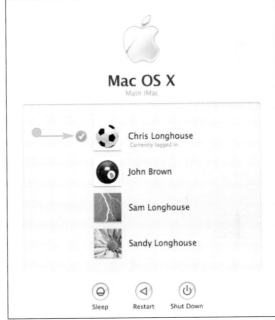

TIPS

What is the quickest way to switch to my user account?

If another user has left her user session displayed, you do not need to go to the login window.

① Click the current user's user name.

② Click your user name on the menu.

How can I log another user out so that I can shut down?

From the login window, you can see which other users are logged in to the iMac. If possible, ask each user to log in and then log out before you shut down. If you must shut down the iMac, and you are an administrator, click **Shut Down** in the login window. Mac OS X warns you that there are logged-in users. Type your name and password, and click **Shut Down**.

Turn On Parental Controls for an Account

Parental controls are settings you as an administrator can apply to limit the actions that a user can take on the iMac. For example, you can prevent the user from running certain applications, allow her only to e-mail and chat with specific people, or prevent her from using the iMac at night.

Turn On Parental Controls for an Account

① Click 🍎.

   The Apple menu opens.

② Click **System Preferences**.

● The System Preferences window opens.

③ Click **Accounts**.

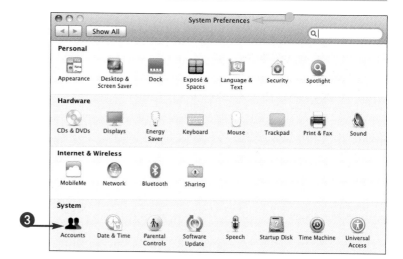

   The Accounts preferences pane opens.

④ Click 🔒.

   The Authenticate dialog opens.

⑤ Type your password.

⑥ Click **OK** or press Return.

- The Authenticate dialog closes (🔒 changes to 🔓).

7 Click the account to which you want to apply parental controls.

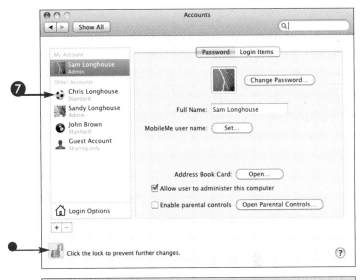

The settings for the account appear.

8 Click **Enable parental controls** (☐ changes to ☑).

You can now choose parental control settings as described in the following four sections.

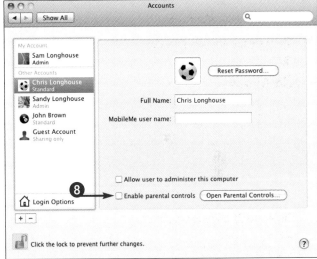

TIP

Can I apply parental controls to any user account?
You can apply parental controls to any Standard user account. To apply parental controls to an account, you must use an Administrator account. You cannot apply parental controls to an Administrator account, but you can downgrade an Administrator account to a Standard account, and then apply the controls to the Standard account. Your iMac must always have one Administrator account to manage the other user accounts.

Standard
~~Administrator~~
Account
Parental Controls in Place

Choose Which Applications a User Can Run

An effective way of limiting the actions users can take is by letting them use only some of the applications and utilities installed on the iMac. Parental controls let you choose exactly which applications the user can run. For example, if the user may not communicate via instant messaging, you can make iChat unavailable.

Choose Which Applications a User Can Run

① In the Accounts preferences pane, click the user account you want to change.

Note: *To open the System Preferences window and unlock the settings, see the section "Create a User Account for Another User," earlier in this chapter.*

② Click **Open Parental Controls**.

The Parental Controls preferences pane opens.

③ Click **System**.

The System pane appears.

④ Click **Only allow selected applications** (☐ changes to ☑).

⑤ In the Select the Applications to Allow list, click ▶ next to a category of applications (▶ changes to ▼).

The list of applications appears.

⑥ Click ☑ for each application you want to prevent the user from using (☑ changes to ☐).

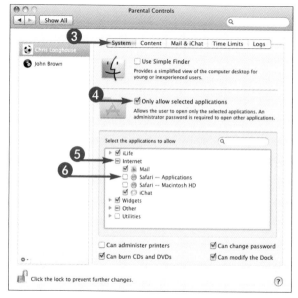

Note: *To prevent the user from using an entire category of applications, click* ☑ *next to the category (*☑ *changes to* ☐ *).*

7 Add other restrictions as needed:

● Click **Can administer printers** (☐ changes to ☑) if the user may administer printers — for example, resuming stuck print jobs.

● Click **Can burn CDs and DVDs** (☑ changes to ☐) if the user may not burn discs.

● Click **Can change password** (☑ changes to ☐) to prevent users changing their password.

● Click **Can modify the Dock** (☑ changes to ☐) if you want to prevent the user from rearranging the Dock icons, adding icons, or removing icons.

8 Set further parental controls as described on the next pages.

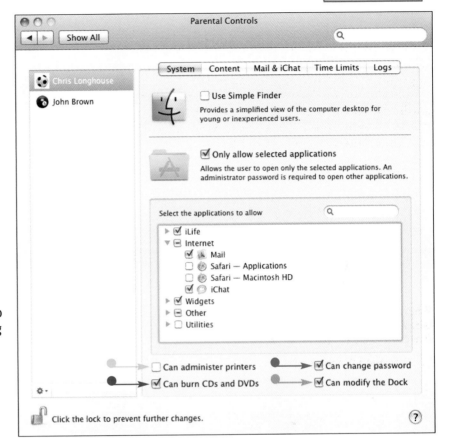

TIP

What is Simple Finder and when should I make a user use it?

Simple Finder is a simplified version of the Finder designed for use by younger, older, or less experienced computer users. Simple Finder provides a more streamlined look with fewer choices, making it easier to find applications and folders, and prevents the user from changing important settings. Some users benefit from using Simple Finder in the long term, whereas for others it is a step toward using the regular Finder after more computing experience.

Prevent a User from Seeing Inappropriate Content

The Web includes sites containing almost every known depravity, and even the Mac OS X Dictionary contains words some people find offensive. Parental controls include settings for preventing a user from seeing inappropriate content in the Dictionary or on the Web.

① In the Accounts preferences pane, click the user account you want to change.

Note: *To open the System Preferences window and unlock the settings, see the section "Create a User Account for Another User," earlier in this chapter.*

② Click **Open Parental Controls**.

The Parental Controls preferences pane opens.

③ Click **Content**.

The Content pane appears.

④ If you want to suppress offensive words in the dictionary, click **Hide profanity in Dictionary** (☐ changes to ☑).

⑤ In the Website Restrictions area, click **Try to limit access to adult websites automatically** if you want to prevent access to adult Web sites (○ changes to ◉). For more control, go to step **10**.

⑥ Click **Customize**.

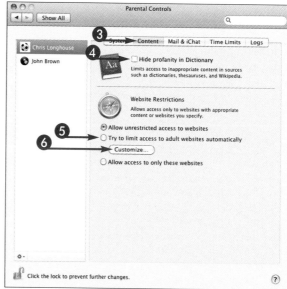

7 In the Customize dialog, click ⊞.

8 Type the Web address to disallow and press **Return**.

Note: You can also add permitted addresses to the Always Allow These Websites field.

9 Click **OK**.

10 To allow the user to visit only certain Web sites, click **Allow access to only these websites** (○ changes to ⊙).

A list of inoffensive Web sites appears.

11 To add a site, click ⊞ and then click **Add bookmark**.

12 In the dialog that appears, type the descriptive name for the Web site.

13 Type the Web site's address.

14 Click **OK**, and the site appears in the list.

15 To remove a site, click it and then click ⊟.

Note: When you permit a user to visit only certain Web sites, those sites appear on the Bookmarks bar in Safari.

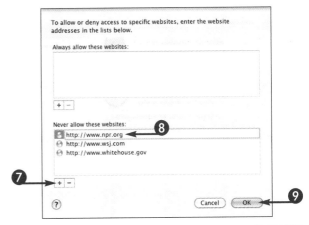

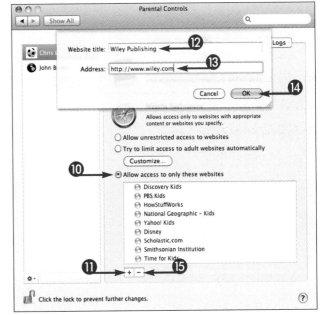

How effective is the blocking of adult Web sites?

The blocking of adult Web sites is only partly effective. Mac OS X can block sites that identify themselves as adult sites using standard rating criteria, but many adult sites either do not use ratings or do not rate their content accurately. Because of this, do not rely on Mac OS X to block all adult material. It is much more effective to choose **Allow access to only these websites** and provide a list of acceptable sites. You can add to the list by vetting and approving extra sites when the user needs to access them.

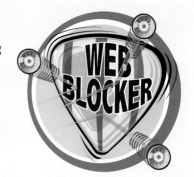

Control Whom a User Can E-mail and Chat With

When you have applied parental controls to an account, you can control the people with whom the user can exchange e-mail messages and chat. This capability is useful for protecting children and other vulnerable individuals from unsuitable e-mail messages and chat.

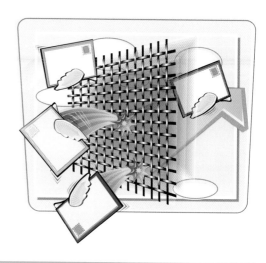

① In the Accounts preferences pane, click the user account you want to change.

② Click **Open Parental Controls**.

Note: To open the System Preferences window and unlock the settings, see the section "Create a User Account for Another User," earlier in this chapter.

The Parental Controls preferences pane opens.

③ Click **Mail & iChat**.

The Mail & iChat pane appears.

④ Click **Limit Mail** (☐ changes to ☑) if you want to allow e-mail to only the addresses you specify.

⑤ Click **Send permission requests to** if you want messages to non-allowed addresses to trigger a message to you.

⑥ Type your e-mail address for the permission requests.

⑦ Click **Limit iChat** (☐ changes to ☑) if you want to allow chat only with addresses you specify.

⑧ Click ⊞.

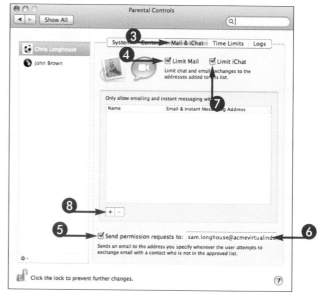

A dialog for adding allowed addresses appears.

9 If the address does not appear in your address book, add it like this:

● Type the first name.

● Type the last name.

● Type the address.

● Click ⬍ and click the address type: **Email**, **AIM**, or **Jabber**.

● If you need to add another address, click ⊞ and repeat the steps.

● Click **Add person to my address book** if you want to add the person.

10 If the address appears in your address book, click ▾.

The dialog expands to show the addresses in your address book.

11 Click the address.

12 Click **Add**.

The name appears in the list.

Note: To remove a name from the Only Allow E-mailing and Instant Messaging With list, click the name and then click ⊟.

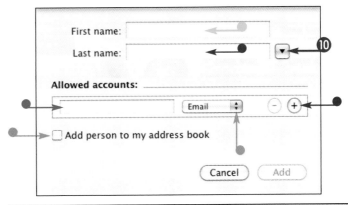

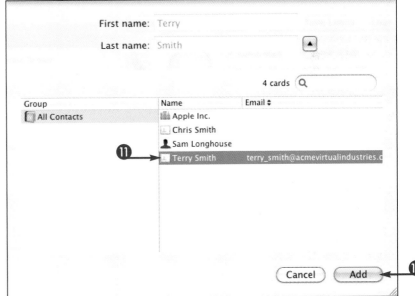

TIP

How effective is the blocking of e-mail and chat?
Mac OS X's blocking of e-mail and chat requests is highly effective for Mail and iChat. As long as you create a suitable list of allowed e-mail and chat addresses, you can give the user solid protection against unwanted messages and chat requests. Mac OS X does not block other e-mail and instant-messaging applications, however, so you must make sure that none are available for the user to circumvent the blocking.

Set Time Limits for Logging On

After turning on parental controls, you can limit the times during which a controlled user can log on to the Mac. You can set the permitted number of hours for weekdays and weekends and define the hours during school nights and weekend nights when the user may not use the Mac.

Set Time Limits for Logging On

① In the Accounts preferences pane, click the user account you want to change.

Note: To open the System Preferences window and unlock the settings, see the section "Create a User Account for Another User," earlier in this chapter.

② Click **Open Parental Controls**.

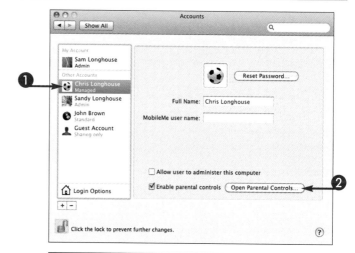

The Parental Controls preferences pane opens.

③ Click **Time Limits**.

The Time Limits pane appears.

④ To set a weekday time limit, click **Limit computer use to** in Weekday time limits (☐ changes to ☑).

⑤ Click and drag the slider to set the limit.

Note: You can set a weekday time limit of between 30 minutes and 8 hours a day.

6 To set a weekend time limit, click **Limit computer use to** in Weekend time limits (☐ changes to ☑).

7 Click and drag the slider to set the limit.

Note: You can set a weekend time limit of between 30 minutes and 8 hours a day.

8 To set a block of time when the Mac is not available on school nights, click **School nights** (☐ changes to ☑).

Note: Parental controls go strictly by the days of the week and make no exceptions for holidays and vacations.

9 Set the start and end time for school nights.

10 To set a block of time when the Mac is not available on weekend nights, click **Weekend** (☐ changes to ☑).

11 Set the start and end time for weekend nights.

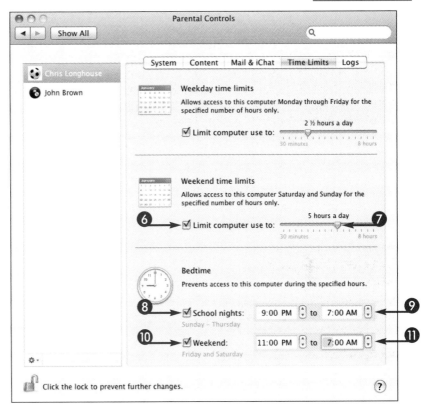

TIPS

What happens if a controlled user tries to log in outside the allowed times?

If a controlled user tries to log on during blocked night hours, Mac OS X displays the Computer Time Expired dialog. An administrator can allow the user an extra period of time, from 15 minutes to the rest of the day, by typing the administrator user name and password.

What happens if a controlled user is still logged on when the time limit arrives?

Mac OS X displays the Your Computer Time Is Almost Up dialog to warn the user that he needs to log out. If the user does not have an administrator add time, log out, or switch the user by the deadline, Mac OS X switches users if Fast User Switching is turned on, or logs the user out if it is not.

See What a Controlled User Has Done on the iMac

Your iMac tracks the actions of each user to whose account you have applied parental controls. You can review the logs of each user's actions to decide whether the parental controls are effective, whether you need to adjust them, or whether it is time to remove them completely.

See What a Controlled User Has Done on the iMac

1 In the Accounts preferences pane, click the user account you want to change.

Note: To open System Preferences and unlock the settings, see "Create a User Account for Another User."

2 Click **Open Parental Controls**.

The Parental Controls preferences pane opens.

3 Click **Logs**.

The Logs pane appears.

4 Click **Websites Blocked**.

The list of blocked Web sites appears.

5 Click 🔽 next to Show Activity For, and choose the length of time.

6 Click 🔽 next to Group By, and choose **Website** or **Date**.

7 Click ▶ to expand a category (▶ changes to 🔽).

8 Click a site.

● Click **Open** to open the site in Safari.

● Click **Allow** if you want to add the site to the Allowed list.

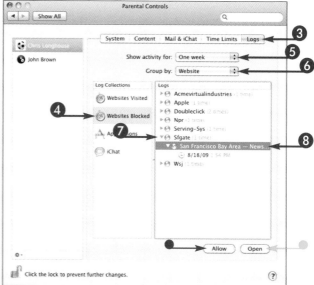

9 Click **Applications**.

The list of blocked applications appears.

10 Click 🔼 next to Show Activity For, and choose the length of time.

11 Click 🔼 next to Group By, and choose **Application** or **Date**.

12 Click ▶ to see the times the user used it.

13 Click **Restrict** to restrict an application.

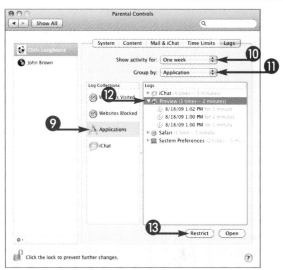

14 Click **iChat**.

The list of iChat contacts appears.

15 Click 🔼 next to Show Activity For, and choose the length of time.

16 Click 🔼 next to Group By, and choose **Contact** or **Date**.

17 To view details of a contact, double-click the contact in the log.

18 To view a chat, click the chat's date and time, and then click **Open**.

19 To prevent the user from communicating with the contact, click the contact's name, and then click **Restrict**.

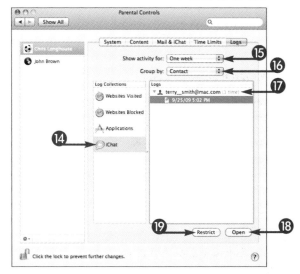

 TIP

Why do the restrictions I apply not take effect immediately?

Most of the restrictions you apply using parental controls do take effect immediately, but others may not take effect until the next time the user logs on and starts the application. So if the user is currently logged in using Fast User Switching, the restrictions may not take effect immediately. For best effect, apply the restrictions when the user is logged out.

Running Applications and Creating Documents

Mac OS X includes many applications, such as the TextEdit word processor, the Preview viewer for PDF files and images, and the iTunes player for music and videos. You can use these applications to create and open documents, but you will very likely need to install other applications as well.

Open and Close an Application 50

Install an Application 52

Switch Quickly to Other Applications 54

**See All the Windows Open on
  Your iMac** 56

Create and Save a Document 58

Close and Open a Document 60

Edit a Document 62

Use Mac OS X's Help System 64

Open and Close an Application

To use an application, you must first open it. You can open an application from the Dock if the application's icon appears there or from the Applications folder if it does not. When you have finished using an application, you close it by giving a Quit command.

Open an Application from the Dock

1 Click the application's icon on the Dock.

Note: If you do not recognize an application's icon, position the mouse pointer over it to display the application's name.

The application opens.

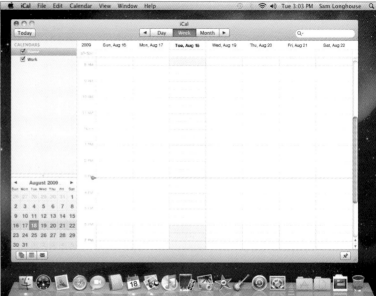

Open an Application from the Applications Folder

1 Click **Finder** (🖥) on the Dock.

A Finder window opens.

2 Click **Applications** in the left column.

An icon appears for each application.

3 Double-click the application you want to run.

The application opens.

Close an Application

1 Click the application's menu, the menu with the application's name — for example, **Dictionary**.

The menu appears.

2 Click the Quit command. This command has the application's name — for example, **Quit Dictionary**.

Note: *If any document that you have opened in the application contains unsaved changes, the application prompts you to save them. Normally you should click **Save**, but you can click **Do Not Save** if you want to discard the changes since you last saved.*

TIPS

Can I add an application to the Dock so that I do not need to open the Applications folder?

You can click an application in the Applications folder and drag it to the Dock. Drop the application to the left of the divider line between applications and files. Alternatively, open the application, Control-click or right-click its Dock icon, highlight **Options** on the shortcut menu, and click **Keep in Dock**.

Can I close an application by closing its window?

Most Mac OS X applications enable you to open multiple windows, and even when you close the last window, the application remains open. But some applications quit automatically when you close the last window or the only window that the application lets you use. After closing a window, see if the application's menu bar is still active. If so, quit the application.

Install an Application

To get your work or play done, you will most likely need to install applications on your iMac. You can install an application or a suite of related applications either from a CD or DVD or from a file that you have downloaded from the Internet.

Install an Application

① Open the disc or file that contains the application.

If the application is on a CD or DVD, insert the disc in your iMac's optical drive.

If the application is in a file you have downloaded, double-click the file.

A Finder window opens showing the contents of the disc or file.

② If there is a file containing installation instructions, open it, read the instructions, and then follow them. Otherwise, double-click the Installer icon.

A dialog opens prompting you to type your password.

Note: *To install most applications, you must have an Administrator account or provide an Administrator's password.*

③ Type your password.

④ Click **OK**.

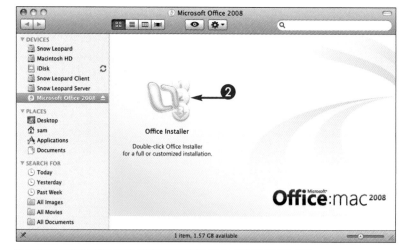

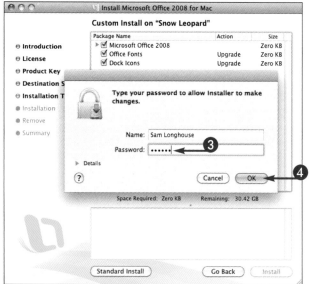

The installation continues. When it is complete, Installer displays a screen telling you that the install succeeded.

⑤ Click **Close**.

Installer closes.

⑥ Click **Finder** (📄) on the Dock.

A Finder window opens.

⑦ Click **Applications** in the sidebar.

The list of applications appears.

⑧ Double-click the application you just installed.

Note: *Some application suites place a folder in the Applications folder. Click this folder in Column view, or double-click it in any other view, to see the applications.*

The application opens.

Note: *Installer places icons for some applications on the Dock. You can click the application's icon to open the application.*

TIP

How do I install an application that has no installer or installation instructions?

If the application does not have an installer or specific installation instructions, use the standard method of installing an application on Mac OS X. Click the icon in the Finder window for the application's disc or file, and then drag the application's icon to the Applications folder in the sidebar. If the sidebar does not appear, click the rounded button at the right end of the window's title bar.

Switch Quickly to Other Applications

When you work with several applications at the same time, it is often useful to switch quickly from one application to another. In Mac OS X, you can switch quickly by using either the mouse or the keyboard.

Switch Applications Using the Mouse

① If you can see a window for the application you want to switch to, click anywhere in that window.

② If you cannot see a window you want to switch to, click the application's icon on the Dock.

All the windows for that application appear in front of the other applications' windows.

③ Click **Window** on the menu bar.

The Window menu opens.

④ Click the window you want to bring to the front.

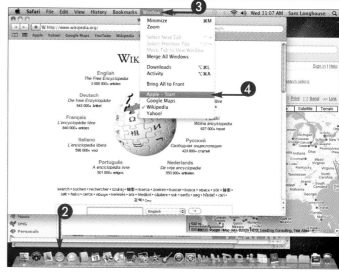

Switch among Applications Using the Keyboard

1 Press and hold ⌘ and press Tab.

Application Switcher opens, showing an icon for each open application.

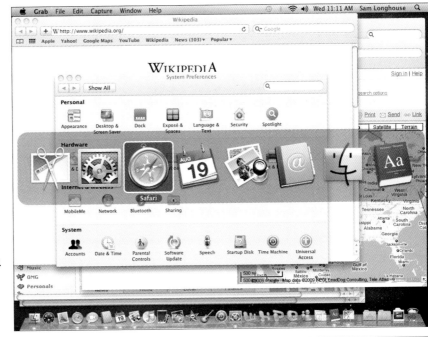

2 Still holding down ⌘, press Tab one or more times to move the highlight to the application you want.

Note: Press and hold ⌘ + Shift and press Tab to move backward through the applications.

3 When you reach the application you want, release ⌘.

Note: To return to the application that was active before you opened Application Switcher, press Esc or . . You can also keep pressing Tab until the application is selected again in Application Switcher.

Application Switcher closes, and the selected application comes to the front.

4 If necessary, switch to a different window in the application as described on the previous page.

Are there other ways of switching among applications?

You can switch among applications by using the keyboard and the mouse together. Press and hold ⌘, press Tab once to open Application Switcher, and then click the application you want to bring to the front.

Can I do anything else with Application Switcher apart from switch to an application?

You can also hide an application or quit an application from Application Switcher. Press and hold ⌘, press Tab to open Application Switcher, and then select the application you want to affect. Press H to hide the application. Press Q to quit the application.

See All the Windows Open on Your iMac

Another way of switching among windows is by using the Exposé feature, which shrinks down open windows so that you can see all those you need. You can display all open windows in all applications or just the windows in a particular application.

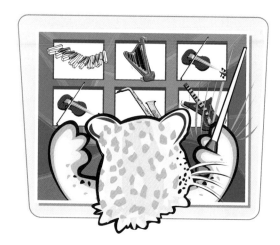

See All the Windows Open in All Applications

① After opening various windows, press F3 to display all windows.

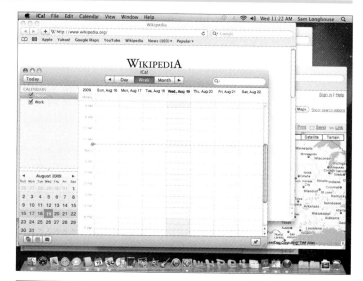

Mac OS X shrinks and repositions each window so that you can see all windows. The desktop background darkens to make the windows more visible.

② Click the window you want to use.

Mac OS X restores the windows to normal size and displays the window you clicked at the front.

You can now work with the window you clicked.

See All the Windows in the Active Application

1 Activate the application whose windows you want to see. For example, click a window from that application.

2 Press Control + F3.

Mac OS X tiles the windows of the application you chose so that you can see them all, and hides all other applications' windows.

3 Click the window you want to see.

Mac OS X restores all the windows from all the applications, placing the window you clicked at the front.

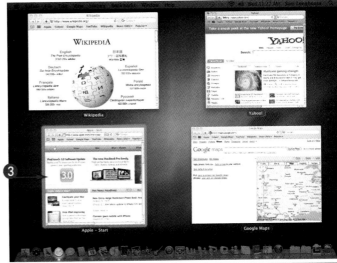

 TIPS

Does Exposé have any other tricks I should know about?

After pressing Control + F3 to show all windows of the current application, you can press Tab to show all windows of the next application. Press Shift + Tab to show all windows of the previous application. You can press ⌘ + F3 to move all open windows to the sides of the desktop to reveal the desktop. Press ⌘ + F3 when you want to see the windows again.

Can I trigger Exposé with the mouse instead of the keyboard?

Yes, you can run Exposé with the mouse. What you need to do is set up a hot corner on the screen for Exposé. You then move the mouse pointer to that corner to trigger Exposé. See Chapter 12 for instructions.

Create and Save a Document

After opening an application, you can create a document and work with it. Mac OS X stores the document temporarily in your iMac's memory as you work. To keep the document permanently, you save the document to your iMac's hard disk.

Create a Document

1 Click **File**.

The File menu opens.

2 Click **New**.

*Note: Some applications display a New dialog to let you choose among different types of documents. Click the type you want, and then click **OK**.*

A new document opens.

3 Start working in the document. For example, start typing text in a TextEdit document.

Save a Document

1 Click **File**.

The File menu opens.

Note: You can also save a document by pressing ⌘ + S . This shortcut is quick and convenient when you are working with the keyboard.

2 Click **Save**.

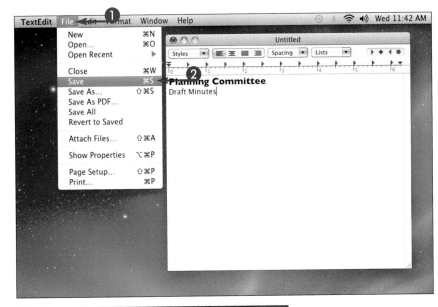

The Save As dialog appears.

3 In the Save As field, type the name you want to give the document.

4 If you want to change the folder, click ⬙ next to the Where list and choose the folder.

5 Click **Save**.

The application saves the document.

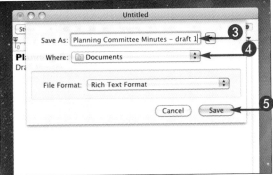

TIPS

When and how often should I save a document?

To avoid losing data, save each document as soon as you create it. After you have chosen the document's folder and given it a name, you can save it in moments by pressing ⌘ + S or choosing **File** and then **Save**. In case your Mac has software or hardware problems, save every time you make changes to a document that you do not want to make again.

How do I save a document under another name?

After you give a document a name, the application keeps saving changes to it under that name. To save the latest version of the document with a different name, click **File** and then click **Save As** (●). The Save As dialog opens. You can then save the document under another name.

Close and Open a Document

After creating and saving a document, close it when you have finished working with it. You can then reopen the document whenever you need to work with it.

Close a Document

1 Click **File**.

The File menu opens.

2 Click **Close**.

Note: *You can also press* ⌘ *+* W *to close a document.*

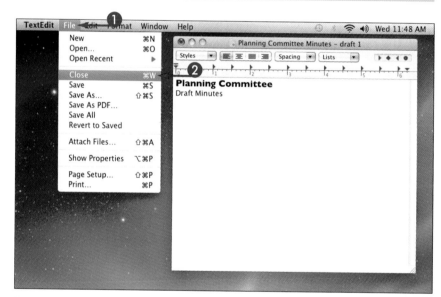

If the document contains unsaved changes, a dialog opens asking if you want to save changes.

3 Click **Save** if you want to save the changes. Click **Don't Save** if you want to discard the changes.

The document closes.

Note: *When you tell an application to quit, the application automatically closes each open document. If any document contains unsaved changes, the application displays a dialog asking if you want to save the changes. The application does not quit until you dismiss the dialog.*

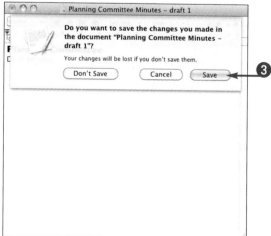

Open a Document

1. In the application you will use to view or edit the document, click **File**.

   The File menu opens.

   Note: *You can also press ⌘+O to display the Open dialog.*

2. Click **Open**.

   The Open dialog appears.

3. Click the document.

   ● If the document is in a different folder, click ▤ in the From list, and then click the folder that contains the document.

4. Click **Open**.

   A window opens showing the document.

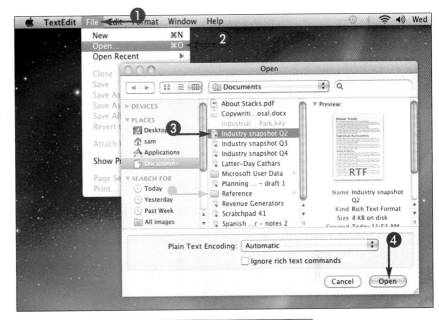

TIP

Are there other ways of opening documents?

If you have opened the document recently, choose **File** and then **Recent Files**, and then click the document. In a Finder window, double-click the document, or select it and press ⌘+O, to open the document in the default application. To use another application, Control-click or right-click a document in a Finder window, highlight **Open With**, and then click the application (●).

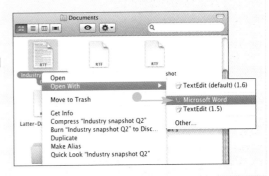

Edit a Document

Many types of documents are based on text — for example, word processing documents, text files, and e-mails. To edit such documents, you can use standard techniques of selecting, copying, moving, and deleting text.

Select Text

1 Click at the beginning of the text you want to select, and then drag to the end.

Note: You can also select by clicking at the end of the text and dragging to the beginning. Sometimes this is easier.

2 When you have selected all the text you want, release the mouse button.

The application highlights the selected text, and you can then work with it.

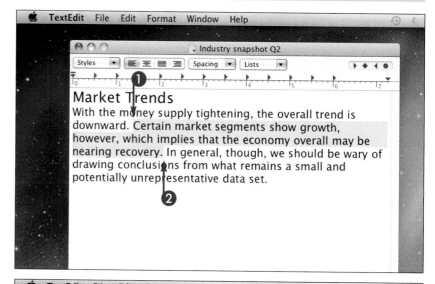

Delete a Selection

1 Select the text you want to delete.

2 Press Delete.

The text disappears.

Note: To delete text without selecting it first, click after the last character of the text, and then press Delete until the text disappears.

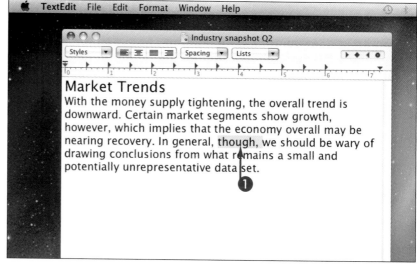

Copy or Move Text

1 Select the text you want to copy or move.

Note: You can also press ⌘ + C to copy or ⌘ + X to cut.

2 Control-click or right-click anywhere in the selection.

3 Click **Copy** if you want to copy the text. Click **Cut** if you want to move it.

Note: The Cut and Copy commands both place the text on the Mac OS X Clipboard, an area of memory that can hold one item at a time. Cut also removes the text from the document.

4 In the document, Control-click or right-click where you want to insert the text.

Note: You can also click to place the insertion point where you want it and press ⌘ + V to paste where the insertion point is.

The shortcut menu opens.

5 Click **Paste**.

The application inserts the text where you clicked.

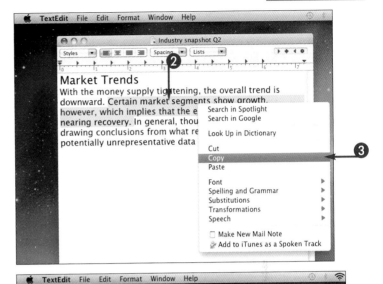

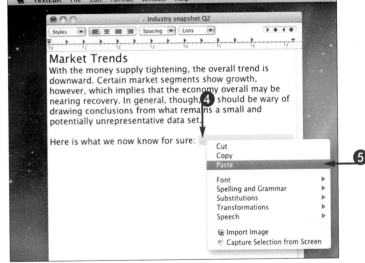

TIP

Is there a way to control scrolling when I click and drag to select text that continues off the screen?

When you need to select past the end of the text on the screen, it is usually easier to use a different method than clicking and dragging. Click to place the insertion point where you want to begin selecting. Scroll until you can see the end of the text you want to select. Press and hold **Shift** and click. The application selects from where you placed the insertion point to where you click.

Use Mac OS X's Help System

Mac OS X includes a built-in help system that you can use to solve problems that this book does not cover. You can launch the help system from the Finder toolbar or by clicking a Help button in a dialog. You can then either browse or search to find the information you need.

Use Mac OS X's Help System

① Click anywhere on the desktop.

The Finder becomes active.

② Click **Help**.

The Help menu opens.

③ Click **Mac Help**.

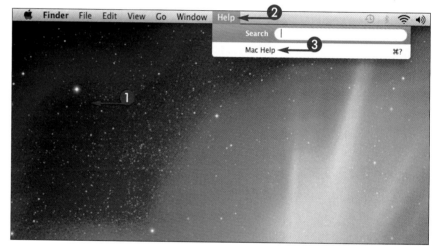

The Mac Help window opens and displays the Mac Help screen.

④ Click the search box.

⑤ Type a question or some keywords.

⑥ Press Return.

The Mac Help window shows a list of topics related to what you searched for.

⑦ Click the topic you want to view.

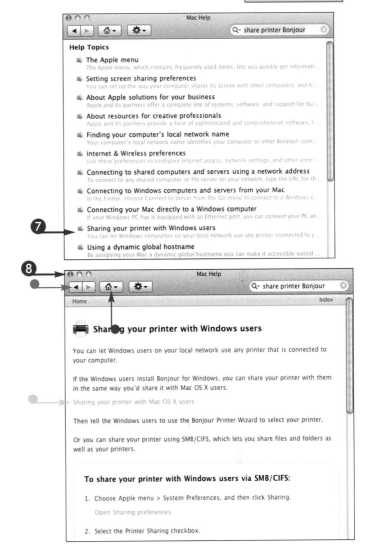

Mac Help displays the detailed help for the topic.

● Click a link to open another topic, an application or utility, or a Web page.

● Click the **Home** button (🏠) to return to the Mac Help screen.

● Click the **Back** button (◀) to return to the previous screen you viewed.

⑧ When you have finished using Mac Help, click 🔴.

The Mac Help window closes.

 TIPS

Can I print out a Help topic for reference?

To print the current topic, click **Action** (⚙️), and then click **Print** (●) on the pop-up menu. This menu also includes commands for making the text in the Mac Help window larger or smaller and for searching for text in the current topic.

How do I get help for other applications?

Each application has its own Help menu. Activate the application, click **Help** to open the Help menu, and then click the Help topic for the application or type your search terms and press Return.

CHAPTER 4

Managing Your Files and Folders with the Finder

The Finder is Mac OS X's built-in tool for managing files, folders, and drives. The Finder runs all the time Mac OS X is running, and is a vital tool for getting things done in Mac OS X. This chapter shows you how to perform essential tasks in the Finder.

Understanding Where to Store Files on Your iMac 68

Using the Finder's Four Views Effectively 70

Look Through a File without Opening It 72

Search for a File or Folder 74

Save a Search in a Smart Folder 76

Create and Name a New Folder 78

Copy a File from One Folder to Another 80

Move a File from One Folder to Another 82

Rename a File 84

View the Information about a File or Folder 86

Compress Files for Easy Transfer 88

Burn Files to a CD or DVD 90

Erase a CD or DVD 92

Throw a File in the Trash 94

Understanding Where to Store Files on Your iMac

For each user account you set up, Mac OS X automatically creates a structure of folders for storing files. The key folder is the Home folder, which contains the Desktop, Documents, Downloads, Library, Movies, Music, Pictures, Public, and Sites folders.

You can create extra folders of your own as needed, but for most people the built-in folders are plenty to start with.

Go to the Home Folder

① Click **Finder** (📖) on the Dock.

A Finder window opens to your default folder.

Note: *The default folder may be your Home folder. If so, skip step* **2**.

② Click your user name in the sidebar.

The Finder window shows your Home folder.

Note: *You can also go to the Home folder by clicking the desktop and then choosing* **Go** *and* **Home** *from the menu bar.*

Open the Documents Folder

① Click **Documents**.

The contents of the Documents folder appear.

Note: *The Documents folder is your storage place for word processing documents, spreadsheets, and similar files. Most applications that create these types of documents use the Documents folder automatically.*

② Click ◀.

The Finder window displays the previous folder, the Home folder.

Look in the Music Folder

① Click **Music**.

The contents of the Music folder appear.

● The GarageBand folder appears if your iMac has iLife installed. GarageBand automatically stores your compositions in this folder.

● The iTunes folder is where iTunes stores songs you buy or import from CD.

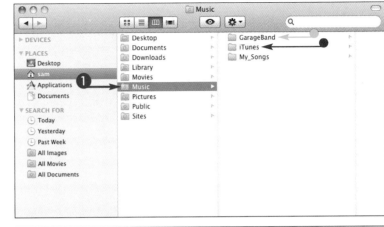

Meet the Movies Folder and the Pictures Folder

① Click **Movies**.

● The contents of the Movies folder appear. iMovie stores your movie projects here.

Note: If you have not yet used iMovie, the iMovie Projects folder does not appear in the Movies folder.

② Click **Pictures**.

The Pictures folder appears. This folder contains an iChat Icons folder and your iPhoto Library.

③ Click .

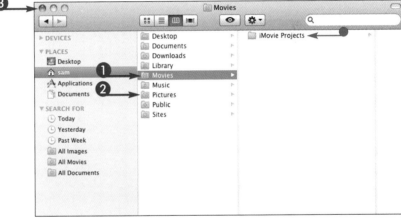

TIPS

What are the Library folder and the Sites folder?

The Library folder in your Home folder contains files and settings for your user account. For example, the Mail folder contains details of your e-mail accounts. Normally you change the contents of the Library folder by using applications rather than directly through the Finder. The Sites folder is for any Web sites you host on your iMac using the Web Sharing feature.

What is the Public folder in my Home folder for?

When you place files in your Public folder, other users of your iMac and other computers on your network can see them, open them, and copy them, but not change them. Your Public folder contains a Drop Box folder (●) in which others can place files they want to give to you. Only you can see the contents of the Drop Box.

Using the Finder's Four Views Effectively

To help you find and identify your files, the Finder has four different views. Icon view shows each file or folder as a large icon, whereas List view shows folders as a collapsible hierarchy. Column view lets you navigate quickly through folders and see where each item is located, and Cover Flow view is great for identifying files visually by looking at their contents.

Using the Finder's Four Views Effectively

Icon View

1 Click **Finder** (🖥️) on the Dock.

A Finder window opens showing your default folder.

2 Click **Icons** (▦) on the toolbar.

The files and folders appear in Icon view.

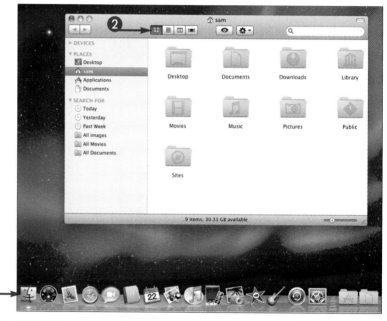

List View

1 In the Finder window, click **List** (☰) on the toolbar.

The files and folders appear in List view.

2 Click ▷ (▷ changes to ▽) next to a folder.

The folder's contents appear.

Note: In List view, you can expand the contents of multiple folders at the same time.

3 When you need to hide the folder's contents again, click ▽ (▽ changes to ▷).

Column View

1 Click **Columns** (▥).

The files and folders appear in Column view.

2 Click a folder in the first column after the sidebar.

The folder's contents appear in the next column.

3 Click a document.

● A preview of the document appears.

Cover Flow View

1 Click **Cover Flow** (▦).

The files and folders appear in Cover Flow view.

2 Click a file; a preview appears in the Cover Flow area.

● Click to show the previous document.

● Click to show the next document.

● Click and drag to scroll quickly through documents.

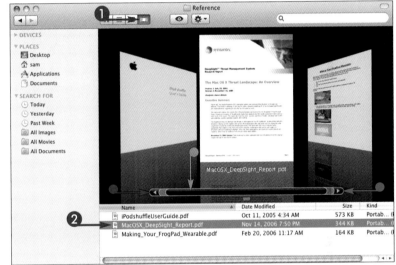

TIPS

Can I change the size of icons used in Icon view?

Click and drag the slider in the lower-right corner of a Finder window in Icon view to set the size for that folder. To set a default size in Icon view, choose **View** and **Show View Options**. Click and drag the **Icon size** slider (●) until the icons are the size you want. Click **Use as Defaults**. Click ▣.

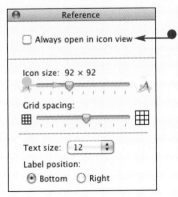

Is there an easy way to use different views for different folders?

You can tell the Finder to use a particular view for any folder. Click the folder and choose **View** and **Show View Options**. In the main window, click the view icon you want and then click the **Always open** option (☐ changes to ☑) — for example, **Always open in list view** (●).

Look Through a File without Opening It

When you have many files with similar names or contents, it can be difficult to identify the document you need without opening the document and looking at its contents. To help you find the right document, Mac OS X's Quick Look feature enables you to look quickly inside many widely used types of documents right from the Finder without opening the document in an application.

Look Through a File without Opening It

1 Click **Finder** (⬚) on the Dock.

A Finder window opens to your default folder.

2 Click the file you want to see.

3 Click ⚙-.

The Action pop-up menu opens.

4 Click **Quick Look**.

Note: *You can also click ⬚ on the Finder toolbar to open Quick Look for the selected file or files.*

A Quick Look window opens showing a preview of the file.

Note: *When you use Quick Look on a video file, Mac OS X starts playing the file.*

5 If you need to scroll to see more of the file, click and drag the scroll bar.

6 To see the file full screen, click ⬚.

The Quick Look window expands to fill the screen.

Note: *To see more of the file in full-screen view, click and drag the scroll bar, or press* Page down .

⑦ Click when you have finished using full-screen view.

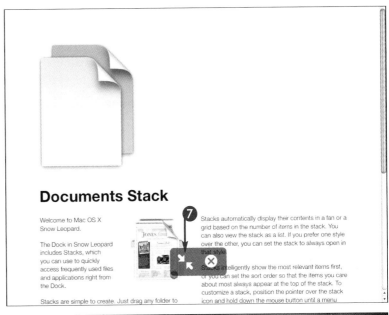

⑧ Click ⊗ to close the Quick Look window.

Note: *Instead of closing the Quick Look window, you can press* ➡, ⬅, ⬆, *or* ⬇ *to display another file or folder.*

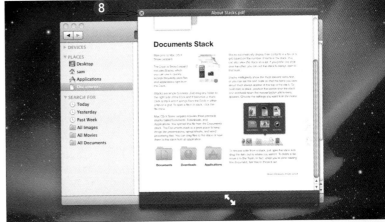

TIPS

Why does the Quick Look preview of a file look different from the actual file?

Quick Look does not actually open the file fully, so the Quick Look preview of the file may look somewhat different from the actual file. Normally, all text and objects such as graphics are visible, but the layout and formatting may be different. When Quick Look is not accurate enough to identify a file visually, open the file in an application to see it better.

Can I use Quick Look on more than one file at a time?

You can use Quick Look on as many files as you want. Select the files and then launch Quick Look. Click ▶ to play each preview for a few seconds, or click ➡ and ⬅ to move from preview to preview. Click ▦ to see the index sheet showing all previews, and then click the item you want to see.

Search for a File or Folder

To help you find the files and folders you need to work with, Mac OS X includes a powerful search feature called Spotlight. You can search quickly from the desktop or from a Finder window, using either straightforward search keywords or complex search criteria.

Search Quickly from the Desktop

1 Click 🔍.

The Spotlight search field opens.

2 Type one or more keywords in the search field.

Note: *Spotlight searches automatically for the keywords within the contents of files as well as in the names of files.*

Spotlight displays a list of matches as you type.

3 Click the result you want to see.

The file opens in the application associated with it.

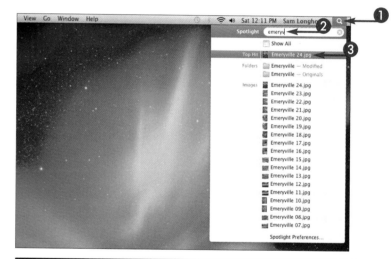

Search from a Finder Window

1 Click **Finder** (🖼️) on the Dock.

A Finder window opens to your default folder.

2 If you want to search a different folder, click it.

3 Click in the search field.

4 Type the keywords for your search.

The Finder window's title bar changes to Searching, and the list of search results appears.

5 To change where Spotlight is searching, click a button.

6 To search file names instead of file contents, click **File Name**.

7 To quickly view a file, Control -click or right-click it and choose **Quick Look**.

8 To open a file, double-click it.

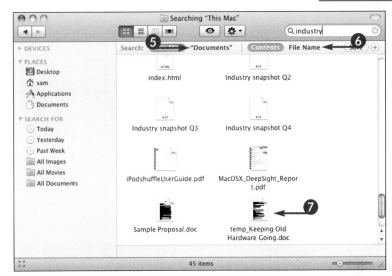

9 To refine the search, click ▲ and choose **Kind**, **Last opened date**, **Last opened date**, **Created date**, **Name**, or **Contents**.

10 Click ▲ and choose search criteria — for example, *Created date is within last 3 days*.

11 If you need to add more search criteria, click ⊕, and another line of controls appears.

12 Set up another condition as described in steps **9** and **10**.

The search results appear.

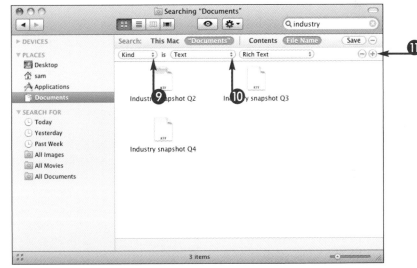

TIPS

How can I tell the difference between two search results that seem to be the same?

When you have two or more files with the same name in different folders, it can be hard to tell them apart in the Spotlight search results. For a quick check, position the mouse pointer over a search result for a moment. A ScreenTip (●) opens showing the folder that contains the file.

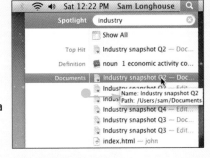

Can I change where Spotlight searches for files?

You can customize the list of folders that Spotlight searches. See Chapter 12 for instructions on customizing Spotlight.

Save a Search in a Smart Folder

After a successful search, you can save the search in a smart folder so that you can use it again quickly and easily. Unlike a regular folder, a smart folder does not actually contain the items it shows because each item remains in its original folder. The smart folder gives you a way to locate items swiftly by their characteristics.

Save a Search in a Smart Folder

① Click **Finder** ( ) on the Dock.

A Finder window opens.

② Set up a search as described on the previous pages.

Your search results appear in the Finder window.

③ Click **Save**.

The Specify a Name and Location for Your Smart Folder dialog opens.

Note: *Mac OS X automatically saves your smart folders in the Saved Searches folder in your Library folder. You can choose another folder if you want.*

④ Type the smart folder name.

⑤ Click **Add to Sidebar** (☑ changes to ☐) if you do not want to add the smart folder to the sidebar.

⑥ If you want to save the search in a different folder, click .

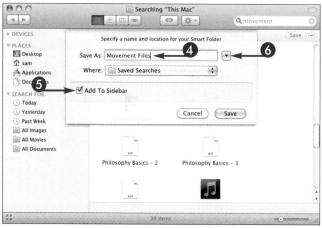

The Specify a Name and Location for Your Smart Folder dialog expands.

⑦ Choose the folder in which to store the smart folder.

⑧ Click **Save**.

The Specify a Name and Location for Your Smart Folder dialog closes.

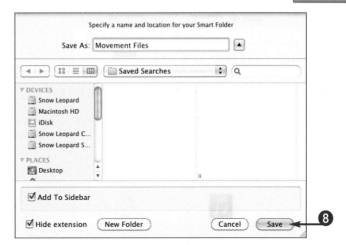

If you left Add to Sidebar selected, Mac OS X adds the smart folder to the Search For category in the Finder's sidebar.

⑨ Click the smart folder when you need to display matching items.

Note: *To use a smart folder that you did not add to the sidebar, open a Finder window to the folder in which you stored the smart folder.*

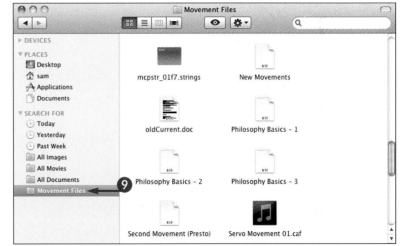

 TIPS

Should I add my smart folders to the sidebar?

If you create only a few smart folders, adding them to the sidebar is usually helpful. If you create many smart folders, you may prefer to keep them in different folders. Alternatively, add each smart folder to the sidebar, and then remove those you do not need to keep. To remove a smart folder from the sidebar, Control -click or right-click the folder, and then click **Remove from Sidebar**.

How do I change a smart folder?

Click the smart folder in the sidebar or in the folder in which you saved it. Click ✿ and choose **Show Search Criteria** (●) from the Action pop-up menu. The

controls for changing the criteria appear. You can then change the smart folder by using the same techniques you used to set it up.

Create and Name a New Folder

Mac OS X builds a hierarchy of folders in your user account, but you will normally need to create other folders to keep different types of files or different projects organized. You can create as many folders as needed, and you can create subfolders within other folders.

Create and Name a New Folder

① Click **Finder** (🖥️) on the Dock.

A Finder window opens to your default folder.

② Click or double-click, depending on the view you are using, the folder in which you want to create the new folder.

③ Click 🔅▾ on the toolbar.

The Action pop-up menu opens.

④ Click **New Folder**.

● A new folder appears in the Finder window.

The new folder shows an edit box around the default name, Untitled Folder.

⑤ Type the name you want to give the folder.

⑥ Press Return.

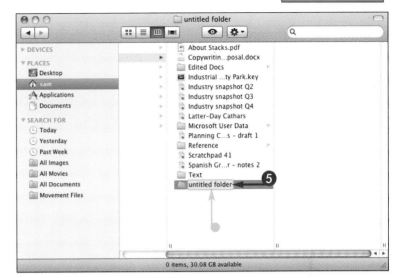

The folder takes on the new name.

⑦ Click or double-click the folder, depending on the view you are using.

The folder opens. You can now add files to the folder or create subfolders inside it.

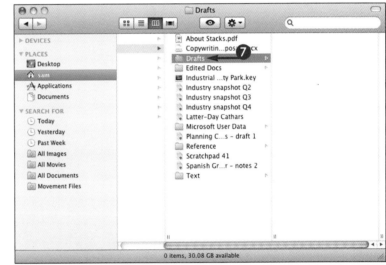

 TIPS

Are there other ways of creating a new folder?

You can also create a new folder in three other ways. In a Finder window in any view, press ⌘+Shift+N or choose **File** and **New Folder** from the Finder menu bar. In Icon view or Column view, Control-click or right-click in open space inside the folder and then click **New Folder** (●) on the shortcut menu.

Why can I not create a new folder inside some other folders?

Most likely, you do not have permission to create a folder in that folder. Each user can create new items in the folders in his or her user account, and administrators can create folders in some other folders. But Mac OS X protects other folders, such as the System folder and the Users folder, from anybody creating new folders.

Copy a File from One Folder to Another

Mac OS X makes it easy to copy a file from one folder to another. Copying is useful when you need to share a file with other people or when you need to keep a copy of the file safe against harm.

You can copy one or more files at a time either by clicking and dragging or by using the Copy and Paste commands.

Copy a File from One Folder to Another

Copy a File by Clicking and Dragging

1. Click **Finder** (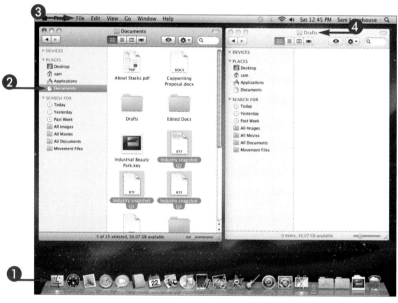) on the Dock.

   A Finder window opens to your default folder.

2. Open the folder that contains the file you want to copy.

3. Choose **File** and **New Finder Window**.

   A new Finder window opens.

4. In the second Finder window, open the folder to which you want to copy the file.

5. Click and drag the Finder windows so that you can see both.

6. Select the file or files you want to copy.

7. Press and hold Option while you click the file and drag it to the destination folder.

   Note: When you Option -drag a file, ➤ changes to ➤ to indicate that you are making a copy.

   A copy of the file appears in the folder.

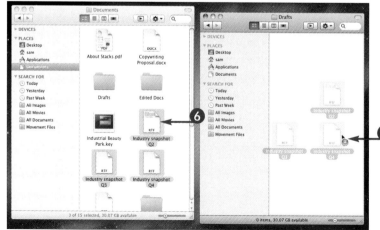

Copy a File by Using Copy and Paste

1 Click **Finder** ( ) on the Dock.

A Finder window opens to your default folder.

2 Open the folder that contains the file you want to copy.

3 Click the file to select it.

4 Click .

The Action pop-up menu opens.

5 Click **Copy**.

Mac OS X copies the file's details to the clipboard.

6 Open the folder in which you want to create the copy.

7 Click .

The Action pop-up menu opens.

8 Click **Paste Item**.

A copy of the file appears in the destination folder.

Note: You can use the Paste command in either the same Finder window or another Finder window — whichever you find more convenient.

TIPS

How do I copy a folder?

You can copy one or more folders by using either of the techniques for copying files: Either Option-click and drag the folder or folders to the destination folder, or use the Copy command to copy the folder and the Paste command to paste it into the destination folder.

Can I make a copy of a file in the same folder as the original?

To make a copy of a file in the same folder as the original, click the file, click , and then click **Duplicate** ( ) from the Action pop-up menu. Finder automatically adds *copy* to the end of the copy's file name to distinguish it from the original.

Move a File from One Folder to Another

When organizing your files, you will often need to move a file from one folder to another.

You can move files quickly by selecting the file or files and then clicking and dragging. But you must use a different technique if the destination folder is on a different drive from the source folder than if it is on the same drive.

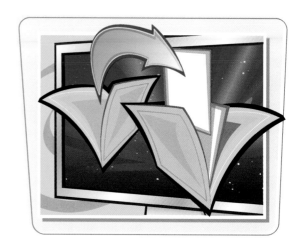

Move a File from One Folder to Another

Move a File between Folders on the Same Drive

① Click **Finder** (🖼️) on the Dock.

A Finder window opens to your default folder.

② Open the folder that contains the file you want to move.

③ Choose **File** and **New Finder Window**.

A new Finder window opens.

④ In the second Finder window, open the folder to which you want to move the file.

⑤ Click and drag the Finder windows so that you can see both.

⑥ Click the file and drag it to the destination folder.

The file appears in the destination folder and disappears from the source folder.

Move a File from One Drive to Another

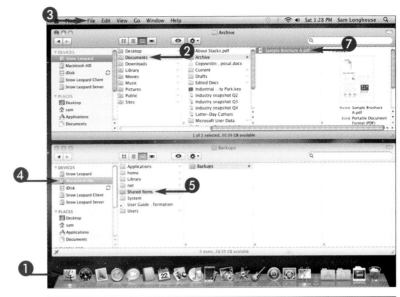

① Click **Finder** ( ) on the Dock.

A Finder window opens to your default folder.

② Open the folder that contains the file you want to move.

③ Choose **File** and **New Finder Window**.

A new Finder window opens.

④ In the second Finder window, open the drive to which you want to copy the file.

⑤ Open the destination folder on that drive.

⑥ Click and drag the Finder windows so that you can see both.

⑦ Select the file or files you want to move.

⑧ Press and hold while you click the file or files and drag them to the destination folder.

The file appears in the destination folder and disappears from the source folder.

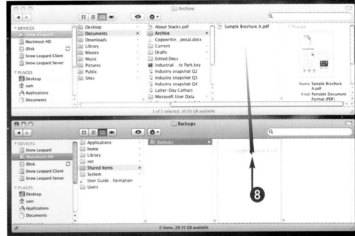

TIP

Can I move files by using menu commands instead of clicking and dragging?

If you find it awkward to click and drag files from one folder to another, you can use a two-stage process with menu commands. First, use the Copy and Paste commands to copy the files to the destination folder. Second, delete the original files from the source folder. This method is workable and effective if a little cumbersome.

Rename a File

When you create a new file or folder, you normally give it a name that describes its contents or what you intend it to be.

To keep your iMac's file system well organized, you will often need to rename files and folders after creating them. You can rename a file or folder in seconds by using the Finder.

Rename a File

1 Click **Finder** (icon) on the Dock.

A Finder window opens to your default folder.

2 Open the folder that contains the file you want to rename.

3 Click the file to select it.

4 Press Return.

Note: You can also display the edit box by clicking the file's name again after selecting it. Be careful to pause between the clicks, or Mac OS X registers a double-click and opens the file.

An edit box appears around the file name.

5 Edit the file's current name, or simply type the new name over the current name.

6 Press Return.

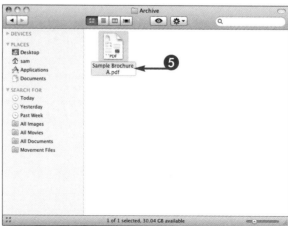

● The file takes on the new name.

You can now open the file by double-clicking it or pressing ⌘+O, or rename another file or folder.

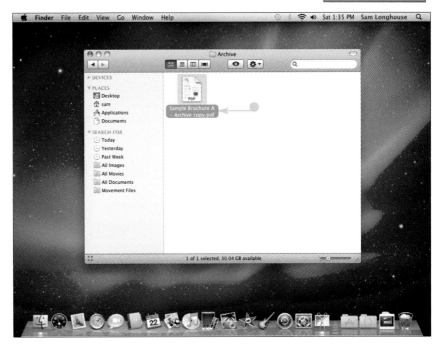

 TIPS

Can I rename any file or folder in Mac OS X?

You can rename many items within your Home folder. It is best not to rename the folders that Mac OS X creates for you, such as Desktop, Documents, Downloads, and Library, but you can freely rename any folders you create. In addition, you can safely rename your iMac's hard disk, but do not rename any of the system folders. For example, do not rename the Applications folder, the System folder, the Users folder, or your Home folder, because renaming these folders may cause Mac OS X problems.

Can I rename several files at once?

There is no convenient way to rename several files at once from the Finder manually. Each file in a folder must have a unique name, so you cannot apply the same name to two or more files at once. Some applications and scripts have features for renaming multiple files at once, usually by giving them sequential names using numbers appended to a base name — for example, Photo01, Photo02, Photo03, and so on.

View the Information about a File or Folder

When you click a file or folder in a Finder window, the Finder displays its file name in all views. In all views but Icon view, the Finder displays basic information, such as the file's kind, size, and date last modified. To see extra information about the file or folder, and to add information, you can open the Info window.

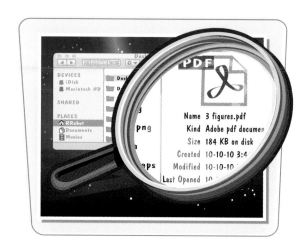

View the Information about a File or Folder

① Click **Finder** (🖼) on the Dock.

② In the Finder window, open the folder that contains the file whose info you want to view.

③ Click the file.

④ Click **⚙▾**.

⑤ Click **Get Info**.

The Info window for the file opens.

Note: *The Info window has several sections. You can expand each section by clicking ▶ or collapse it by clicking ▼.*

⑥ Click ▶ next to General.

⑦ Review the general information for the file:

Kind shows the file's type. *Size* shows the file's size on disk. *Where* shows the folder that contains the file. *Created* shows when the file was created. *Modified* shows when the file was last changed.

⑧ Click ▶ next to Spotlight Comments.

⑨ To make the file easier to find with Spotlight, type keywords in the Spotlight Comments field.

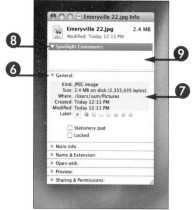

⓾ Click ▸ next to Open With.

The Open With area appears.

⓫ To change the application with which this file opens when you double-click it in the Finder, click ⬍, and then click the application.

⓬ Click ▸ next to Preview.

The Preview area appears, and you can see a preview of the file.

⓭ Click ▸ next to Sharing & Permissions.

The Sharing & Permissions area appears.

⓮ If necessary, click 🔒, type your password, and then change the permissions.

Note: *Normally, it is best not to change the permissions Mac OS X has set for a file.*

⓯ Click ⊗.

The Info window closes.

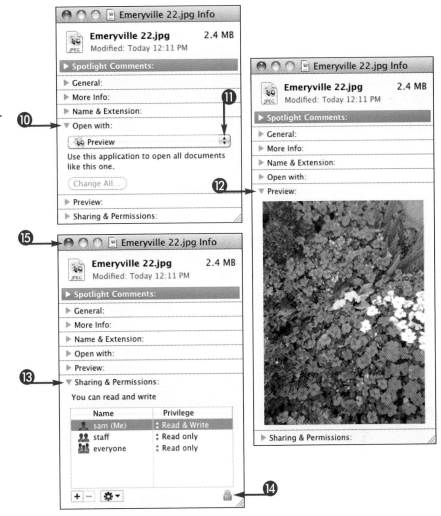

 TIPS

What does the Locked setting in the Info pane do?

You can click **Locked** (☐ changes to ☑) in the General section of the Info window to lock the file against changes. When someone tries to save changes to the file, a dialog opens to warn him that the file is locked. The user can overwrite the lock, so locking provides only modest protection against changes.

What does the More Info section of the Info window contain?

The information in the More Info section (●) of the Info window depends on the type of file or folder you have selected. For example, the More Info section for a photo contains details of the photo's dimensions, the make and model of the camera that took the photos, and the aperture used for the lens.

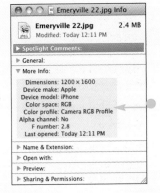

Compress Files for Easy Transfer

To transfer files faster and more easily across the Internet, or to fit more files onto a CD, DVD, or removable disk, you can compress the files. Compressing creates a compressed file in the widely used zip format, often called a "zip file," that contains a copy of the files. The original files remain unchanged in their folder.

Compress Files to a Zip File

① Click **Finder** (⌘) on the Dock.

A Finder window opens to your default folder.

② Open the folder that contains the file or files you want to compress.

③ Select the file or files.

④ Click ⚙▾.

The Action pop-up menu opens.

⑤ Click **Compress**.

● The compressed file appears in the folder.

Note: *If you selected one file, Mac OS X gives the file the same name with .zip added to the end. If you selected two or more files, Mac OS X names the zip file Archive.zip.*

⑥ If you want to rename the file, click it and press Return.

An edit box opens around the file name.

⑦ Type the new name and press Return.

The file takes on the new name.

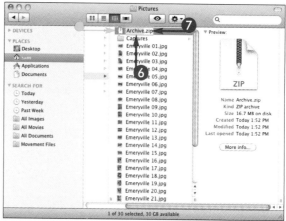

Extract Files from a Zip File

1 Open a Finder window to the folder that contains the zip file.

Note: If you receive the zip file attached to an e-mail message, save the file as explained in Chapter 6.

2 Double-click the zip file.

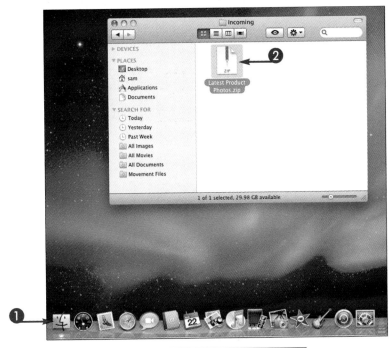

Archive Utility unzips the zip file, creates a folder with the same name as the zip file, and places the contents of the zip file in it.

3 Double-click the new folder to see the files from the zip file.

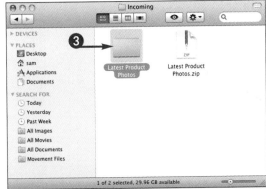

TIPS

Can I exchange zip files with Windows users?

The zip file is a standard format used by Macs, Windows PCs, and other operating systems. This means that you can normally exchange zip files with users of Windows or other operating systems without needing to worry about compatibility.

When I compress a music file, the zip file is bigger than the original file. What have I done wrong?

You have done nothing wrong. Compression removes extra space from the file, and can squeeze some graphics down by as much as 90 percent. But if you try to compress a file that is already compressed, such as an MP3 audio file or an MPEG video file, Archive Utility cannot compress it further — and the zip file packaging adds a small amount to the file size.

Burn Files to a CD or DVD

A CD or DVD is a useful means of storing files and folders, either for transferring them to another computer or keeping a copy as a backup. Mac OS X enables you to easily copy files and folders to a CD or DVD. The process of creating a CD or DVD is called *burning*.

Burn Files to a CD or DVD

① Insert a blank CD or blank DVD in your iMac's optical drive.

A dialog opens asking what you want to do with the disc.

Note: *If you always want to burn this type of disc using the Finder, click **Make this action the default** (☐ changes to ☑).*

② Click ⬍.

The Action pop-up menu opens.

③ Click **Open Finder**.

④ Click **OK**.

The blank CD or blank DVD appears on your desktop.

⑤ Double-click the icon for the CD or DVD.

● A Finder window opens showing the CD's or DVD's contents — nothing so far.

⑥ Choose **Finder** and **New Finder window**.

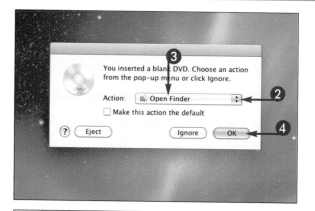

⑦ Position the new Finder windows so that you can see both of them.

⑧ Drag files from the new Finder window to the CD or DVD window.

Note: *When you drag files to the CD or DVD, Mac OS X adds aliases, or shortcuts, to the files. It does not add the files to the CD or DVD yet.*

⑨ Click **Burn**.

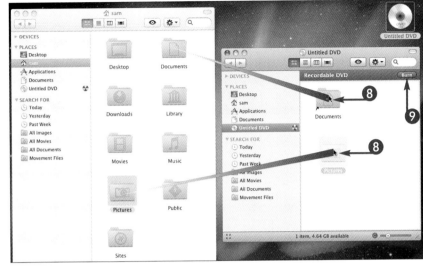

A dialog opens.

⑩ Type a name.

⑪ Click ⬩ and choose the speed at which to burn the disc.

Note: *The Maximum Possible speed is usually the best choice.*

⑫ Click **Burn**.

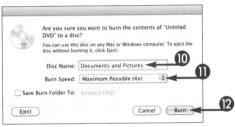

The iMac starts burning the CD or DVD.

The Burn dialog shows you the progress of the burn.

When the burn has completed, your iMac ejects the disc.

Note: *Before labeling and storing the disc, it is a good idea to reinsert it in your iMac and check that the disc's contents are as you intended them to be.*

 TIPS

Should I use a CD or a DVD for my files?

Use a CD when you have only a modest amount of data to store. Most recordable CDs can hold 650 MB or 700 MB. Use a DVD when you need to store more data than this. A single-layer DVD holds 4.7GB, whereas a dual-layer DVD holds 9.4GB.

Is it better to use rewriteable discs or single-use discs?

Use single-use recordable discs when you want to make a permanent copy of data — for example, on a backup that you intend to keep indefinitely. Use rewriteable discs for data you plan to store for only a short time. For example, if you back up documents to DVD each day, keep a rewriteable DVD for each day of the week.

Erase a CD or DVD

After you have burned a rewriteable CD or DVD, you can erase its contents so that you can use the disc again. To erase a rewriteable disc like this, you use the Disk Utility tool, which also works with hard disks and removable disks.

Erase a CD or DVD

1 Insert the CD or DVD in your iMac's optical drive.

● The CD or DVD appears on your desktop.

2 Click the desktop.

The Finder becomes active.

3 Choose **Go** and **Utilities**.

A Finder window opens showing the Utilities folder.

4 Press and hold **Option** and double-click **Disk Utility**.

Note: *Pressing and holding down* **Option** *while you double-click a file makes the Finder window close when the file opens.*

The Finder window closes and Disk Utility opens.

5 Click the CD or DVD in the sidebar.

6 Click **Erase**.

The Erase pane opens.

7 If the disc has not been working normally, click **Completely** (○ changes to ◉). Otherwise, leave **Quickly** selected.

8 Click **Erase**.

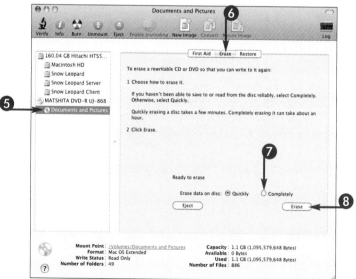

A dialog opens to confirm that
you want to erase the disc.

9 Click **Erase**.

● Disk Utility erases the disc and
shows a readout of its progress.

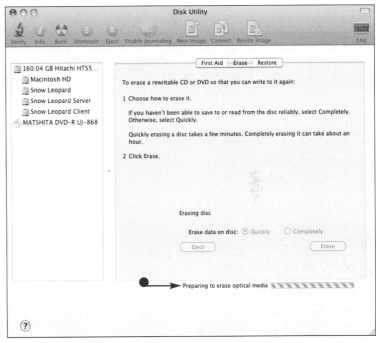

When Disk Utility finishes erasing
the disc, a dialog opens.

10 Click ⬍ and choose the
application to open. For example,
choose **Open Finder** if you want
to burn files to the disc.

11 Click **OK**.

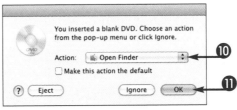

How many times can I reuse a rewriteable CD or DVD?
You should be able to reuse a rewriteable CD or DVD several dozen times
before needing to replace it. However, if the disc suffers wear and tear, or
if it is several years old, it is better to err on the side of caution and
replace the disc. Similarly, if the disc gives errors but is not scratched, try
using the Completely option in Disk Utility to erase it thoroughly and
make it work properly again — but if your data is valuable, it is safer to
replace the disc instead.

Throw a File in the Trash

When you do not need a file any more, you can throw it in the Trash. The Trash is a special folder in which Mac OS X keeps files and folders you intend to dispose of.

Like a real-world trash can, the Trash retains files until you actually empty it. So if you find you have thrown away a file that you need after all, you can recover the file from the Trash.

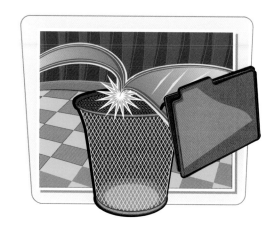

Throw a File in the Trash

Throw a File in the Trash

1 Click **Finder** (🖥️) on the Dock.

A Finder window opens to your default folder.

2 Open the folder that contains the file you want to throw in the Trash.

3 Click ⚙️.

The Action pop-up menu opens.

4 Click **Move to Trash**.

● The file disappears from the folder and moves to the Trash.

Note: *You can also throw a file in the Trash by clicking and dragging it to the Trash icon on the Dock. From the keyboard, press* ⌘ + Delete.

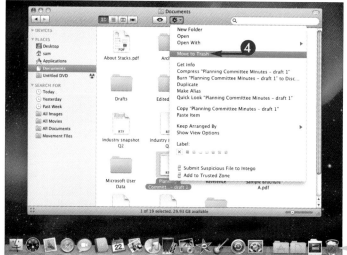

Recover a File from the Trash

① Click **Trash** on the Dock.

The Trash window opens.

② Choose **File** and **New Finder window**.

Note: If you want to restore the file to the folder it was in, you do not need to open a new Finder window. Just click the file in the Trash and then choose **File** and **Put Back**.

A new Finder window opens.

③ Open the folder to which you want to restore the file or files.

④ Position the Finder windows so that you can see both the Trash and the destination folder.

⑤ Select the file or files in the Trash.

⑥ Click and drag the file or files from the Trash to the destination folder.

You can now work with the file again.

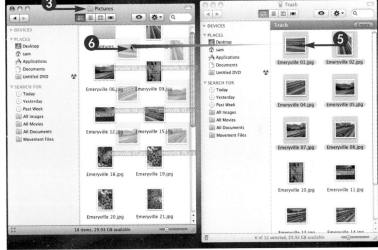

TIPS

When and how do I get rid of the Trash?

You can empty the Trash at any time you find convenient. Chapter 15 shows you how to empty the Trash. Unless you need to dispose of sensitive files immediately, it is normally a good idea to leave files in the Trash until you are certain that you never need them again.

What else do I need to know about the Trash?

When you click a CD, DVD, or removable disk and drag it toward the Trash, the Trash icon changes to an Eject icon (⏏). Drop the item on the Eject icon to eject it. When you click and drag a recordable CD or DVD to which you have added files toward the Trash, Mac OS X displays a Burn icon (☢). Drop the disc on the Burn icon to start burning it.

Surfing the Web with Safari

If your iMac is connected to the Internet, you can browse or *surf* the sites on the World Wide Web. For surfing, Mac OS X provides the Safari browser, which enables you to quickly move from one Web page to another, search for interesting sites, and download files to your iMac.

Open and Close Safari..98

Open a Web Page...100

Follow a Link to a Web Page..........................101

Open Several Web Pages at Once...............102

Find Your Way from One Page to
    Another..104

Return to a Recently Visited Page...............106

Change the Page Safari Opens at First......108

Keep Bookmarks for Web Pages
    You Like..110

Find Interesting Web Sites.............................112

Download a File from the Internet.............114

Keep Up to Date with News Feeds.............116

Choose Essential Security Settings.............118

Open and Close Safari

To start surfing the Web, you open the Safari browser.

Open and Close Safari

Open Safari

1 Click **Safari** () on the Dock.

Note: *If the Safari icon does not appear on the Dock, click the desktop. Choose **Go** and **Applications**, and then double-click the Safari icon in the Applications folder.*

The Safari window opens and shows your default page.

Note: *The default page may be the Top Sites page, which shows the pages you have visited most recently, your home page, or another page.*

You can then browse to another page as explained later in this chapter.

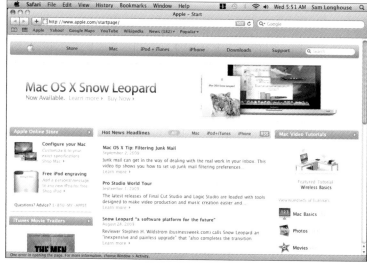

Close Safari

1 Click **Safari**.

The Safari menu opens.

2 Click **Quit Safari**.

The Safari window closes.

TIPS

Are there quicker ways of opening and closing Safari?

The quickest way to launch Safari is to have your iMac launch it when you log in. Control-click or right-click **Safari** ( ) on the Dock, highlight **Options**, and then click **Open at Login**. Mac OS X puts a check mark next to this option to show it is on. To quit Safari quickly, press + when Safari is active.

Can I use other another Web browser instead of Safari?

Safari is a fast and responsive browser, but you can use another Web browser instead if you prefer. The next most popular browser for Macs is Firefox, which you can download for free from www.mozilla.com. Camino, free from www.caminobrowser.org, is another fast and easy-to-use browser for Macs.

Open a Web Page

Each Web page has a unique address called a *uniform resource locator* or *URL*. The most straightforward way to go to a particular Web page is by typing its URL into the address box in Safari.

This technique works well for short addresses but is slow and awkward for complex addresses.

Open a Web Page

① In Safari, triple-click anywhere in the address box.

Safari selects all of the current address.

Note: *If you find triple-clicking difficult, press* ⌘ *+* L *to select the whole address.*

② Type the URL of the Web page you want to visit.

Note: *You do not need to type in the http:// part of the address. Safari adds this automatically for you when you press* Return.

③ Press Return.

Safari opens the Web page and displays its contents.

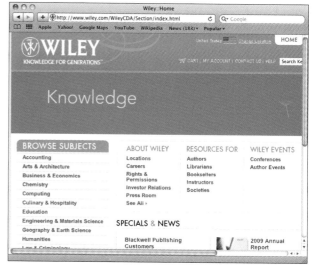

Once you have opened a page in Safari, you can use the easier way of navigating to a Web page: Clicking a link on a page to go to another page.

Most Web pages contain links to other pages. Some links are underlined, whereas others are attached to graphics or to different-colored text. When you position the mouse pointer over a link, it changes from ▶ to ☝.

Follow a Link to a Web Page

① In Safari, position the mouse pointer over a link (▶ changes to ☝).

● The address of the linked Web page appears in the status bar.

*Note: If the Safari window is not showing the status bar, choose **View** and **Show Status Bar** to display it.*

② Click the link.

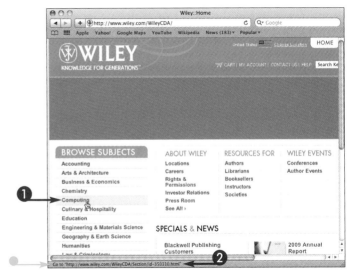

Safari shows the linked Web page.

● The address of the linked Web page appears in the address box.

Open Several Web Pages at Once

To browse quickly and easily, you can open multiple Web pages at the same time. In Safari, you can open multiple pages on separate tabs in the same window or in separate windows.

Use separate tabs when you need to see only one of the pages at a time. Use separate windows when you need to compare two pages side by side.

Open Several Web Pages at Once

Open Several Pages on Tabs in the Same Safari Window

1. Go to the first page you want to view.

Note: *You can also click **Add** (✱) or press ⌘ + T to open a new tab showing your default page. Type a URL in the address box, and then press* Return *to go to the page.*

2. Control-click or right-click a link.

   The shortcut menu opens.

3. Click **Open Link in New Tab**.

● Safari opens the linked Web page in a new tab.

Note: *You can now repeat steps **2** and **3** to open further pages on separate tabs.*

4. To change the page Safari displays, click the tab for the page you want to see.

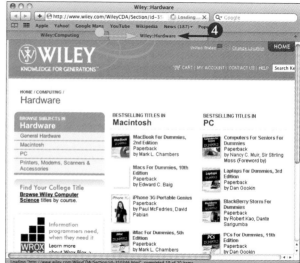

Open Several Pages in Separate Safari Windows

1. Go to the first page you want to view.

2. **Control**-click or right-click a link.

   The shortcut menu opens.

3. Click **Open Link in New Window**.

Note: *You can also open a new window by pressing ⌘+N.*

● Safari opens the linked Web page in a new window.

4. To move back to the previous window, click it.

Note: *You can also move back to the previous window by closing the new window you just opened.*

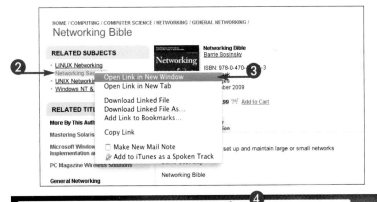

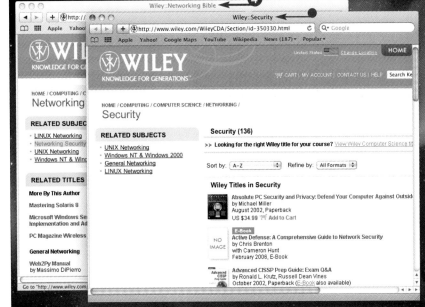

Can I change the way that Safari tabs and windows behave?

Choose **Safari** and **Preferences** to open the Preferences window, and then click **Tabs** (○). Select **⌘-click opens a link in a new tab** (☑) to use ⌘-click for opening a new tab. Select **When a new tab or window opens, make it active** (☑) if you want to switch to the new tab or window on opening it. Clear **Confirm before closing multiple tabs or windows** (☐) if you want to prevent Safari double-checking that you want to quit the application with multiple tabs or windows open. Click ⊗ to close the Preferences window.

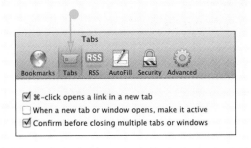

Find Your Way from One Page to Another

As you browse, Safari tracks the pages that you visit, so that the pages form a path. You can go back along this path to return to a page you viewed earlier; after going back, you can go forward again as needed.

Safari keeps a separate path of pages in each open tab or window, so you can move separately in each.

Find Your Way from One Page to Another

Go Back One Page

① Click **Previous Page** (◀).

Safari displays the previous page you visited in the current tab or window.

Go Forward One Page

① Click **Next Page** (▶).

Note: The Next Page button is available only when you have gone back. Until then, there is no page for you to go forward to.

Safari displays the next page for the current tab or window.

Go Back Multiple Pages

1 Click **Previous Page** (◀) and keep holding down the mouse button.

A pop-up menu opens showing the pages you have visited in the current tab or window.

2 Click the page you want to display.

Safari displays the page.

Go Forward Multiple Pages

1 Click **Next Page** (▶) and keep holding down the mouse button.

A pop-up menu opens showing the pages further along the path for the current tab or window.

2 Click the page you want to display.

Safari displays the page.

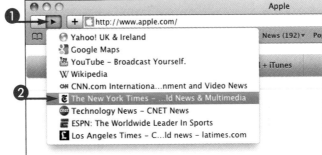

TIP

Can I navigate from page to page, or tab to tab, by using the keyboard?
You can use the following keyboard shortcuts to move quickly from page to page and from tab to tab in Safari:

- Press ⌘ + [to display the previous page.
- Press ⌘ +] to display the next page.
- Press ⌘ + Shift + H to display your home page.
- Press ⌘ + Shift + [to display the previous tab.
- Press ⌘ + Shift +] to display the next tab.
- Press ⌘ + W to close the current tab and display the previous tab. If the window has no tabs, this command closes the window.
- Press ⌘ + Shift + W to close the current window and display the previous window, if there is one.

Return to a Recently Visited Page

To help you return to Web pages you have visited before, Safari keeps a History list of all the pages you have visited recently.

If you share a user account with other people, you can clear the History list to prevent them from seeing what Web pages you have visited. You can also shorten the length of time for which History tracks your visits.

Return to a Recently Visited Page

Return to a Page on the History List

1 In Safari, click **History**.

The History menu opens.

2 Highlight or click the day on which you visited the Web page.

Note: If the item for the Web page you want appears on the top section of the History menu, before the day submenus, simply click the item.

The submenu opens, showing the sites you visited on that day.

3 Click the Web page to which you want to return.

Safari displays the Web page.

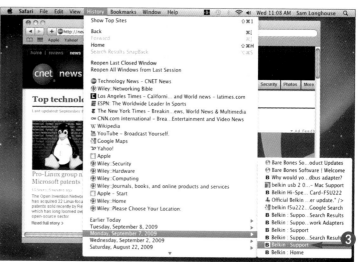

Clear Your Browsing History

① Click History.

The History menu opens.

② Click Clear History.

The Are You Sure You Want to Clear History? dialog opens.

③ Click Also reset Top Sites (☐ changes to ☑) if you want to reset the list of sites you visit most frequently.

④ Click Clear.

Safari clears the History list.

What does the Show All History command do?

Choose **History** and **Show All History** to open a History window for browsing and searching the sites you have visited. Type a term in the search box (●) to search. Below the previews (●), click **Previous** (◀) to bring the previous page to the front, or click **Next** (▶) to bring the next page to the front. Drag the scroll bar to move quickly through the history pages. Click a page in the Bookmark list (●) to bring it to the front. Double-click a page to open it.

Change the Page
Safari Opens at First

When you launch Safari, it automatically opens a page called your *home page*, the page from which it is set to start. Safari also opens your home page each time you open a new window.

You can set your home page to any Web page you want by using the technique explained here.

Change the Page Safari Opens at First

1 In Safari, navigate to the Web page that you want to make your home page.

2 Click **Safari**.

The Safari menu opens.

3 Click **Preferences**.

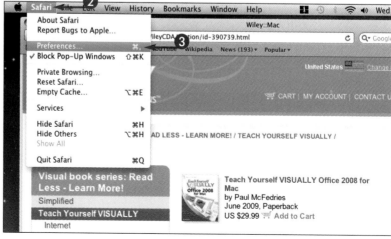

The Preferences window opens.

④ Click **General**.

The General pane opens.

⑤ Click **Set to Current Page**.

Safari changes the Home Page text field to show the page you chose.

⑥ Optionally, choose other General preferences as discussed in the tip.

⑦ Click .

The Preferences window closes.

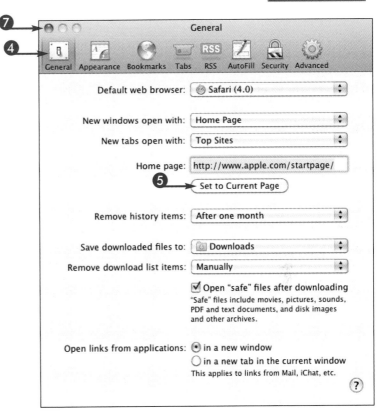

Are there other General preferences I can benefit from changing?

In the New Windows Open With pop-up menu (●), choose what you want new windows to show. A good choice is **Empty Page** because you can then choose the History item or bookmark you want. You can also choose **Same Page** if you want a new window showing the same page that your current window shows. The New Tabs Open With pop-up menu (●) gives you similar choices for what you see when you open a new tab. The Remove History Items pop-up menu (●) lets you tell Safari when to delete History items: **After one day**, **After one week**, **After two weeks**, **After one month**, **After one year**, or **Manually** (when you choose **History** and **Clear History**).

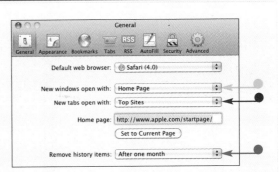

Keep Bookmarks for Web Pages You Like

History is handy for revisiting Web pages, but you can also create markers called *bookmarks* for sites you want to revisit. The advantage of bookmarks over History is that you can organize your bookmarks and put the ones you use most frequently on the Bookmarks bar so that you can access them with a single click.

Keep Bookmarks for Web Pages You Like

Create a New Bookmark

1. In Safari, navigate to a Web page you want to bookmark.

2. Click **Bookmarks**.

   The Bookmarks menu opens.

3. Click **Add Bookmark**.

   The Add Bookmark dialog opens, with the Web page's title added to the upper box.

4. Type a new name for the bookmark if you want.

5. Click ▣.

   The pop-up menu opens.

6. Click the location or folder in which to store the bookmark.

7. Click **Add**.

   Safari closes the Add Bookmark dialog and adds the bookmark to the location or folder you chose.

Organize Your Bookmarks

1. Click **Show All Bookmarks** (▭).

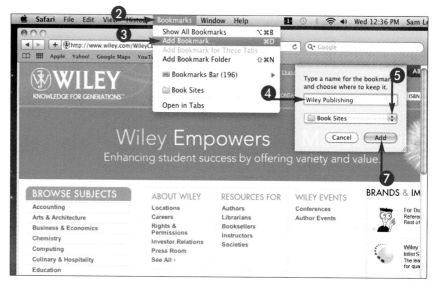

Safari opens a list of all your bookmarks.

② Click the bookmarks collection you want to organize.

Note: *The Bookmarks bar collection contains the bookmarks that appear on the Bookmarks bar below the address bar.*

③ Click **Add** (⊞).

Safari adds a new bookmarks folder to the list.

④ Type the name for the new folder and press Return .

⑤ Click and drag a bookmark to the new folder.

Note: *You can click and drag the bookmarks folders into a different order. You can also place one folder inside another folder.*

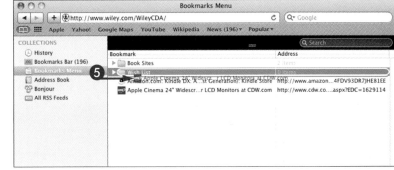

How do I go to a bookmark I have created?

If you placed the bookmark on the Bookmarks bar, click the bookmark. If you put the bookmark on the Bookmarks menu, click **Bookmarks**, and then click the bookmark on the Bookmarks menu or one of its submenus (●). Otherwise, click **Show All Bookmarks**, locate the bookmark, and then double-click it.

Find Interesting Web Sites

Perhaps the best aspect of the Web is that you can search it for exactly the information you need.

Safari has a built-in search capability for searching with Google, the Internet's biggest search engine. You can also open a different search engine and search from it.

Find Interesting Web Sites

Search with the Built-in Google Search Feature

① Click in the search box.

② Type keywords, a phrase, or a whole question into the search box.

③ Press Return.

Safari displays a page of search results from the Google search engine.

④ Click a link to open a Web page.

The Web page opens.

Note: When examining search results, it is often useful to Control *-click or right-click a link and choose* **Open in New Tab** *or* **Open in New Window***. This way, the page of search results remains open, and you can follow other linked results as needed.*

Search with a Search Engine other than Google

1 Triple-click in the address box to select the current address.

2 Type the address of the search engine you want to use.

Note: Other search engines include Microsoft's Bing (www.bing.com), Yahoo! (www.yahoo.com), and Cuil (www.cuil.com).

3 Press Return.

Safari displays the search engine you chose.

4 Click in the search box.

5 Type the terms for which you want to search.

6 Press Return or click the **Search** button (🔍).

The site displays a page of search results.

7 Click a link you want to open.

Safari opens the linked Web page.

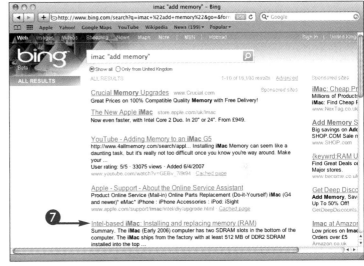

How can I get more useful search results?
Here are three ways to make your search results more accurate and helpful:

- To keep two words together as a phrase instead of searching for them separately, put them in double quotes. For example, use "add memory" to search for that phrase rather than for add and for memory separately.

- To exclude a word from a search, put a – sign before it. For example, – g5 tells Google not to return search results that include the term "G5."

- To make sure each search result includes a particular term, put a + sign before it. For example, +upgrade tells Google to return only search results that include the term "upgrade."

SEARCH TIPS

Download a File from the Internet

Many Web sites contain files that you can download and use on your iMac. For example, you can download applications to install on your iMac, pictures to view on it, or songs to play.

Mac OS X includes applications that can open many file types, including music, graphic, movie, document, and PDF files. To open other file types, you may need to install extra applications.

① In Safari, go to the Web page that contains the link for the file you want to download.

② Click the link.

● Safari starts the download and opens the Downloads window to show its progress.

③ When the download is complete, `Control`-click or right-click the file in the Downloads window.

The shortcut menu opens.

④ Click **Open**.

Note: *Depending on the file type and the preferences you have set, Safari may open the file automatically for you.*

The file opens.

Depending on the file type, you can then work with the file, enjoy its contents, or install it.

Note: *If the file is an application, you can install it as discussed in Chapter 3. If the file is a data file, such as a document or a picture, Mac OS X opens the file in the application for that file type.*

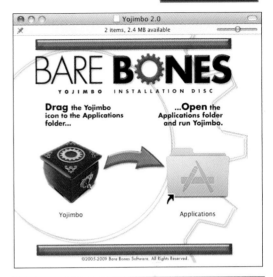

⑤ If the file disappears from the Downloads window and Safari does not open the file for you, click **Downloads** on the Dock.

The Downloads stack opens.

⑥ Click the file you downloaded.

The file opens.

Can downloading files from the Internet be dangerous to my iMac?

Files available on the Internet for download can contain software that attempts to attack your iMac or compromise your privacy. For safety, download files only from Web sites that you trust, and use antivirus software as discussed in Chapter 14.

What should I do when clicking a download link opens the file instead of downloading it?

Control-click or right-click the link, and then click **Download Linked File** (●). To save the file in a different folder or under a different name of your choice, click **Download Linked File As**. Safari opens a dialog in which you can choose the folder and file name.

Keep Up to Date with News Feeds

If you like to keep up to the minute with what is happening, use Safari's news feeds to bring you the latest news. The news feeds use a technology called Really Simple Syndication, or RSS, to enable you to subscribe to Web sites and to receive the latest information when it becomes available.

Open a News Feed from Safari

1 In Safari, click **News**.

The News pop-up menu opens.

2 Click **View All RSS Articles**.

Safari displays a page showing the headlines of the available articles.

3 Click and drag the **Article Length** slider if you want to change the amount of information displayed for each article.

4 Click the article you want to read.

Safari opens the article.

Note: To find articles on a particular topic, click in the Search Articles box and type one or more keywords.

Open a News Feed from a Web Site

1 On a page that shows the RSS button (RSS) in the address box, click the button.

If multiple news feeds are available, a menu opens.

2 Click the news feed you want.

Safari opens the news feed.

3 Click the article you want to read.

Note: You can bookmark a news feed by choosing **Bookmarks** *and* **Add Bookmark**.

 TIP

How can I get the latest news feeds in Safari?
Choose **Safari** and **Preferences**. The Preferences window opens. Click **RSS** (●) to display the RSS pane. In the Automatically Update Articles In area, select **Bookmarks bar** (☑) to update news feeds on the Bookmarks bar or **Bookmarks menu** (☑) to update news feeds on the Bookmarks menu. Click ⬍ next to **Check for updates** and choose how often to check for updates — **Every 30 minutes**, **Every hour**, or **Every day**. Click ⬤ to close the Preferences window.

Choose Essential Security Settings

The Web is packed with fascinating sites and useful information, but it is also full of criminals who want to attack your iMac and steal your valuable data.

Safari comes with several important security settings. It is a good idea to make sure all the protective settings you need are turned on.

Choose Essential Security Settings

① Click **Safari**.

The Safari menu opens.

② Click **Preferences**.

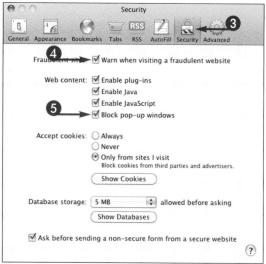

The Preferences window opens.

③ Click **Security**.

The Security pane opens.

④ Make sure that **Warn when visiting a fraudulent website** is checked (☑).

⑤ Make sure that **Block pop-up windows** is checked (☑).

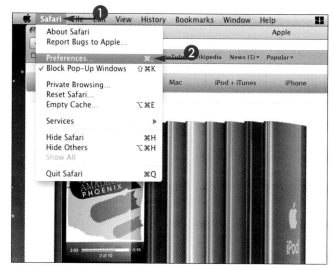

⑥ In the Accept Cookies area, click **Only from sites I visit** (○ changes to ⦿).

⑦ Make sure that **Ask before sending a non-secure form from a secure website** is checked (☑).

⑧ Click **AutoFill**.

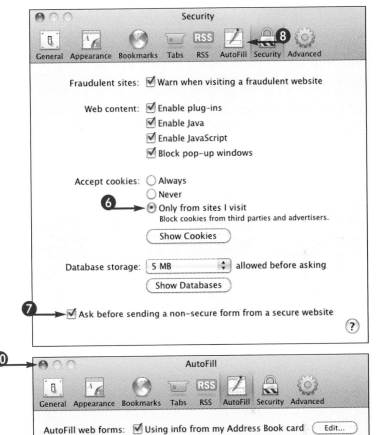

The AutoFill pane opens.

⑨ Make sure that **User names and passwords** is cleared (☐).

⑩ Click ⊗.

The Preferences window closes.

Should I allow pop-up windows for certain Web sites?

Pop-up windows can be dangerous. Some shopping sites need pop-up windows to function properly, but many malicious Web sites use pop-up windows to distribute malevolent software. For safety, keep pop-up windows blocked until you know a particular site requires them. Then choose **Safari** and **Block Pop-up Windows** to temporarily allow pop-ups, removing the check mark from the command. When you have finished, click the command again to restore the blocking.

What are cookies, and should I accept them?

A *cookie* is a small text file that a Web site uses to store information about what you do on the site — for example, what products you have browsed or added to your shopping cart. Cookies from sites you visit are usually helpful to you. Cookies from third-party sites, such as those that advertise on sites you visit, may threaten your privacy. For this reason, choose **Only from sites I visit** rather than **Always** in the Accept Cookies area.

Sending and Receiving E-mail and Files

Your iMac includes Apple Mail, a powerful but easy-to-use e-mail application. After setting up an e-mail account, you can send and receive not only e-mail messages but also files across the Internet. Mail also includes features for creating notes and to-do items.

Open and Close Apple Mail 122

Set Up Your E-mail Account 124

Send an E-mail Message 126

Get Your Messages and Read Them 128

Reply to a Message 130

Send a Message on to Someone Else 132

Send a File via E-mail 134

Receive a File via E-mail 136

Get Your E-mail on Any Computer 138

Create Notes 140

Create To-Do Items 142

Reduce the Amount of Spam
    You Receive 144

Open and Close Apple Mail

To use Mail, you must first open the application either from the Dock or from your iMac's Applications folder.

Unless you entered your e-mail account information when setting up Mac OS X, you must set up an e-mail account the first time you open Mail. See the next two pages for details of the setup process.

Open Mail

1 Click **Mail** () on the Dock.

Note: *If Mail does not appear on the Dock, click the desktop, and then choose **Go** and **Applications**. In the Finder window that opens, double-click **Mail**.*

The Mail window opens.

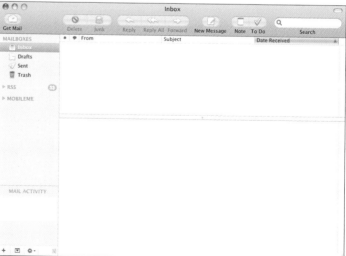

Close Mail

① Click **Mail**.

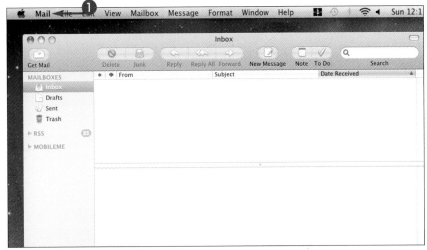

The Mail menu opens.

② Click **Quit Mail**.

Mail closes.

TIPS

How can I make my iMac open Mail automatically for me?

You can make your iMac open Mail automatically each time you log in. To do so, Control-click or right-click the **Mail** icon (▨) on the Dock, highlight or click **Options**, and then click **Open at Login** (●). Mac OS X puts a check mark next to Open at Login. Next time you log in, Mail opens automatically.

Is it okay to leave Mail running all the time?

Many people like to leave Mail running all the time that they are using their Macs. If you set Mail to check automatically for new messages, you receive the messages soon after they reach your ISP's mail server. The disadvantage to keeping Mail running is that new messages may distract you from your other tasks.

Set Up Your E-mail Account

Unless you gave the Mac Setup Assistant your account information while setting up Mac OS X, you must set up Mail with your e-mail account. Mail works with most types of e-mail account, including Apple's MobileMe service and industry-standard POP mail servers and IMAP mail servers.

To set up your account, you need to know your e-mail address and password. You may also need to know the addresses and types of your provider's mail servers.

Set Up Your E-mail Account

① Click **Mail** (🖾) on the Dock.

The first time you open Mail, the Welcome to Mail assistant opens to its first screen.

*Note: If you have already set up an e-mail account, open the Add Account dialog by choosing **File** and **Add Account** and follow the remaining steps.*

② Change the name if necessary. Mail uses your Mac OS X account name.

③ Type your e-mail address.

④ Type your e-mail account password and click **Continue**.

Note: If you are setting up a MobileMe e-mail account, you need provide no further information.

⑤ In the Incoming Mail Server screen, click the **Account Type** 🔽 and choose the account type; this example uses **POP**.

⑥ Type a name for this e-mail account.

*Note: See the tips for more information on steps **5** and **6**.*

⑦ Type the name of your provider's incoming mail server.

⑧ Check your user name and password and click **Continue**.

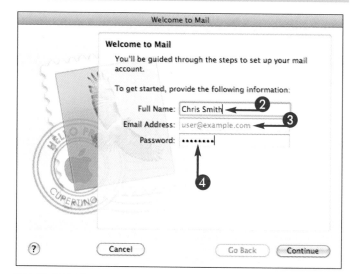

⑨ In the Incoming Mail Security screen, make sure that **Use Secure Sockets Layer (SSL)** is checked (☑) if your ISP uses SSL.

⑩ Click the **Authentication** 🔽 and choose the authentication for receiving messages, usually **Password**, and click **Continue**.

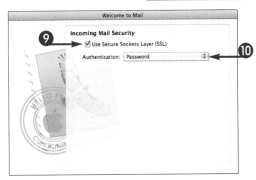

⑪ In the Outgoing Mail Server screen, type a name for this outgoing server.

⑫ Type the server address.

⑬ If your provider requires authentication for sending messages, click **Use Authentication** (☐ changes to ☑). Type your e-mail user name and password and click **Continue**.

⑭ In the Outgoing Mail Security screen, click **Use Secure Sockets Layer (SSL)** (☐ changes to ☑) if your provider requires SSL.

⑮ Click the **Authentication** 🔽 and choose the authentication for sending messages, usually **Password**, and click **Continue**.

⑯ In the Account Summary screen, click **Continue**, and Mail sets up the e-mail account

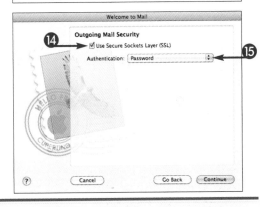

TIPS

Which account type should I choose for my incoming mail server?

If you do not know which type of e-mail server your ISP uses, check the ISP's Web site or call customer service to find out. Most ISPs use POP (Post Office Protocol) servers for incoming mail, but some use IMAP (Internet Mail Access Protocol). Exchange 2007 and Exchange IMAP are mostly used within companies rather than by ISPs that provide accounts to consumers.

POP?
IMAP?
EXCHANGE?

What should I write as a description for my incoming and outgoing mail servers?

When setting up an e-mail account, you have to type almost all the information exactly as your mail provider gives it. But in the description fields for the incoming mail server and outgoing mail server you can type any name you want. The name is to help you identify the mail servers, which becomes important when you set up more than one e-mail account.

Send an E-mail Message

After setting up an e-mail account, you can send an e-mail message to anybody whose e-mail address you know. You can either type the e-mail address directly into the message or pick it out of your Address Book.

You can create either unformatted text messages or messages that include formatting and pictures. Mail includes stationery templates for creating graphical messages.

Create and Send a Text-based E-mail Message

① In Mail, click **New Message** (🖊).

② In the message window, type the name of the recipient.

Note: To send the message to two or more recipients, type a comma after the first address, and then type the next address.

③ To send a copy of the message to another person, type the e-mail address in the Cc field.

Note: If you start typing an e-mail address that is in Address Book, Mail offers to complete the address for you.

④ Type the subject or heading of the message.

⑤ Type the body of the message.

⑥ Click **Send** (🖅).

Mail sends the message and stores a copy in your Sent folder for reference.

Create a Formatted Message Using Stationery

① With a message window open, click **Show Stationery** (🖼).

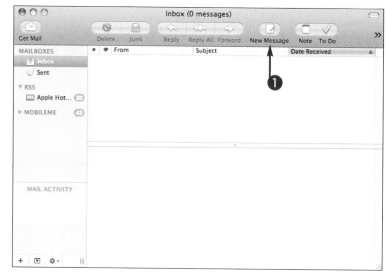

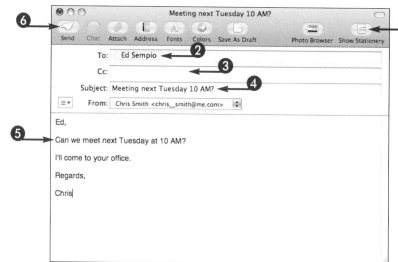

② In the Stationery pane, click a category of stationery.

③ Click a stationery design.

Mail applies the stationery design to the message.

④ Click **Hide Stationery** () to close the Stationery pane.

⑤ Type the recipient's address.

⑥ Type the subject of the message.

⑦ Replace the sample text with your own text.

Note: *You can change the font formatting of the message by clicking* **Fonts** *( ) and using the Fonts window.*

⑧ If the stationery includes photo placeholders, click **Photo Browser** ( ).

⑨ In the Photo Browser window, click and drag a photo to each placeholder.

⑩ Click to close the Photo Browser window.

⑪ Click **Send** ( ), and Mail sends the message.

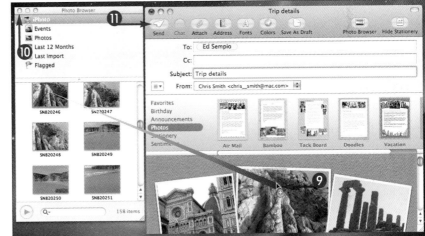

TIP

How do I send a message to many people at once?

To send the same message to many people at once, you can simply add each name to the To field. When you are sending a message to people who may not know each other, be discreet. Type your own e-mail address in the To field. Then click **Customize** ( ), and click **Bcc Address Field** ( ) on the pop-up menu. A Bcc field appears below the Cc field. Add each address to the Bcc field, and then send the message. Each recipient then sees only your address in the To field, not the addresses of the other recipients.

Get Your Messages and Read Them

When someone sends you an e-mail message, it goes to your mail provider's e-mail server. To receive the message, you make Mail connect to the e-mail server and retrieve the message.

Mail comes set to check for new messages when you launch the application and at five-minute intervals after that. You can set Mail to check at different intervals if you prefer.

Get Your Messages and Read Them

Get Your Messages from the E-mail Server

1 In Mail, click **Get Mail** ( ).

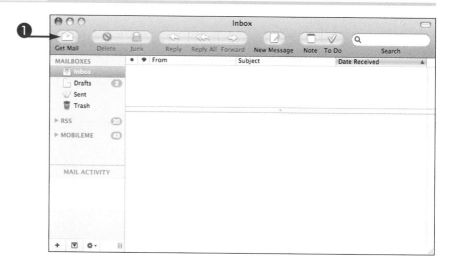

Mail connects to the e-mail server and downloads any messages.

● The Mail Activity pane shows information about incoming messages.

● The new messages appear in your Inbox.

● A blue dot indicates that you have not read a message yet.

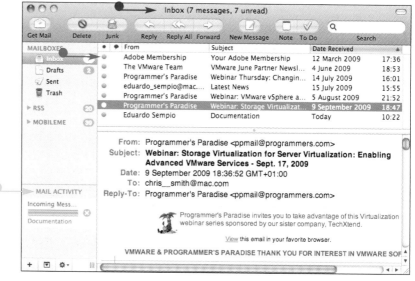

Read a Message in the Preview Pane

① Click the message in the message list.

The message's text and contents appear in the preview pane.

② Read the message.

Read a Message in a Separate Window

① Double-click the message in the message list.

A window opens showing the message.

② Read the message.

③ Click .

The message window closes.

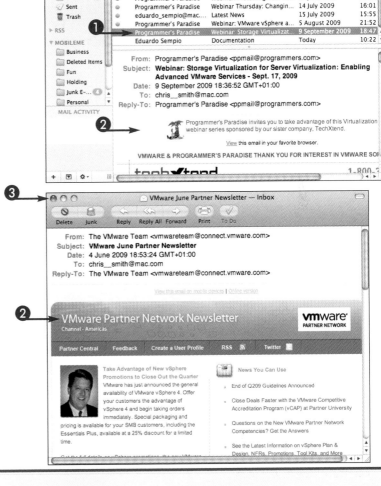

Is there an easy way to tell whether I have new messages?

If you have unread messages, the Mail icon on the Dock shows a red circle containing the number of messages (🖼). If you usually read all your e-mail messages, you can use this telltale as a quick way of checking whether you have new messages.

How can I change Mail's frequency of checking for new messages?

Choose **Mail** and **Preferences** to open the Preferences window, and then click **General**. Click ⬍ next to **Check for new messages**, and then click the interval (●): **Every minute**, **Every 5 minutes**, **Every 15 minutes**, **Every 30 minutes**, **Every hour**, or **Manually**. Click 🖼 to close the Preferences window.

Default email reader:	Mail (4.1)
	Every minute
Check for new messages	✓ Every 5 minutes ←
	Every 15 minutes
New messages sound	Every 30 minutes
	Every hour
	Manually
Dock unread count	

Reply to a Message

After reading an e-mail message you receive, you can reply to it.

If you are one of several recipients of the message, you can choose between replying only to the sender or replying to the sender and the other recipients.

① In the Inbox, click the message to which you want to reply.

Note: *You can also double-click the message to open it in a separate window.*

② Click **Reply** (　).

Note: *If the message has multiple recipients, you can click **Reply All** (　) to reply to the sender and to all the other recipients.*

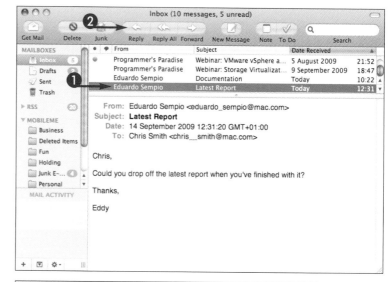

Mail creates the reply and opens it in a window.

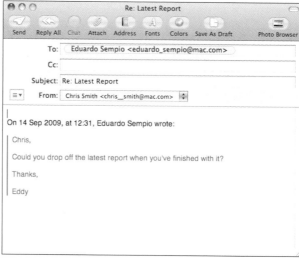

3 Type the text of your reply.

It is usually best to type your text at the beginning of the reply rather than after the message you are replying to.

Note: *You can also add other recipients to the message as needed. If you have chosen to reply to all recipients, you can also remove any recipients as necessary.*

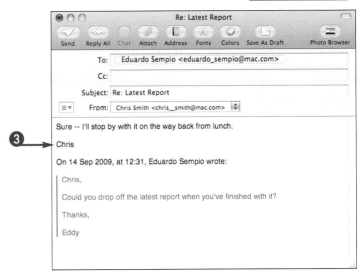

4 Click **Send** ().

Mail sends the reply and saves a copy in your Sent folder.

TIPS

Can I reply to only part of a message rather than send the whole of it?

To reply to only part of a message, select the part you want to include, and then click **Reply** ( ) or **Reply All** ( ), as appropriate. Mail creates a reply containing only the part you selected. Use this technique to keep replies concise and make them easy to read.

What are the Send Again, Redirect, and Bounce commands on the Message menu for?

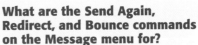

Choose **Message** and **Send Again** to send the same message again — for example, because a mail server returns it. Choose **Message** and **Redirect** if you receive a message in error; this command lets you send it on to the correct recipient, if you know who that is. Choose **Message** and **Bounce** to return a message to a sender and make it appear that your e-mail address was invalid.

Send a Message on to Someone Else

When you receive a message that you want to share with someone else, you can forward it to that person. You can add your own comments to the forwarded message — for example, to explain to the recipient who sent the original message or why you are forwarding it.

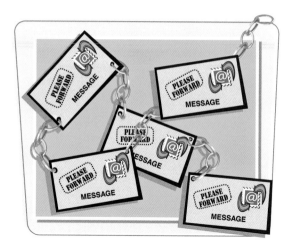

1 In the Inbox, click the message you want to forward.

The preview pane shows the contents of the message.

Note: You can also forward a message that you have opened in a separate message window.

2 Click **Forward** (⬚).

A window opens showing the forwarded message.

The subject line shows Fwd: and the message's original subject, so that the recipient can see it was forwarded.

3 Type the recipient's e-mail address.

4 Edit the subject line of the message if necessary.

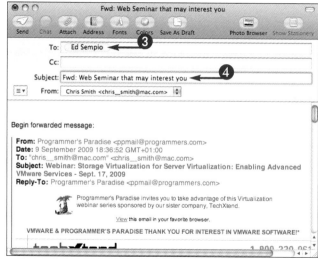

5 Optionally, edit the forwarded message to make it more useful to the recipient.

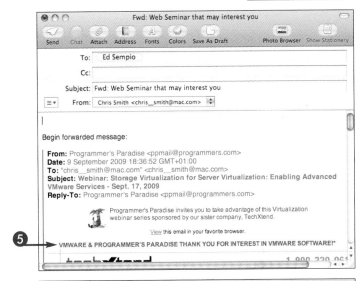

6 Type any message you want to include to the recipient.

7 Click **Send** (◌).

Mail sends the forwarded message to the recipient.

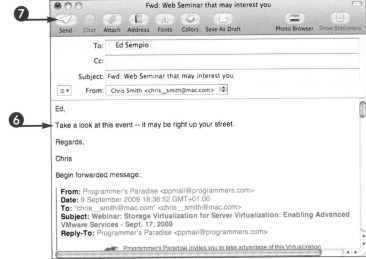

TIPS

What does the Forward as Attachment command on the Message menu do?

The Forward as Attachment command enables you to send a copy of a message as an attachment to a message rather than in the message itself. This command is useful when you want to send a forwarded message that includes formatting in a plain text message.

Can I forward only part of a message rather than all of it?

To forward only part of a message, select the part you want to forward, and then click **Forward** (◌). Mail includes only the part you selected. This trick is often quicker than creating a forwarded message containing the full text of the message and then deleting the parts you do not want to send.

Send a File via E-mail

E-mail also provides an easy way to send files to other people. You can attach one or more files to an e-mail message so that the files travel as part of the message.

You can send any kind of file, from a document to a photo or movie. The recipient can then save the file on her computer and open it.

① In Mail, click **New Message** ().

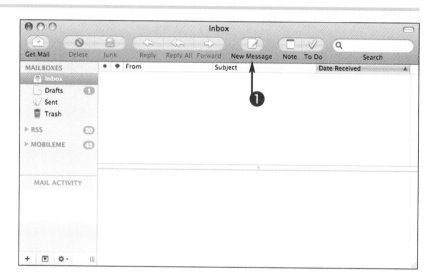

A message window opens.

② Add the recipient's name.

③ Type the subject for the message.

④ Type any message body that is needed.

⑤ Click **Attach** ().

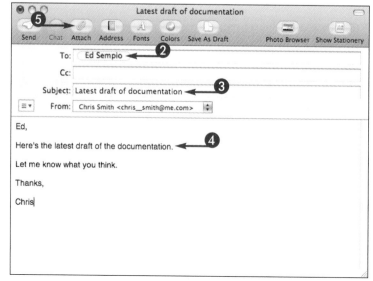

A dialog opens.

6 Click the file you want to attach to the message.

7 Click **Choose File**.

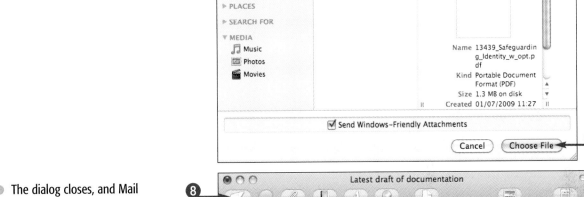

- The dialog closes, and Mail attaches the file to the message.

Note: Depending on the file type, the attachment may appear as an icon in the message or as a picture.

8 Click **Send** (📨).

Mail sends the message with the file attached.

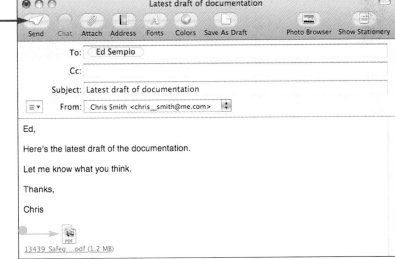

TIPS

How big a file can I attach to a message?

The size limit depends on your e-mail provider and the recipient's e-mail provider, so it is hard to determine. Generally, it is wise to limit attachments to 5MB total, either a single file or multiple files. If you need to transfer many files, use a file transfer site such as Dropbox (www. getdropbox.com) or an FTP server.

Are there other ways to attach files to a message?

You can also attach a file to a message by clicking the file in a Finder window and then dragging it to the message window (●). To attach photos from iPhoto, select the photos in iPhoto, and then click the **Email** button (📧) on the toolbar. Mail then creates a new message containing the photos.

Receive a File via E-mail

A file you receive via e-mail appears as an attachment to a message in your Inbox. You can use Quick Look to examine the file and decide whether to keep it or delete it.

To keep the file, you can save it to your iMac's hard disk. From there, you can open it in a suitable application.

① Click a message in your Inbox.

The contents of the message appear.

● The number of attachments appears below the To line.

● The attachments appear where the sender positioned them in the message.

② Click ▶ (▶ changes to ▼).

The details of the attachments appear.

③ Click **Quick Look**.

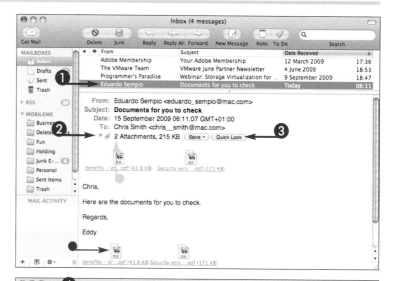

A Quick Look window shows the beginning of the first attachment.

● Click to scroll down through the attachment.

● Click to display the next attachment.

④ When you have decided whether the attachments are worth saving, click ⊗.

The Quick Look window closes.

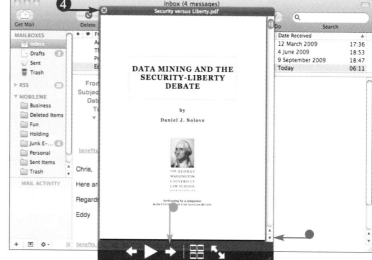

5 Click **Save** and keep pressing and holding the mouse button until the Save menu appears.

6 Click **Save All**.

Note: To save just one of the attachments, click the attachment's name. By doing this, you can save the attachments in different folders.

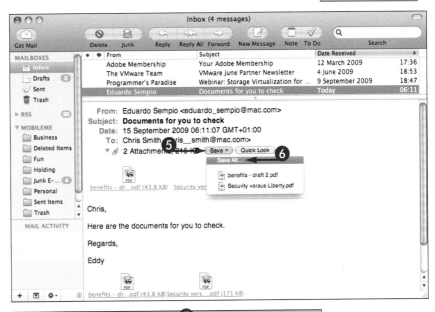

The Save As dialog opens.

7 Navigate to the folder in which you want to save the files.

8 Click **Save**.

The Save As dialog closes.

9 If you want to remove the attachments from the message, choose **Message** and **Remove Attachments**.

Note: After saving the attachments, it is a good idea to remove them from the message if you plan to keep the message. If you leave the files in the message, your mailbox can quickly grow to a large size.

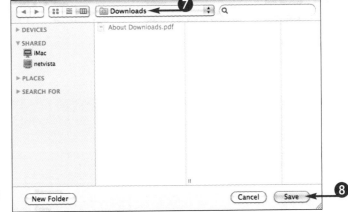

 TIPS

Do I need to check incoming files for viruses and malevolent software?

Yes, you should always check incoming files with antivirus software. Even though Mac OS X generally has fewer problems with viruses and malevolent software than Windows PCs, it is possible for a file to cause damage, steal data, or threaten your privacy.

Is there a quick way to see which messages have attachments?

In the Inbox, Control-click or right-click a column heading (●). On the shortcut menu that opens, click **Attachments**. Mail displays a column headed with a paperclip icon (✐) showing how many attachments each message has.

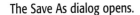

Get Your E-mail on Any Computer

If you have a subscription to Apple's MobileMe service, you can send and receive e-mail using any computer, not just your iMac. All you need is an Internet connection and a full-featured Web browser, such as Safari or Internet Explorer.

Get Your E-mail on Any Computer

Log In to MobileMe Mail and Read Your Mail

1 Open your Web browser. For example, on a Mac, click **Safari** (🧭) on the Dock.

2 Select the address in the address box. For example, in Safari, triple-click in the address box.

3 Type the address **me.com** and press Return.

The MobileMe Login page opens.

4 Type your login name.

5 Type your password.

6 Click **Log In**.

MobileMe shows your Inbox.

Note: If MobileMe shows another part of your user account, such as your photos or calendar, click **Mail** (✉).

7 Click a message header.

MobileMe displays the message's content.

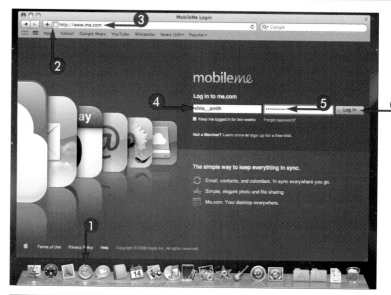

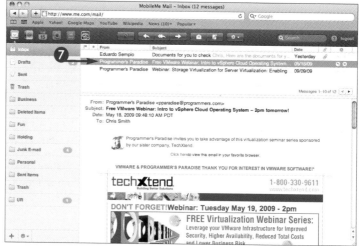

Send an E-mail Message

① Click **Compose new message** ().

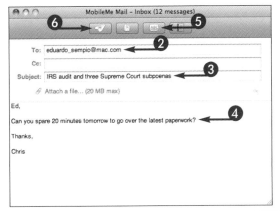

A New Message window opens.

② In the To field, type the recipient's e-mail address.

*Note: You can click **Add contacts to this message** ( ) and then choose an address from your Contacts list.*

③ Type the subject for the message.

④ Type the body text of the message.

⑤ Click **Check the spelling of this message** ( ) if you want to check your spelling.

⑥ Click **Send message** ( ).

MobileMe sends the message.

TIPS

Should I check the Keep Me Logged In for Two Weeks box when I log into MobileMe?

Check the **Keep me logged in for two weeks** check box (changes to) only when you are using one of your own Macs to access MobileMe. Using this setting on another computer increases the risk that someone else will be able to access your MobileMe mail.

✓ **Keep me logged in for two weeks**

How can I get a MobileMe account?

You can sign up for a MobileMe account either on the MobileMe Web site (www.me.com) or from System Preferences. Click , and then click **System Preferences**. In the System Preferences window, click **MobileMe** to open the MobileMe pane. Click **Learn More** to open your Web browser to the page for signing up for a 60-day free trial of MobileMe.

Create Notes

As well as e-mail messages, Mail also enables you to create notes. Notes are useful for jotting down information or for planning what you need to do.

You can paste a note's contents into another document, or you can create an e-mail from the contents of a note.

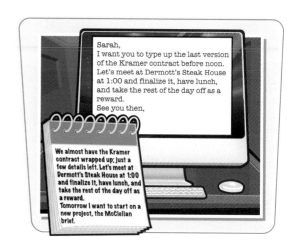

Create Notes

Create a Note

① In Mail, click **Note** (⬜).

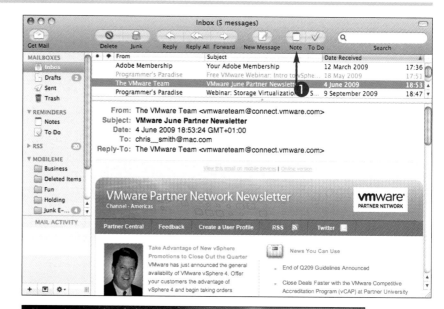

Mail opens a note window.

② Type the text of the note.

Note: *You can also paste text into the Note window.*

③ When you have finished creating the note, click **Done** (⬜).

Mail closes the note window.

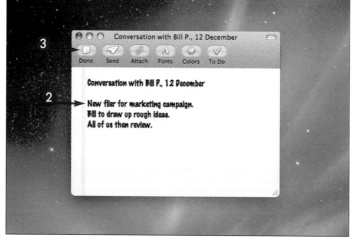

View Your Notes

1 If ▶ appears next to Reminders, click ▶ (▶ changes to ▼).

2 Click **Notes**.

The list of notes appears.

3 Click a note to display it in the preview pane, or double-click a note to display it in a window.

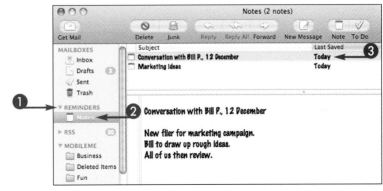

Send a Note

1 In Mail, double-click the note to open it in a note window.

2 Click **Send** (✉).

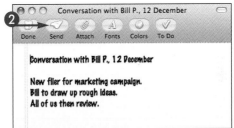

Mail opens a new message containing the note.

3 Type the recipient for the note.

4 Edit the subject as needed. Mail inserts the note's title as the subject.

5 Edit the note if necessary.

6 Click **Send** (✉).

Mail sends the note.

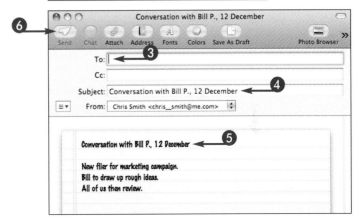

 TIPS

How can I send just the text of a note?

After creating a message containing the note, choose **Format** and **Make Plain Text**. Mail removes the note formatting, leaving only the text.

What does the To Do button in the note window do?

Click **To Do** (✓) to create a to-do item from the current paragraph in the note. Mail adds a check box (●) to the paragraph, enabling you to create a to-do list within the note. Mail also adds the to-do item to your To Do list (see the next section for more about your To Do list).

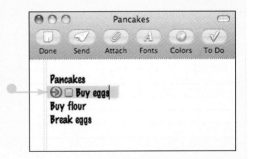

Create To-Do Items

Mail also provides a To Do list for tasks you need to complete. You can create, edit, and delete to-do items easily while working in Mail. You can either type a to-do item from scratch or create it from existing text in a note or message in Mail.

Create To-Do Items

Create a To-Do Item

① In Mail, click **To Do** (☑).

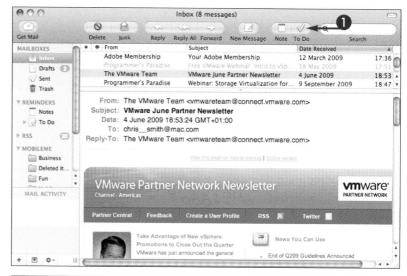

Mail displays the To Do list under Reminders and adds a new to-do item.

② Type the text for the to-do item.

③ Click ▾.

The Date Due pop-up menu opens.

④ Click the date on which the to-do item is due.

Note: To use a date that does not appear on the list, click **Other**. A dialog opens. Choose the date, and then click **OK**.

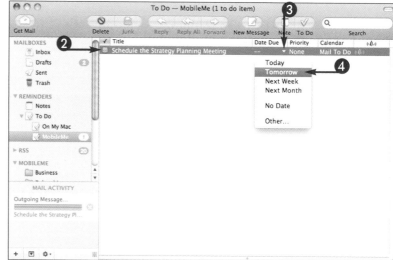

5 Click ⊡.

The Priority pop-up menu opens.

6 Click the appropriate priority:
Low, **Medium**, **High**, or **None**.

7 To set an alarm, click ⊡.

The alarm pop-up panel opens.

8 Choose options for the alarm, and
then click in empty space in the
window.

Mail creates the to-do item.

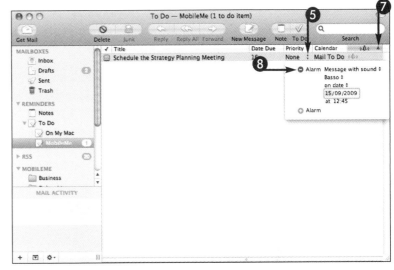

Mark a To-Do Item as Complete

1 If ▶ appears next to Reminders,
click ▶ (▶ changes to ▼).

2 Click **To Do**.

The list of to-do items appears.

3 Click ☐ next to the to-do item
(☐ changes to ☑).

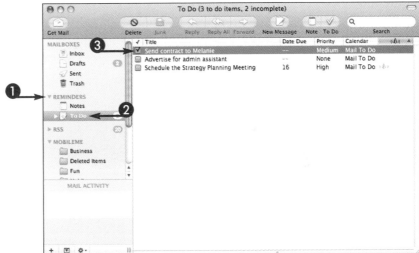

TIP

**How do I create a to-do item from existing text in
a message or note?**

To create a to-do item from a message or note, click and
drag through the text from which you want to create the
item. Click **To Do** (☑) on the toolbar. Mail creates a new
to-do item (●) within the note or message and links it to
a to-do item in the To Do list.

•	◆	From	Subject
		Adobe Membership	Your Adobe Membership
		Programmer's Paradise	Free VMware Webinar: Intro
		Programmer's Paradise	Webinar: Storage Virtualizati
		Eduardo Sempio	Documents for you to check

⊙☐ **Storage Virtualization for Server Virtualization:**
September 17, 2009
○

Reduce the Amount of Spam You Receive

Spam is unwanted e-mail messages, also called *junk mail*. Spam ranges from messages offering stimulating pharmaceuticals — real or fake — to attempts to steal your financial details, passwords, or identity.

It is almost impossible to avoid spam completely, but you can reduce the amount you receive by setting Mail to identify junk mail automatically and by learning to spot identifying features of spam messages.

Reduce the Amount of Spam You Receive

Set Mail to Identify Junk Mail Automatically

1. Click **Mail**.

2. Click **Preferences**.

3. In the Preferences window, click **Junk Mail**.

4. In the Junk Mail pane, make sure **Enable junk mail filtering** is checked (☑).

5. Click **Mark as junk mail, but leave it in my Inbox** (◉) if you want to review junk mail in your Inbox. Click **Move it to the Junk mailbox** (◉) if you prefer to review it in your Junk mailbox.

6. Make sure **Sender of message is in my Address Book**, **Sender of message is in my Previous Recipients**, and **Message is addressed using my full name** are all checked (☑).

7. Verify that **Trust junk mail headers set by my Internet Service Provider** is checked (☑).

8. Click ⬛ to close the Preferences window.

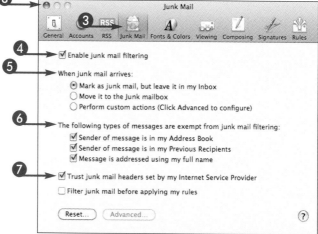

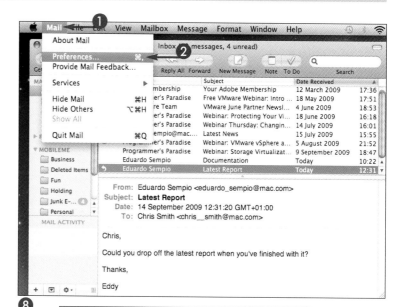

chapter 6

Review Your Junk Mail

① Click **Inbox** or **Junk E-mail** — wherever you told Mail to put your junk mail in step **5** on the previous page.

The list of messages in the mailbox appears.

② Click a message title.

The contents of the message appear.

③ Look to see whether Mail has identified the message as junk mail.

④ Look at the To field to see if the message is addressed to you.

⑤ Check whether the message greets you by name or with a generic greeting, such as "Dear customer."

⑥ Read the message's content and see if it is obviously spam or an offer too good to be true.

⑦ If the message appears to be spam, and Mail has not identified it as junk, click **Junk** ().

⑧ Click **Delete** () to delete the message.

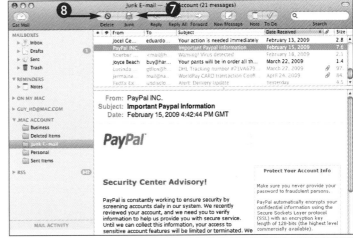

TIPS

How can I tell whether a message is genuine or spam?

Does the message show your e-mail address and your name? If not, it is most likely spam. If it does, read the content and decide whether it is likely true. If the message calls for action, such as reactivating an online account that you have, do not click a link in the message. Instead, open Safari, type the address of the Web site, log in as usual, and see if there is an alert for you.

How can I make a spammer remove me from his mailing list?

You cannot make a spammer remove you from his mailing list. Never click a "Remove Me" link in a message, because it confirms to the spammer that your e-mail address is "live" and makes it worth selling to other spammers. For the same reason, never reply to spam either.

CHAPTER

7

Keeping Yourself Organized with iCal and Address Book

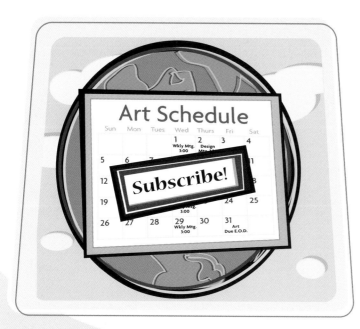

To help you keep your daily life organized, your iMac includes the iCal and Address Book applications. iCal is a calendar application that you can use to note down and manage your appointments and tasks. Address Book is a digital address book in which to store your contact information.

Open and Close iCal...148

Find Your Way around the Calendar 150

Create a New Calendar.....................................152

Create a One-Shot Appointment 154

Create a Repeating Appointment 156

Create a To-Do Item...158

Share Your Calendar with Other People....160

Subscribe to a Calendar Someone
     Is Sharing...162

Open and Close Address Book.....................164

Add Someone to Your Address Book 166

Change the Information for a Contact 168

Organize Your Contacts into Groups 170

iCal is a sleek and streamlined calendar application that makes it easy to enter and track your appointments, events, and tasks. You can launch iCal either from the Dock or from the Applications folder.

Open and Close iCal

Open iCal

1 Click **iCal** () on the Dock.

Note: *If iCal does not appear on the Dock, click the desktop, and then choose* **Go** *and* **Applications**. *In the Finder window that opens, double-click* **iCal**.

The iCal window opens, showing your existing calendars.

Close iCal

① Click **iCal**.

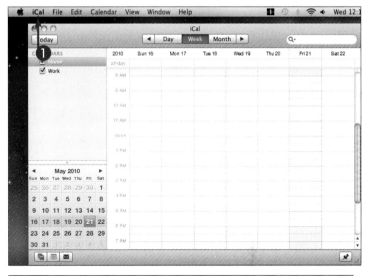

The iCal menu opens.

② Click **Quit iCal**.

iCal closes.

How can I make iCal run each time I log in?

If you use iCal in every computing session, set the application to launch automatically when you log in to your iMac. Control-click or right-click **iCal** ( ) on the Dock, highlight or click **Options**, and then click **Open at Login** ( ). Mac OS X puts a check mark next to this item to indicate it is turned on. Next time you log in, iCal opens automatically.

Find Your Way around the Calendar

iCal has a streamlined user interface that makes it easy to move from month to month and day to day. You can use the month readout to choose the month or the Go to Date dialog to jump directly to a specific date.

Find Your Way around the Calendar

Navigate to the Month You Need

① If the mini calendar does not appear, click **Mini Calendar** (▦) to display it.

② Click **Next Month** (▶) to move to the next month or **Previous Month** (◀) to move to the previous month.

iCal displays the month you chose.

③ Click the day you want to display.

iCal displays the day in the appointments area.

④ Click **Day**, **Week**, or **Month** to control the number of days that appear in the appointments area.

⑤ Click **Today** when you want to switch to today's date.

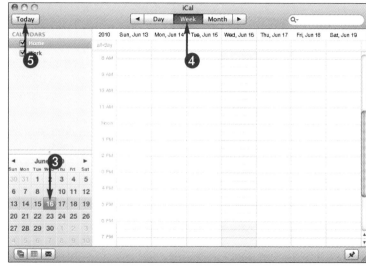

Jump to a Specific Date

1 Click **View**.

The View menu opens.

2 Click **Go to Date**.

The Go to Date dialog opens.

3 Click the day, month, or year, and then click ⬍ to increase or decrease the number.

Note: *You can also type the date into the Go to Date dialog.*

4 Click **Show**.

iCal closes the Go to Date dialog and shows the date you chose.

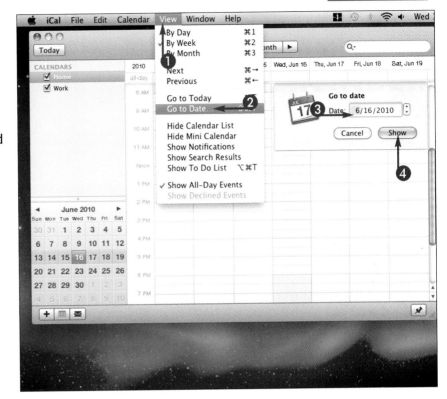

Which keyboard shortcuts can I use to navigate in iCal?

Press ⌘+1 to display the calendar by day, ⌘+2 by week, or ⌘+3 by month. Press ⌘+→ to move to the next day, week, or month, or ⌘+← to move to the previous one. Press ⌘+Shift+T to open the Go to date dialog. Press ⌘+T to jump to today's date.

How else can I move quickly around the calendar?

If you have only a few calendars, click the divider bar (●) above the month display and drag it upward. By giving the month display more space, you can fit two months or more in the space. This makes it easier to click the day you need to display.

Create a New Calendar

iCal comes with two calendars already created for you, the Home calendar and the Work calendar. You can create new calendars as needed. For example, you can create a calendar specifically for sports or for family events.

If you have a MobileMe subscription, you can choose between storing a new calendar on your iMac and storing it on the MobileMe Web site.

① In iCal, click **Add** (⊞).

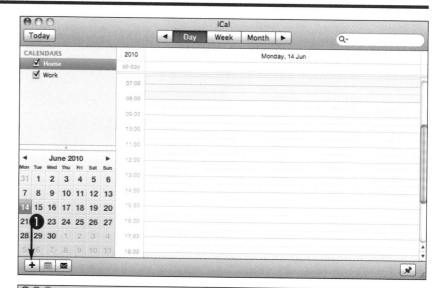

iCal creates a new calendar and displays an edit box around its name.

② Type the name for the calendar and press Return.

③ **Control**-click or right-click the calendar's name.

The shortcut menu opens.

④ Click **Get Info**.

A dialog opens showing information for the calendar.

⑤ Click ⬛.

The pop-up menu opens.

⑥ Click the color you want the calendar to use.

⑦ Type a description for the calendar.

Note: *Click **Ignore alarms** (☐ changes to ☑) if you want to suppress alarms for the calendar.*

⑧ Click **OK**.

The dialog closes.

You can now add events to the calendar.

TIPS

How do I create a new calendar on MobileMe?

To create a new calendar on MobileMe, do not click **Add** (⊞). Instead, click **File**, highlight or click **Calendar**, and then click **MobileMe**. The new calendar appears in the MobileMe section of the Calendars pane. Type the name for the new calendar and press **Return**.

How can I organize my many calendars?

You can organize your calendars by creating calendar groups. **Control**-click or right-click in the Calendars pane and then click **New Group**. Type the name for the new group and press **Return**. You can then click a calendar and drag it into the group (●).

Create a One-Shot Appointment

To organize your time commitments, create an *event* in iCal for each appointment, meeting, or trip. iCal displays each event as an item on its grid, so you can easily see what is supposed to happen when.

You can create an event either for a specific length of time, such as one or two hours, or for an entire day.

Create a One-Shot Appointment

① Use the mini calendar to go to the day for which you want to create the event.

② Click the calendar to which the event belongs.

③ If the appointments area is in Month view, click **Day** to switch to Day view or **Week** to switch to Week view.

④ In the appointments area, click the time the event starts, and then drag to the time at which it ends.

iCal creates an event where you clicked and selects its default name, *New Event*.

⑤ Type the name for the event and then press Return.

⑥ Double-click the event.

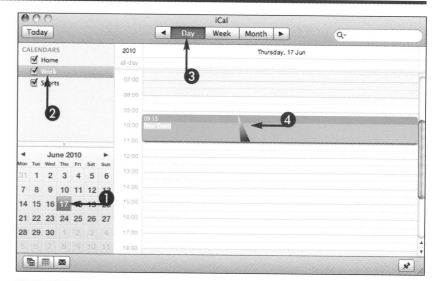

A panel opens showing the details of the event.

7 Click **location** and type the location for the event.

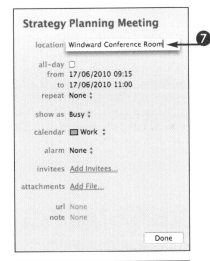

Strategy Planning Meeting

location Windward Conference Room

all-day ☐
from 17/06/2010 09:15
to 17/06/2010 11:00
repeat None ⇕

show as Busy ⇕

calendar ☐ Work ⇕

alarm None ⇕

invitees Add Invitees...

attachments Add File...

url None
note None

Done

8 If you want a reminder, click **alarm** and choose the details of the alarm.

9 To add further information, click **note** and type the note.

10 Click **Done**.

The panel closes.

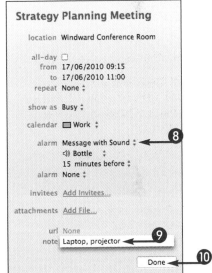

Strategy Planning Meeting

location Windward Conference Room

all-day ☐
from 17/06/2010 09:15
to 17/06/2010 11:00
repeat None ⇕

show as Busy ⇕

calendar ☐ Work ⇕

alarm Message with Sound ⇕
🔊 Bottle ⇕
15 minutes before ⇕
alarm None ⇕

invitees Add Invitees...

attachments Add File...

url None
note Laptop, projector

Done

How do I create an all-day event?

To create an all-day event, click the calendar that will contain the event, and then double-click in the all-day area at the top of the day (●). iCal creates a new event, gives it the name *New Event*, and displays an edit box around the name. Type the name for the event and press Return.

2010	Mon, 14 Jun	Tue, 15 Jun	Wed,
all-day	New Event		
07:00			
08:00			

iCal

◀ Day Week

Create a Repeating Appointment

Many events occur only once, but others occur repeatedly on a schedule — for example, once a week, once every two weeks, or once a month.

iCal enables you to set up repeating appointments for your events that recur regularly. iCal then maintains and updates each repeating event until the stop date you choose or until you delete the event.

Create a Repeating Appointment

1. In the mini calendar, click the day on which to start the repeating event.

2. Click the calendar to which the repeating event belongs.

3. If the appointments area is in Month view, click **Day** to switch to Day view or **Week** to switch to Week view.

4. In the appointments area, click the time the event starts, and then drag to the time at which it ends.

   iCal creates an event where you clicked and selects its default name, *New Event*.

5. Type the name for the repeating event and then press Return.

6. Double-click the repeating event.

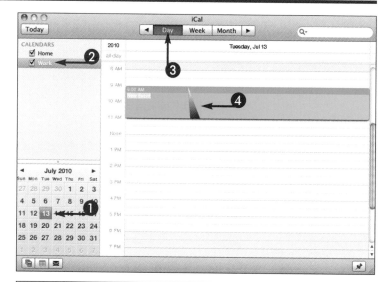

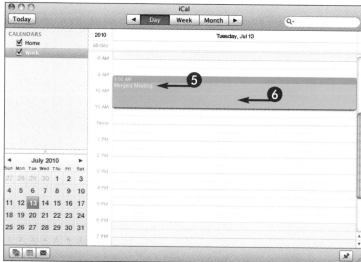

A panel opens showing the details of the event.

7 Click ⬍ next to **repeat**.

The pop-up menu opens.

8 For a simple repetition, click **Every day**, **Every week**, **Every month**, or **Every year**, as appropriate. Skip to step **12**.

9 For a complex repetition, click **Custom**.

A dialog opens.

10 Click ⬍ next to **Frequency** and choose **Daily**, **Weekly**, **Monthly**, or **Yearly**, as appropriate.

The controls in the dialog change to show options for that frequency.

11 Choose the frequency or schedule. For example, you can choose **Every 1 month(s) On the second Tuesday** to repeat the event on the second Tuesday of each month.

12 Click **OK**.

The dialog closes.

13 Click **Done**.

The panel closes.

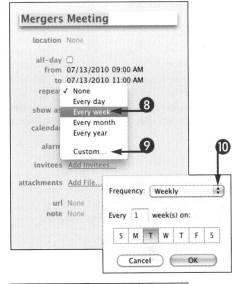

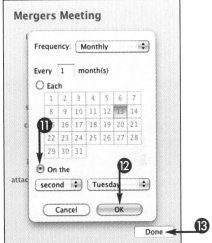

TIP

How do I make a repeating event end?

After your set up the repeat schedule, click ⬍ next to **end** in the event panel. You can then choose **After** (⬤) and set the number of times — for example, **13 times** (⬤) — or choose **On date** and set the date on which the repeating event will end.

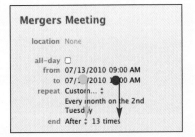

Create a
To-Do Item

As well as events, iCal enables you to track your tasks — *to-do items*, as iCal calls them. You can add to-do items to iCal, assign them priorities, and sort them into order.

When you have completed a to-do item, you mark it as complete, and iCal removes it from the list of uncompleted tasks.

Create a To-Do Item

① Click the calendar in which you want to create the to-do item.

② Click **File**.

The File menu opens.

③ Click **New To Do**.

Note: *You can also press* ⌘ + K *to start creating a new to-do item.*

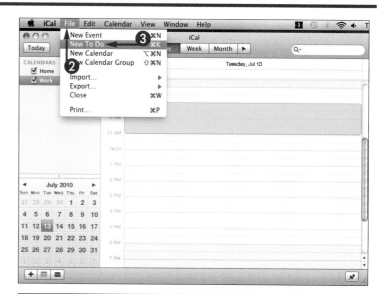

iCal opens the To Do list at the right side of the window and adds a new to-do item, putting an edit box around its name.

④ Type the name you want to give the to-do item and press Return.

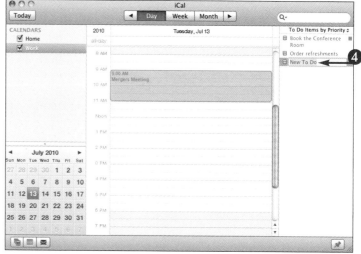

The to-do item takes on the name.

⑤ Click the **Set Priority** button to the right of the to-do item.

A pop-up menu opens.

⑥ Click the priority for the to-do item: **Low**, **Medium**, **High**, or **None**.

⑦ To set further details, double-click the to-do item.

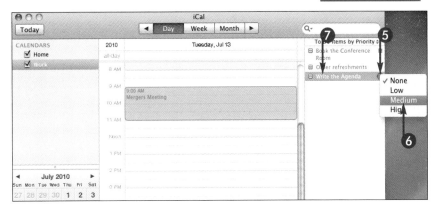

A pop-up panel opens.

⑧ To apply a due date, click **due date** (☐ changes to ☑).

⑨ Choose the due date.

⑩ Optionally, set an alarm for the to-do item.

⑪ Add any notes needed.

⑫ Click **Close**.

⑬ If you want to hide the To Do list, click **View or Hide To Dos** (📌).

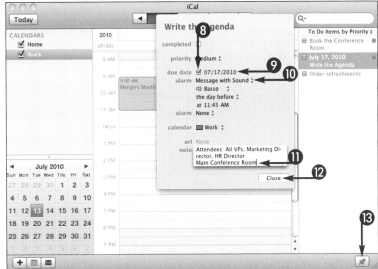

TIPS

How do I mark a to-do item as completed?

When you have done a to-do item, click the **Completed** check box to its left (☐ changes to ☑).

How can I sort my to-do items differently?

Click ⬍ at the top of the To Do list. A pop-up menu opens. Click the way you want to sort the items: **Sort by Due Date**, **Sort by Priority**, **Sort by Title**, **Sort by Calendar**, or **Sort Manually**. If you choose **Sort Manually** (●), click and drag the items into the order in which you want them to appear.

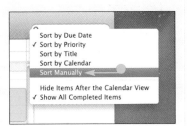

Share Your Calendar with Other People

As well as keeping your calendar on your iMac, iCal enables you to share your calendar with other people so that they know when you are busy.

The easiest way to share your calendar is by publishing it to your MobileMe account. You can also publish your calendar to a private calendar server — for example, a server that your company runs.

Share Your Calendar with Other People

1 Click the calendar you want to share.

2 Click **Calendar**.

3 In the Calendar menu, click **Publish**.

4 In the Publish Calendar dialog, type the name under which you want to publish the calendar.

Note: *Make your calendar's name descriptive so that people can identify it easily. For example, publish it as John Brown's Work Calendar rather than just Work.*

5 Click ⬍ next to **Publish on**.

6 In the Publish On pop-up menu, click **MobileMe** to publish the calendar on MobileMe.

Note: *To publish the calendar on a private server, see the tip.*

7 Click **Publish changes automatically** (☐ changes to ☑) for iCal to automatically update your published calendar.

8 Click **Publish alarms** (☐ changes to ☑) to include alarms.

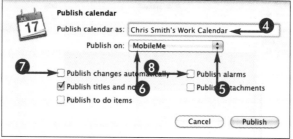

9 Click **Publish attachments**
(☐ changes to ☑) to include
attached items.

10 Click **Publish to do items**
(☐ changes to ☑) to include
to-do items.

Note: Make sure **Publish titles and notes** is checked (☑) unless you do not want others to see the names of your events.

11 Click **Publish**, and iCal publishes
the calendar to the server.

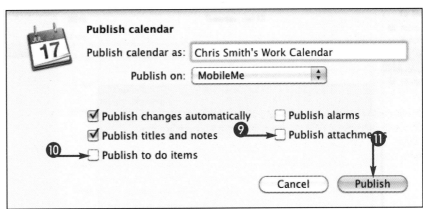

Publish calendar

Publish calendar as: Chris Smith's Work Calendar

Publish on: MobileMe

☑ Publish changes automatically   ☐ Publish alarms
☑ Publish titles and notes   ☐ Publish attachments
☐ Publish to do items

Cancel   Publish

12 In the Calendar Published dialog,
click **Visit Page** to open your
calendar's Web page in Safari and
preview it.

13 Click **Send Mail** to start an e-mail
giving people your calendar's
address so that they can view it or
subscribe to it.

14 Click **OK** to close the Calendar
Published dialog.

Note: To stop publishing a calendar, click the calendar, and then choose **Calendar** and **Unpublish**. In the confirmation dialog that opens, click **Unpublish**.

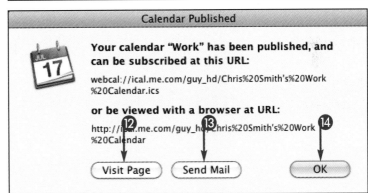

Calendar Published

Your calendar "Work" has been published, and
can be subscribed at this URL:

webcal://ical.me.com/guy_hd/Chris%20Smith's%20Work
%20Calendar.ics

or be viewed with a browser at URL:

http://ical.me.com/guy_hd/Chris%20Smith's%20Work
%20Calendar

Visit Page   Send Mail   OK

 TIP

How do I publish a calendar to a private server?
Ask your network administrator for the server's
base URL and your login name and password.
Then click the calendar and choose **Calendar** and
Publish to open the Publish calendar dialog. Click
☐ (●) next to **Publish on**, and then click **A
private server** in the pop-up menu. An extra
section appears in the dialog. Type the server's
address in the **Base URL** field (●). Type your login
name and password (●). Choose what items to
publish (☐ changes to ☑), and then click
Publish (●).

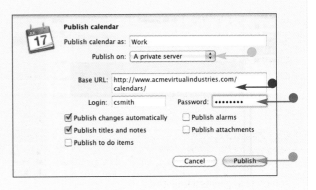

Publish calendar

Publish calendar as: Work

Publish on: A private server

Base URL: http://www.acmevirtualindustries.com/
calendars/

Login: csmith   Password: ••••••••

☑ Publish changes automatically   ☐ Publish alarms
☑ Publish titles and notes   ☐ Publish attachments
☐ Publish to do items

Cancel   Publish

Subscribe to a Calendar Someone Is Sharing

To learn the details of someone else's schedule, you can subscribe to a calendar that person is sharing. After subscribing, you can view the other person's calendar in iCal.

You can subscribe to a calendar either by entering its URL in iCal or by clicking a link in a message that you have received.

Subscribe to a Calendar Someone Is Sharing

1 In iCal, click **Calendar**.

The Calendar menu opens.

2 Click **Subscribe**.

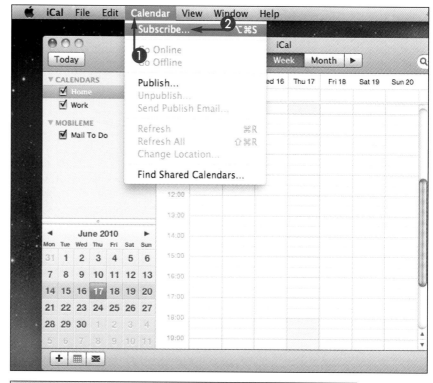

The Enter the URL of the Calendar You Want to Subscribe To dialog opens.

3 Type or paste in the calendar's URL.

Note: If you receive a link to a shared calendar, click the link in Mail. iCal opens and displays the Enter the URL of the Calendar You Want to Subscribe To dialog with the URL inserted. Click Subscribe.

4 Click **Subscribe**.

chapter 7

A dialog opens showing the details of the calendar.

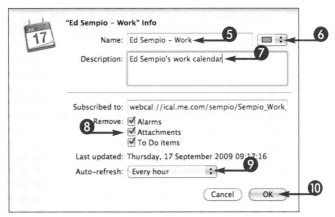

5 Type the name you want to see for the calendar.

6 Click ⬍ and pick the color with which to code the calendar.

7 Optionally, type a description for the calendar.

8 Choose whether to remove alarms, attachments, and to-do items from the calendar.

9 Click ⬍ and choose whether to automatically refresh the calendar: **No**, **Every 5 minutes**, **Every 15 minutes**, **Every hour**, **Every day**, or **Every week**.

10 Click **OK**.

● The calendar appears in the Subscriptions list, and you see its contents.

 TIPS

How do I update a shared calendar?

To update a shared calendar with the latest information the shared has published, Control-click or right-click the calendar, and then click **Refresh** (●). If you subscribe to two or more calendars, you can click **Refresh All** on the shortcut menu to update them all.

How do I unsubscribe from a shared calendar?

Instead of unsubscribing, you delete the calendar from the list. Simply click the calendar and then choose **Edit** and **Delete**.

Open and Close Address Book

Address Book is a powerful but easy-to-use application for tracking and managing your contacts. You can launch Address Book either from the Dock or from the Applications folder.

Open and Close Address Book

Open Address Book

1 Click **Address Book** (🖼) on the Dock.

Note: If Address Book does not appear on the Dock, click the desktop, and then choose **Go** and **Applications**. In the Finder window that opens, double-click **Address Book**.

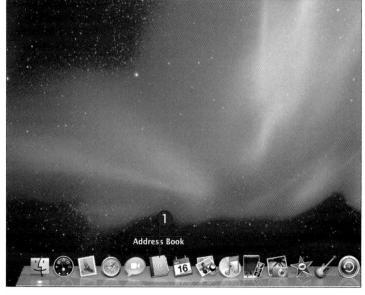

The Address Book window opens.

Close Address Book

1 Click **Address Book**.

The Address Book menu opens.

2 Click **Quit Address Book**.

Address Book closes.

TIP

How can I start an e-mail message to a contact in Address Book?

You can do this in either of two ways.

- In Address Book, click the contact's card (●), and then click the button before the e-mail address — for example, **Work** (●). On the pop-up menu, click **Send Email** (●).

- In Mail, click **New Message** to start a new message, and then click **Addresses**. The Addresses window opens, showing the contacts in Address Book. You can then add one or more contacts to the message.

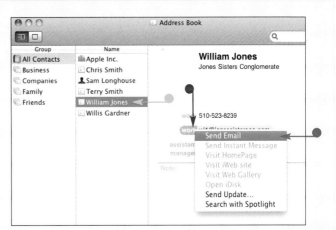

Add Someone to Your Address Book

To add someone to your Address Book, you create a new card and enter the person's data on it.

Address Book provides storage slots for many different items of information, from the person's name, address, and phone numbers to the e-mail addresses, Web site URL, and photo.

Add Someone to Your Address Book

① In Address Book, click **Create a new card** (⊞).

Note: *You can also add a card by pressing* ⌘ + N *or choosing* **File** *and* **New Card**.

Address Book adds a new card with placeholders for the information, and selects the First placeholder.

② Type the person's first name.

Note: *Press* Tab *to move the selection from the current field to the next. You can also click another field to move to it.*

③ Type the person's last name.

④ If the person is with a company, type the company name.

● When creating a card for a company rather than a person, click **Company** (☐ changes to ☑).

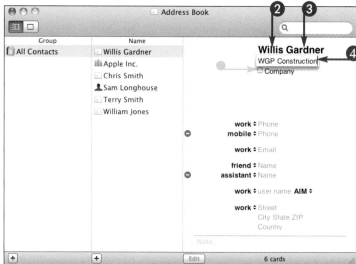

⑤ Click 🔃 next to the first Phone field.

The pop-up menu opens.

⑥ Click the type of phone number — for example, **work**, **home**, or **mobile**.

⑦ Type the phone number.

⑧ Add other phone numbers as needed.

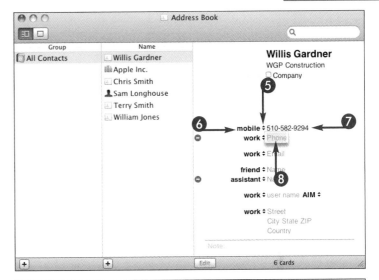

⑨ Click 🔃 next to the Email field.

⑩ Click the type of e-mail address — for example, **work**, **home**, or **MobileMe**.

⑪ Type the e-mail address.

⑫ Add the physical address and other information.

⑬ Click **Edit** to stop editing the card.

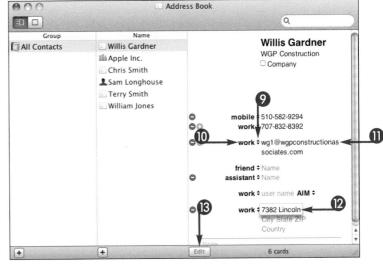

 TIPS

Is there a quicker way of adding a contact to Address Book than typing all the information?

Many people include virtual address cards called vCards with e-mail messages. If you receive a vCard in Mail, Control-click or right-click it, highlight **Open With**, and choose **Address Book** (●). A dialog opens confirming that you want to import the card into Address Book. Click **Import**.

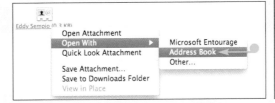

How do I delete a contact from Address Book?

To delete a contact, click the card, and then choose **Edit** and **Delete Card** or press Delete. A confirmation dialog opens. Click **Delete**.

Change the Information for a Contact

People frequently change their phone numbers, e-mail addresses, and even their names, so you will often need to edit your contacts to update their information.

You can add extra fields to a contact record as needed, enabling you to store additional phone numbers, e-mail addresses, or physical addresses. You can even add a photo for a contact.

① In the Name column of Address Book, click the contact you want to change.

② Click **Edit**.

Address Book opens the contact's card for editing.

③ To change an existing field, click it and then type the updated information.

④ To add a field, click ⊕ next to a similar field. Click ⬍ next to the new field, choose the type, and then type the information.

⑤ To remove an existing field, click ⊖.

⑥ To add a photo for the contact, double-click the picture placeholder.

● Address Book opens a dialog for adding a photo.

⑦ Click **iPhoto** (⬛) on the Dock.

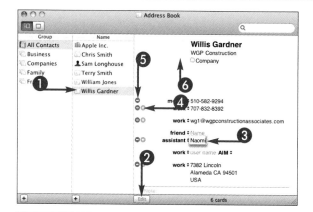

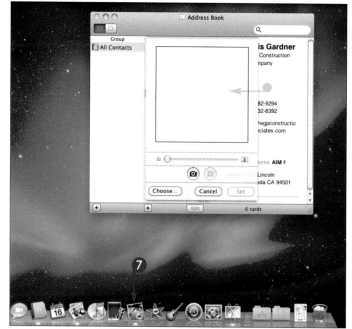

The iPhoto window opens.

8 Click and drag a photo from iPhoto to the Address Book dialog.

Note: You can also click and drag a photo from a Finder window to the Address Book dialog.

9 Choose **iPhoto** and **Quit iPhoto**.

iPhoto closes.

10 Click and drag the slider if you want to zoom the photo.

11 Click and drag the photo if you want to reposition it.

12 Click **Set**.

Address Book closes the dialog and adds the photo to the contact.

How can I add information that does not fit in any of Address Book's fields?

The Notes field is useful for adding extra information, but you can also create a custom field name. Click ⬚ next to an empty field. On the pop-up menu that opens, click **Custom**. The Add Custom Label dialog opens. Type the label you want to use, and then click **OK** (●). Address Book adds the label to the field. Type the data for the field.

Organize Your Contacts into Groups

Like most people, you probably have several different types of contacts — family, friends, colleagues, companies, and so on. Address Book enables you to organize your contacts into separate groups, making it easier to find the contacts you need.

After creating groups, you can view a single group at a time or search within a group. You can also send an e-mail message to all the members of a group.

Organize Your Contacts into Groups

Create a Group of Contacts

1 In Address Book, click **Create a new group** (➕).

Address Book adds a group named *untitled group* and displays an edit box around it.

2 Type the name for the group and press Return.

The group takes on the name.

Add Contacts to the Group

1 Click **All Contacts**.

Address Book displays all your contacts.

2 Click and drag a contact to the new group.

Note: To add multiple contacts to the group, click the first, and then ⌘-click each of the others. Click and drag the selected contacts to the group.

View a Group or Search within It

1 Click the group.

Address Book displays the contacts in the group.

2 To search within the group, click in the search box and type a search term.

Address Book displays matching contacts.

Send an E-mail Message to a Group

1 Control-click or right-click the group name.

The shortcut menu opens.

2 Click **Send Email to *Group Name***.

Address Book launches or activates Mail, which starts an e-mail message addressed to the group.

3 Type the message's subject and text.

4 Click **Send** to send the message.

 TIPS

How do I remove a contact from a group?

Click the group and then click the contact. Choose **Edit** and **Remove from Group**. Address Book removes the contact from the group but does not delete the contact record.

How do I delete a group?

Click the group, and then choose **Edit** and **Delete Group**. Address Book displays a confirmation message. Click **Delete** (⬤). Deleting a group does not affect the contacts it contains; the contacts remain available through the All Contacts group.

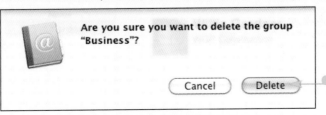

Chatting with Text, Audio, and Video

When you need to communicate instantly on your local network or across the Internet, use iChat, the Mac OS X application for instant messaging. You can choose between chatting using text only and chatting with audio and video. You can even send files while you chat.

Open and Close iChat..........................174

Add Someone to Your Buddy List...............176

Chat with a Buddy Using Text.....................178

**Chat with a Buddy Using Audio
     and Video**..180

Send and Receive Files While You Chat....182

Open and Close iChat

To start using iChat, you open the application from the Dock or from your Applications folder.

The first time you run iChat, you set it up with your instant messaging account. iChat works with Apple's MobileMe service but also with the AIM, Jabber, and Google Talk instant messaging services.

Open and Close iChat

Open iChat

1 Click **iChat** (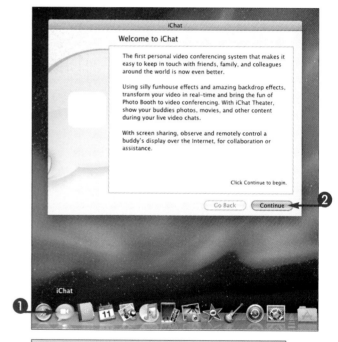) on the Dock.

Note: *If the iChat icon does not appear on the Dock, click the desktop. Click the **Go** menu and click **Applications**. The Applications window opens. Double-click **iChat**.*

The Welcome to iChat dialog opens.

2 Click **Continue**.

The Account Setup dialog opens.

3 Click ⏏ and then choose your account type.

4 Type your account name.

5 Type your password.

6 Click **Continue**.

If you are setting up a MobileMe account, the Encrypted iChat dialog opens.

Note: *The Encrypted iChat account appears only if you pay for a MobileMe subscription.*

7 To encrypt your chats with other MobileMe subscribers, make sure **Enable iChat encryption** is checked (☑).

Note: *Usually it is a good idea to encrypt your chats with other MobileMe subscribers.*

8 Click **Continue**.

Note: *If you leave the Enable iChat encryption check box selected, the iChat Encryption Requested dialog appears. Click **Continue**.*

The Conclusion dialog opens.

9 Click **Done**.

The Conclusion dialog closes.

Close iChat

10 When you have finished using iChat, as described on the following pages, click **iChat** and then **Quit iChat**.

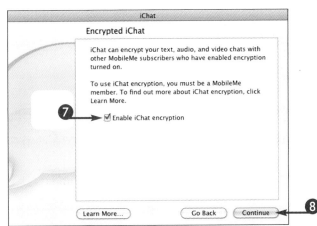

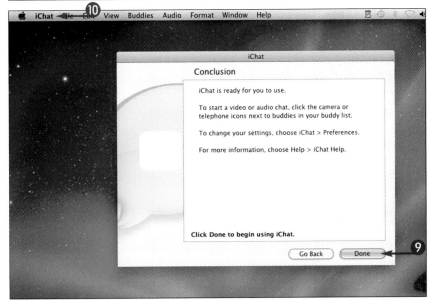

Where can I get an instant messaging account?

If you have a MobileMe subscription, you already have an instant messaging account that uses your MobileMe name. Otherwise, the easiest way to get an instant messaging account is to create an iChat account. This is free and takes only a minute. In the Account Setup dialog, choose **Mac.com** in the Account Type pop-up menu, and then click **Get an iChat Account**. A Safari window opens to the signup form on the Apple Web site.

Can I chat without getting an instant messaging account?

You can chat with people on your local network without getting an instant messaging account. Choose **Window** and **Bonjour List** to display a list of users on your network, and then follow the instructions later in this chapter.

Add Someone to Your Buddy List

After setting up your iChat account, you need to add the people you want to chat with. iChat calls these people *buddies*, and the list to which you add them is your Buddy List. Some other instant messaging services call these people *contacts*.

① Click **Add** (⊞).

The Add menu opens.

② Click **Add Buddy**.

The Enter the Buddy's AIM Account dialog opens.

③ Type the buddy's account name.

④ Click ⬍ and then click the group you want to add the buddy to: **Buddies**, **Family**, or **Co-Workers**.

⑤ Type the first name you want to use for your buddy.

⑥ Type the last name you want to use for your buddy.

⑦ Click **Add**.

iChat adds the buddy to your Buddy List.

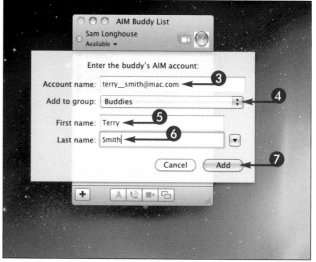

● If your buddy is online, the buddy appears in the section you chose in step **4**.

If your buddy is offline, the buddy appears in the Offline section.

⑧ **Control**-click or right-click the buddy.

The shortcut menu appears.

⑨ Click **Show Info**.

The Info window for the buddy opens.

⑩ Click **Alerts**.

The Alerts pane opens.

⑪ Choose any alerts you want for the buddy:

● Click the Event pop-up menu 🔽 and choose the event. For example, choose **Buddy Becomes Available** or **Buddy Becomes Unavailable**.

● Click the option you want. For example, click **Play a sound** (☐ changes to ☑), click 🔽, and then choose the sound.

⑫ Click 🔘 to close the Info window.

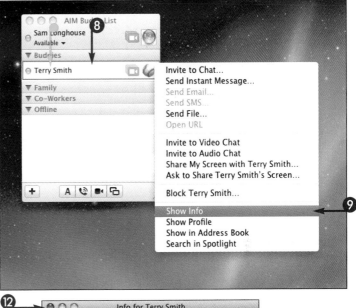

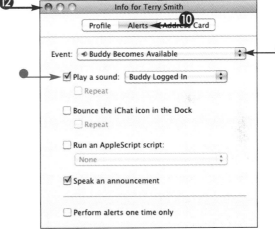

 TIPS

How do I remove a buddy from the Buddy List?

Click the buddy in the Buddy List, and then click **Buddies** and **Remove Buddy**. A confirmation dialog appears. Click **Remove**. iChat removes the buddy.

How do I change the name iChat displays for a buddy?

Control-click or right-click the buddy, then click **Show Info** on the shortcut menu. The Info window opens. Click **Address Card**. The Address Card pane opens. Change the name in the First Name field, Last Name field, or Nickname field (●), and then click 🔘.

Chat with a Buddy Using Text

The easiest way to start using iChat is by exchanging text messages with one or more buddies who are online and available to chat when you are. You send an invitation to text chat to your buddy, and if your buddy accepts the invitation, iChat sets up the chat in a Chat window.

① In iChat, click the buddy in the Buddy List.

② Click **Start a Text Chat** (A).

iChat opens a text chat window.

③ Type a greeting or question.

④ Press Return.

iChat sends the invitation, which opens on your buddy's computer.

When your buddy accepts the invitation, the response appears in the Chat window.

5 Type a reply.

6 If you want to include an *emoticon* or *smiley*, an expressive icon, click ⊙.

The list of smileys opens.

7 Click the smiley you want to use.

8 Press Return.

iChat sends your reply, and the conversation continues.

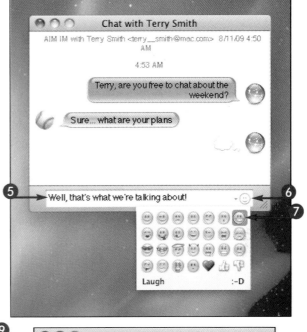

9 When you have finished chatting, click ⊙.

The Chat window closes.

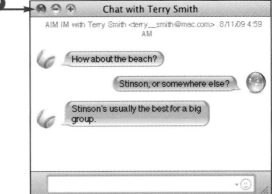

 TIP

How do I prevent people from contacting me?

You can block a buddy from contacting you via instant messaging. When you receive an unwanted invitation from a buddy, click **Block** (●), and then click **Block** in the confirmation message that opens. With the block in place, the buddy cannot see whether you are online and cannot contact you; similarly, you cannot see or contact the buddy. To unblock a buddy, Control-click or right-click the buddy in the Buddy List, and then click **Unblock**.

Chat with a Buddy Using Audio and Video

Your iMac includes a built-in microphone and an iSight Web cam, so you are fully equipped to chat using audio and video as long as your buddy's computer also has a microphone and Web cam.

Start a Video Chat with a Buddy

① In iChat, click the buddy in the Buddy List.

② Click **Start a video chat** (■).

iChat opens a Video Chat window showing your video preview and places a call to your buddy.

③ Adjust your iMac's camera or move so that your preview shows you as you want to appear.

When your buddy accepts the call, the Video Chat window displays your buddy's picture and shrinks your preview to a picture-in-picture video.

④ Chat with your buddy.

● Click **Effects** to open the Effects window, in which you apply visual effects to your video.

● Click to use iChat Theater to share a file or iPhoto.

● Click to mute or unmute the audio.

● Click to switch to Full-Screen mode.

⑤ When you have finished chatting, click 🔲.

Receiving an Invitation to Video Chat

When your buddy calls, iChat displays a Video Chat invitation window.

1 Position the mouse pointer over the Video Chat invitation window.

The Video Chat invitation window expands to show your preview.

2 Click **Accept** if you want to accept the invitation. Otherwise, click **Decline** to decline it, or click **Text Reply** to send a text reply instead.

If you click Accept, iChat makes the connection and displays your buddy's video.

Note: If you are playing music or a movie in iTunes when you accept the call, iTunes automatically pauses playback.

TIP

Can I send video to a buddy whose Mac does not have an iSight Web cam?

If your buddy's Mac does not have an iSight or other Web cam, you can hold a one-way video chat instead of a two-way chat. Start the chat from your iMac rather than from your buddy's Mac. Click your buddy in the Buddy List, and then click **Buddies** and **Invite to One-Way Video Chat**. After accepting the invitation, your buddy sees your video and hears your audio, while you hear your buddy's audio.

Send and Receive Files While You Chat

Text, audio, and video chat are a great way to exchange information, but often you will need to exchange files as well. iChat makes it easy to send files to buddies with whom you are chatting and to receive files from them.

Send and Receive Files While You Chat

Send a File

① Start a text chat with your buddy as described earlier in this chapter.

② Click **Finder** ( ) on the Dock to open a Finder window.

③ Navigate to the folder that contains the file you want to send.

④ Click and drag the file from the Finder window to the Chat window.

iChat adds the file to the Send area.

⑤ Press Return to send the file and any message you have written.

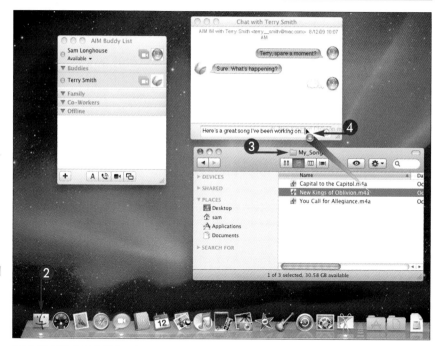

● The file appears in the message, and your buddy receives a prompt to download it.

● The file's name is a link that you can click to open a Finder window to the folder that contains the file.

Receive a File

● When your buddy sends you a file, it appears as a button in the Chat window.

① Click  to download the file.

The File Transfers window opens and transfers the file.

② Click  to open a Finder window to the folder that contains the file.

TIP

Can I change the folder in which iChat puts files I download?
Click **iChat** and then **Preferences**. The Preferences window opens. Click **General** in the upper left corner. The General preferences pane opens. Click **Save Received Files To**, and then click **Other** in the pop-up menu. A dialog opens. Click the folder you want to put your downloaded files in, and then click **Select**. Click to close the Preferences window.

Enjoying Music, Video, and DVDs

Your iMac comes equipped with a full set of applications for enjoying music, video, and DVDs. iTunes enables you to copy songs from CDs, play them back, and watch downloaded videos and movies. DVD Player lets you play back DVDs full screen so that you can enjoy them without distractions.

Open and Close iTunes 186

Add Your CDs to the iTunes Library............188

Buy More Songs Online...................................190

Play Songs..192

Play Videos 194

Create Playlists of Songs You Like..............196

Have iTunes Create Playlists for You..........198

Create a Custom CD of Your Songs.............200

**Listen to Radio Stations over the
    Internet**...202

Enjoy Podcasts..204

Watch a DVD on Your iMac...........................206

Open and Close iTunes

To use iTunes, you must first open the application. If you listen to music or watch videos extensively, you may want to leave iTunes running all the time you use your iMac. But if you have finished using iTunes, you can quit the application to close it and allow Mac OS X to reuse the memory iTunes was using.

Open and Close iTunes

Open iTunes

1 Click **iTunes** ( ) on the Dock.

Note: If the iTunes icon does not appear on the Dock, click **Finder** ( ) on the Dock. In the Finder window that opens, click **Applications**. In the Applications window, press and hold Option and double-click **iTunes**.

The iTunes window opens.

Note: The first time you launch iTunes, the application displays a license agreement and a series of option screens that offer to find your song files. If you consent to the license agreement, you can safely agree to iTunes' suggested options.

Close iTunes

1 Click **iTunes** on the menu bar.

The iTunes menu opens.

2 Click **Quit iTunes**.

The iTunes window closes.

Inquisition Symphony
Apocalyptica

Plays Metallica By Four Cellos
Apocalyptica

Furr
Blitzen Trapper

Greatest Hits
Creedence Clearwater Revival

TIP

iTunes is offering me the Genius sidebar. What is this for, and should I use it?

The Genius sidebar shows songs from the iTunes Store related to the song you have selected. This feature is good if you want to buy more songs or explore related songs; if so, click **Turn On Genius** (●). If you are content to find songs on your own, do not turn on Genius but click **Hide Sidebar** (●).

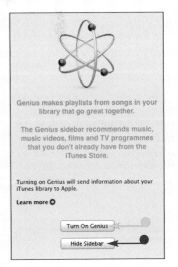

Genius makes playlists from songs in your library that go great together.

The Genius sidebar recommends music, music videos, films and TV programmes that you don't already have from the iTunes Store.

Turning on Genius will send information about your iTunes library to Apple.

Learn more ○

Turn On Genius

Hide Sidebar

Add Your CDs to the iTunes Library

The easiest and least expensive way to add songs to your iTunes music library is to copy the songs from your CDs to iTunes. The copying process is called *ripping*.

iTunes enables you to use different settings to create files using different formats and higher or lower audio quality. The highest-quality files require the most space on your iMac's hard disk.

Add Your CDs to the iTunes Library

① If iTunes is not already running, click **iTunes** ( ) on the Dock.

iTunes launches.

② Insert a CD in your iMac's optical drive.

iTunes recognizes the CD, looks up its title online, and opens a dialog asking if you want to import the CD.

③ Click **No**.

Note: *If you want to prevent iTunes from prompting you to import each audio CD you insert, click **Do not ask me again** (□ changes to ☑) before clicking **No**.*

The dialog closes.

④ Control-click or right-click the CD's name in the Devices list.

The shortcut menu opens.

⑤ Click **Get Info**.

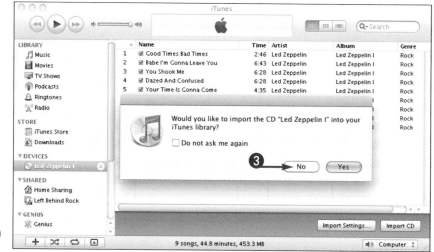

The CD Info dialog opens.

6 Verify that the information is correct. If it is not, correct it.

Note: Many entries for CDs in the online database that iTunes uses contain misspelled or inaccurate information.

7 Click **Compilation CD** (☐ changes to ☑) if the CD is a compilation by various artists.

8 Click **Gapless Album** (☐ changes to ☑) if you want to avoid gaps between songs — for example, on a live album.

9 Click **OK**.

The CD Info dialog closes.

10 Click **Import CD**.

● iTunes imports the songs and adds them to your music library.

11 When iTunes has finished importing, click ▲.

Your iMac ejects the CD.

How can I create MP3 files instead of AAC files?

iTunes comes set to create files in Apple's preferred Advanced Audio Coding format, or AAC. To create MP3 files, click **Import Settings** from the CD screen. The Import Settings dialog opens. Click the **Import Using** ▼ (●) and choose **MP3 Encoder**. Click the **Setting** ▼ (●) and choose the quality you want; **Higher Quality** is the best choice. Check **Use error correction when reading Audio CDs** (●) to ensure you get high-quality files. Click **OK** to close the Import Settings dialog.

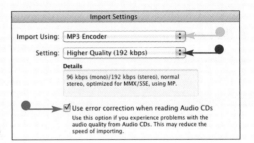

iTunes is tightly integrated with the iTunes Store, Apple's online store that sells songs, videos, games, and more.

To buy items from the iTunes Store, you must set up an account including your credit card details. If you do not already have an account, iTunes prompts you to set one up when you first attempt to buy an item.

Buy More Songs Online

① Double-click **iTunes Store**.

A new iTunes window opens and loads the home page of the iTunes Store.

Note: *You can also browse the iTunes Store in the main iTunes window by clicking **iTunes Store** once. Usually, opening a new window is more convenient because it lets you continue to control your music in the main window.*

② Click **Music**.

The Music pop-up menu opens.

③ Click the type of music you want to browse.

The iTunes Store window displays the kind of music you chose.

④ Click an item to display information on it.

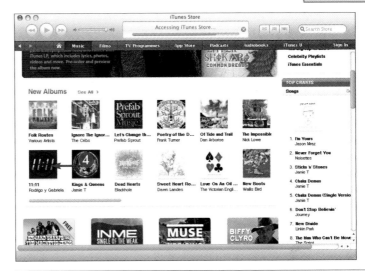

⑤ Highlight a song and click **Play** () next to it to play a sample.

⑥ Click **Buy** to buy the item.

⑦ If the Sign In to Download from the iTunes Store dialog opens, type your user name and password, and then click **Buy**.

iTunes downloads the song and adds it to your library.

⑧ Click **Purchased** in the Store category of the Source list to see your purchases.

TIPS

Are there other online stores that sell songs I can play in iTunes?

Many online stores sell songs in the widely used MP3 format, which you can play in iTunes and on iPods and iPhones. Amazon. com (www.amazon.com) sells a wide variety of songs and albums as MP3 files, as does Wal-Mart Stores, Inc.'s Walmart.com (http://mp3. walmart.com/store/home).

How can I restart a download that fails?

If a download stops partway through a song or other item, choose **Store** and **Check for Available Downloads**. You will need to sign in to the iTunes Store if you are not currently signed in. iTunes then automatically restarts any downloads that were not completed.

Play Songs

You can play any song in iTunes by simply double-clicking it and then using the playback controls.

First, though, you need to find the songs you want to play. To help you browse your songs, iTunes has three different views — List view, Grid view, and Cover Flow view — and a column browser. You can also search for songs.

Play Songs

Play a Song in Grid View

① Click **Grid View** (▦) to see the albums as a grid of covers.

② Double-click the album you want to open.

iTunes opens the album.

③ Double-click the song you want to play.

iTunes starts playing the song.

④ Use the playback controls as needed:

● Click once to go to the beginning of the song. Click again to go to the previous song.

● Click to pause playback. Click again to restart playback.

● Click to go to the next song.

● Drag to change the volume.

Play a Song in List View

① Click **List View** (▤) to see the songs as a list.

② Double-click the song you want to play.

iTunes starts playing the song.

Note: *To navigate quickly from artist to artist in List view, choose* **View** *and* **Show Column Browser.** *iTunes displays a list of the artists. Click the artist whose songs you want to see.*

Play a Song in Cover Flow View

① Click **Cover Flow View** (▥).

② Choose the album you want:

● Click a cover to bring it to the front.

● Click to display the previous cover.

● Click to display the next cover.

● Drag to scroll through the covers.

● Click to switch to full-screen Cover Flow.

The list shows the songs for the selected album.

③ Double-click the song you want to play.

TIPS

How can I search for songs?
Click in the search box and start typing your search term. iTunes shows matching items as you type. To restrict the search, click the arrow (●) and choose **Artist**, **Album**, **Composer**, or **Song** from the pop-up menu. Click ⊗ when you need to clear the search and display all songs.

Can I make iTunes take up less room when it is playing?
You can shrink iTunes down to its Mini Player. Click ⊕ or choose **View** and **Switch to Mini Player** or press ⌘ + Shift + M. To switch back, click ⊕ again, or choose **View** and **Switch from Mini Player**, or press ⌘ + Shift + M again.

Play Videos

Besides playing songs, iTunes also plays videos. You can buy music videos, TV shows, and movies from the iTunes Store or export files of your own movies from iMovie or other applications.

You can watch video content either within the iTunes window or full screen. You can set iTunes to automatically open particular types of video content full screen if you prefer.

1 In iTunes, click **Movies** under Library.

Note: To watch a TV show, click **TV Shows**. To watch a music video you have purchased, click **Purchased** under Store, or locate the video by the artist's name.

The list of movies appears.

2 Position the mouse pointer over the movie you want to play.

The Play Movie button appears.

3 Click **Play Movie**.

iTunes starts playing the movie.

4 Use the controls on the pop-up bar to control playback.

Note: Optionally, click ☐ to switch to full-screen viewing.

5 To stop viewing, click ⊗.

(TIP)

Can I make iTunes always play back movies full screen?

Choose **iTunes** and **Preferences**. The Preferences dialog opens. Click **Playback** (●). Click ▲▼ next to **Play Movies and TV Shows** (●) and choose **full screen**. If you want to play music videos full screen as well, click ▲▼ next to **Play Music Videos** (●) and choose **full screen**. Click **OK** to close the Preferences dialog.

Create Playlists of Songs You Like

The best thing about playing songs on your iMac is that you can play them in any order you want rather than in the order they appear on the CD. iTunes enables you to create playlists that contain the songs you want in your preferred order. You can listen to a playlist, share it with others, or burn it to a CD for listening on a CD player.

Create Playlists of Songs You Like

① In iTunes, click ⊞.

iTunes adds a new playlist to the Playlists section of the Source list and displays an information screen about playlists.

② Type the name for the playlist and press **Return**.

The playlist takes on the new name.

③ Click **Music**.

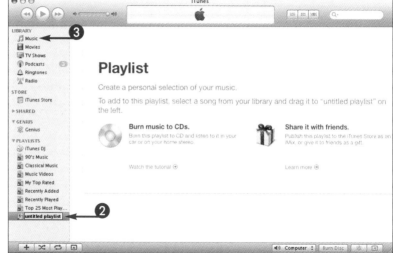

Your songs appear.

④ Click and drag songs to the playlist.

⑤ Click the playlist's name.

The contents of the playlist appear.

⑥ Click and drag the songs in the playlist into your preferred order.

Note: To delete a song from a playlist, click it and then press Delete. The song disappears from the playlist but remains in your iTunes library.

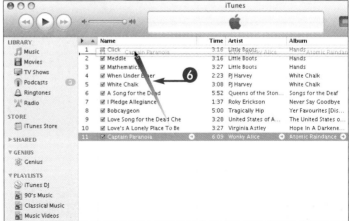

 TIPS

Is there a quick way of creating a playlist?

The quick way of creating a playlist is to select the songs first. Click the first song to include, and then ⌘-click other songs. Choose **File** and **New Playlist from Selection**. iTunes creates a new playlist and displays an edit box around the name. Type the new name and press Return to apply it.

How can I keep my playlists organized?

You can organize your playlists into playlist folders. Choose **File** and **New Playlist Folder**. iTunes creates a folder and displays an edit box around the name. Type the name for the folder and press Return to apply it. You can then click and drag playlists to the folder. Click ▶ to show the playlists in a folder; click ▼ to hide the playlists.

Have iTunes Create Playlists for You

Instead of creating playlists manually as described on the previous pages, you can have iTunes automatically create playlists for you. These playlists are called *smart playlists*.

All you have to do is set up the conditions for the smart playlist. iTunes then creates the playlist for you and automatically updates it when you add songs to your library or remove songs.

Have iTunes Create Playlists for You

① In iTunes, press and hold **Option** and click ⊞.

Note: ⊞ changes to ✷ when you press **Option**.

The Smart Playlist dialog opens.

② Click the first ⬍ and select the item for the first condition — for example, **Genre**.

③ Click the second ⬍ and select the comparison for the first condition — for example, **contains**.

④ Click the text field and type the text for the comparison — for example, **Alternative**, making the condition "Genre contains Alternative."

⑤ To add another condition, click ⊕.

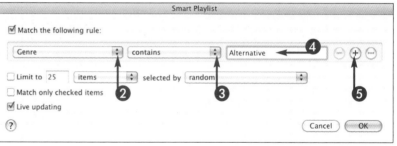

The Smart Playlist dialog adds another line of controls.

⑥ Click and choose **any** to match any of the rules or **all** to match all the rules.

⑦ Set up the second condition by repeating steps **2** to **4**.

Note: You can add as many conditions as you need to define the playlist.

⑧ If you want to limit the playlist, click **Limit to** (☐ changes to ☑). Use the controls on that line to set the limit.

⑨ Make sure that **Live updating** is checked (☑).

⑩ Click **OK**.

iTunes creates the smart playlist and adds it to the Playlists section of the Source list.

⑪ If you want to change the name iTunes gives the playlist, click the name.

An edit box appears around the name.

⑫ Type the name for the smart playlist, and then press Return.

TIPS

How do I produce a playlist the right length for a CD?

To create a playlist the right length for a CD, check **Limit to** (☑). Click the left and choose **minutes**, and set the number before it to **74** or **80**, depending on the capacity of the CD.

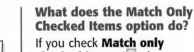
Limit to 60 minutes

What does the Match Only Checked Items option do?

If you check **Match only checked items** (☐ changes to ☑), your smart playlist contains only songs whose check boxes are selected. This means you can uncheck the check box for a song to prevent it from appearing in your smart playlists.

Create a Custom CD of Your Songs

After creating a custom playlist, you can copy it to a CD so that you can play it in any CD player. Creating a CD like this is called *burning* a CD.

You will need a blank recordable CD, or CD-R.

Create a Custom CD of Your Songs

① In iTunes, click the playlist from which you want to create the CD.

The songs in the playlist appear.

② Click **Burn Disc**.

The Burn Settings dialog opens.

3 Make sure that **Maximum Possible** is selected in the Preferred Speed pop-up menu.

Note: If the audio CDs you burn do not play correctly on some CD players, reduce the Preferred Speed setting.

4 Verify that **Audio CD** is selected (⊙).

5 Click ⬍ next to **Gap Between Songs** and choose the gap: **none**, **1 second**, **2 seconds**, **3 seconds**, **4 seconds**, or **5 seconds**. 2 seconds is typical.

6 Click **Use Sound Check** (☐ changes to ☑) if you want iTunes to standardize the audio volume of the songs on the CD.

7 Click **Burn**.

iTunes prompts you to insert a CD.

8 Insert a CD in your iMac's optical drive.

iTunes checks the disc and burns the CD.

● The display shows the progress of the burn.

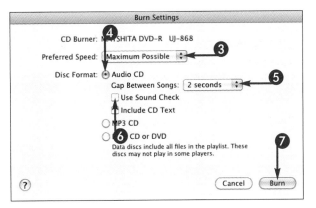

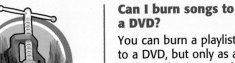

TIPS

Is it a good idea to use Sound Check?

Whether to use Sound Check is entirely up to you. Without Sound Check, songs originally recorded at different levels will play at different volumes from the CD. This can be awkward. Sound Check makes the overall volume more consistent but can rob songs of their dynamic range and power.

Can I burn songs to a DVD?

You can burn a playlist to a DVD, but only as a backup. This is a good way to keep copies of your songs to guard against hardware failure. You cannot create an audio DVD in the same way that you can create an audio CD.

Listen to Radio Stations over the Internet

iTunes enables you to listen to a wide variety of online radio stations that broadcast across the Internet. You listen to the stations in real time as they broadcast, and you cannot pause playback.

If a station does not appear in iTunes' list of stations, you can open it manually.

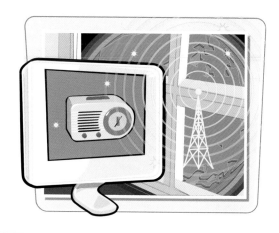

Listen to Radio Stations over the Internet

① In the iTunes Source list, click **Radio**.

A list of radio categories appears in the main window.

② Click ⊡ next to the category you want to display (⊡ changes to ⊡).

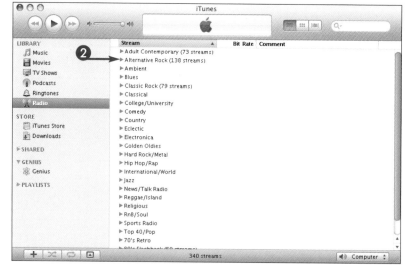

The category expands to show the stations it contains.

3 Double-click the radio station you want to listen to.

Note: If the radio station has two or more entries, try playing the one with the highest bit rate first if you have a broadband Internet connection. The higher the bit rate, the higher the audio quality.

The radio station starts playing.

4 Click **Stop** (■) when you want to stop the radio playing.

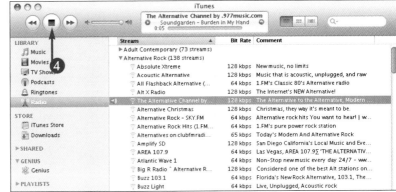

How can I listen to a radio station that does not appear on iTunes' list?

If the station does not appear in iTunes' list, find out the URL of the station's audio stream by consulting the station's Web site. In iTunes, choose **Advanced** and **Open Audio Stream** to display the Open Audio Stream dialog. Type or paste the URL (●) and click **OK**. iTunes starts playing the radio station's audio stream.

How can I record a song from the radio in iTunes?

iTunes does not provide a feature for recording radio. This is because recording a radio station can be a violation of copyright. To record, you need third-party software such as RadioLover from Bitcartel Software (www.bitcartel.com/radiolover/). Before you record, it is a good idea to understand your country's copyright laws about recording.

Enjoy Podcasts

A *podcast* is an audio or video file that you can download from the Internet and play on your iMac or a digital player like the iPod or iPhone.

The iTunes Store makes a wide variety of podcasts available. You can either simply download a podcast or subscribe to a podcast so that iTunes automatically downloads new episodes for you.

Enjoy Podcasts

① In iTunes, double-click **iTunes Store**.

iTunes opens a new window showing the home page of the iTunes Store.

② Click **Podcasts**.

The Podcasts menu opens, showing the different categories of podcasts.

③ Click the category of podcasts you want to see.

The window shows the category you chose.

④ Click the podcast you are interested in.

⑤ Click **Subscribe** if you want to subscribe to the podcast.

A dialog opens to confirm the subscription.

Note: *To download an episode of the podcast without subscribing, click **Get Episode**.*

⑥ Click **Subscribe**.

iTunes subscribes you to the podcast and downloads the available episodes.

How do I watch the podcasts I have downloaded?

In the main iTunes window, click **Podcasts** under Library in the Source list. The list of podcasts appears. Double-click a podcast to see the available episodes, and then double-click the episode you want to listen to or watch. iTunes starts playing the podcast and displays a bar of pop-up controls (●) for handling playback.

Watch a DVD on Your iMac

Mac OS X includes a full-feature DVD player, called simply DVD Player, for enjoying movies.

① Insert the DVD in your iMac's optical drive.

DVD Player automatically launches and starts playing the DVD full screen.

② Move the mouse pointer to the bottom of the screen.

DVD Player displays the control bar for controlling playback.

③ After you use the controls as needed, move the mouse pointer away.

DVD Player hides the control bar again.

④ Move the mouse pointer to near the top of the screen.

DVD Player displays a navigation bar that at first shows the chapters in the DVD.

⑤ Click the chapter to which you want to jump.

DVD Player starts playing that chapter.

⑥ When you have finished watching the DVD, move the mouse pointer to the top of the screen.

The Mac OS X menu bar appears.

⑦ Click **DVD Player**.

The DVD Player menu opens.

⑧ Click **Quit DVD Player**.

DVD Player quits.

TIP

Why does the You Need to Select the Region for Your DVD Drive dialog appear?

To create separate markets, DVDs use eight different region codes: Region 1 is North America, Region 2 is Europe, Region 3 is Southeast Asia, and so on. Most DVDs are tied to one specific region and can play only on players built for that region. This dialog appears when you insert a disc from a different region than your iMac's DVD drive is set to play. You can change the drive's region up to five times; after that, it remains locked to the last region you used. To change region, click ⬍ (●) next to **Change drive region to**, choose the region, and then click **Set Drive Region** (●).

Making the Most of Your Photos

Each new iMac comes with iPhoto, a powerful but easy-to-use application for managing, improving, and enjoying your photos. You can import photos from your digital camera; crop them, straighten them, and perfect their colors; and turn them into albums, slideshows, and online galleries.

Open and Close iPhoto 210

Import Photos from Your Digital Camera ...212

Browse through Your Photos..........................214

Crop a Photo to the Right Size.....................216

Rotate or Straighten a Photo........................218

Remove Red-Eye from a Photo 220

Improve the Colors in a Photo 222

Add an Effect to a Photo 224

Sort Your Photos into Events.........................226

Create Albums of Your Photos.......................228

Create a Slideshow of Your Photos 230

Publish Photos to a MobileMe Gallery 232

Send a Photo via E-mail.................................234

Take Photos or Videos of Yourself...............236

Open and Close iPhoto

To get started with iPhoto, you must first open the application. When you finish using iPhoto, you can leave the application running if you plan to use it again soon, or you can quit the application to close it and make the memory it was using available for other use again.

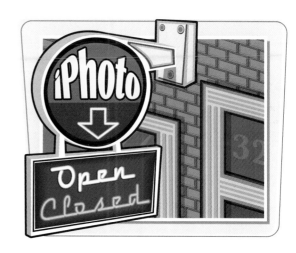

Open and Close iPhoto

Open iPhoto

1 Click **iPhoto** (🖼️) on the Dock.

Note: If the iPhoto icon does not appear on the Dock, click **Finder** (🖥️) on the Dock. In the Finder window that opens, click **Applications**. In the Applications window, press and hold `Option` and double-click **iPhoto** to open iPhoto and close the Finder window.

The iPhoto window opens.

Close iPhoto

1 Click **iPhoto** on the menu bar.

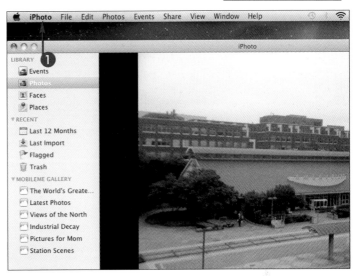

The iPhoto menu opens.

2 Click **Quit iPhoto**.

The iPhoto window closes.

 TIP

When I launch iPhoto, a dialog asks me if I want to use iPhoto when I connect my digital camera. Should I click Yes or No?

If iPhoto displays the Do You Want to Use iPhoto When You Connect Your Digital Camera? dialog, normally it is a good idea to click **Yes** (●). The

exception is if you plan to use another application, such as Mac OS X's Image Capture application or a third-party application supplied by the camera's maker or another software manufacturer, to import your digital photos.

Import Photos from Your Digital Camera

iPhoto enables you to import photos directly from your digital camera's memory or from a memory card. iPhoto can work with a wide variety of types of digital cameras, and normally recognizes a camera automatically when you connect it to your iMac and switch it on.

Import Photos from Your Digital Camera

1 Connect your digital camera to your iMac with a USB cable.

2 Turn on the digital camera.

Note: Some digital cameras turn on automatically when you connect them to a powered USB port, but most cameras need to be turned on manually.

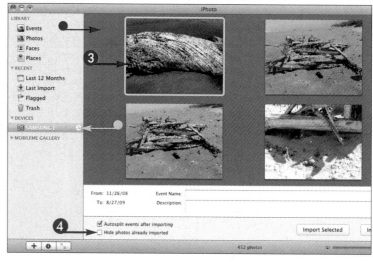

Your iMac launches iPhoto if it is not running, or brings it to the front if it is running.

● The digital camera appears in the Devices category in the Source list.

● iPhoto displays thumbnails of the camera's photos in the viewing area.

3 If you want to import all the photos, you need not select any. To import just some photos, click the first, and then ⌘-click the others.

4 Click **Hide photos already imported** (☐ changes to ☑) if the camera contains photos you have already imported.

iPhoto hides the photos you have already imported.

5 Type a name for the photos.

6 Type a general description.

7 Click **Autosplit events after importing** (☑ changes to ☐) if you want to prevent iPhoto from putting photos in different Events based on their dates and times.

8 Click **Import All**.

Note: If you selected photos in step 2, click Import Selected instead of Import All.

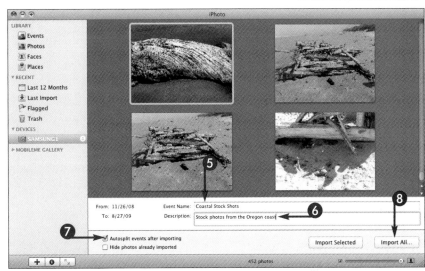

iPhoto copies the photos from the digital camera to your iMac.

The Delete Photos on Your Camera dialog opens.

9 Click **Delete Photos** if you want to delete the photos. To keep the photos, click **Keep Photos**.

10 Click ⏏ next to the camera's entry in the Source list.

iPhoto ejects the camera, and you can safely disconnect it. You can now browse your photos as explained on the following pages.

 TIPS

How can I connect my digital camera to my iMac if I do not have the right kind of connector cable?

If you do not have the right cable to connect your digital camera directly to your iMac, remove the digital camera's memory card and insert it in a memory card reader connected to the iMac. The iMac then recognizes the memory card as a digital camera, and you can import the photos from it as described on these pages.

What is an Event, and what names should I give my Events?

An Event is a way of grouping photos in iPhoto. When you import photos, you assign them to an Event, and you can then browse and organize them through the Event. An Event can be a period of time from a few hours to a week or more, but you can also create Events that have ideas or themes as needed.

Browse through Your Photos

After adding your photos to iPhoto, you can browse them in several ways. Usually the best way to start is by viewing the Last Import category, which contains the photos you most recently imported. You can view the photos either within the iPhoto window or full screen for greater effect.

Browse through Your Photos

1 In iPhoto, click ▶ next to Recent if the Recent category is collapsed.

The contents of the Recent category appear.

2 Click **Last Import**.

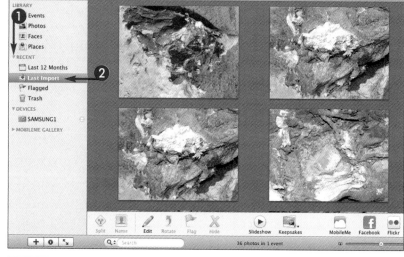

The last batch of photos you imported into iPhoto appear.

Note: *Normally, the Last Import item shows photos from your digital camera. But if you last added photo files from a folder or from a scanner to iPhoto, those photos appear in Last Import.*

3 Click the photo you want to view first.

4 Click **Enter full screen** (⛶) on the toolbar.

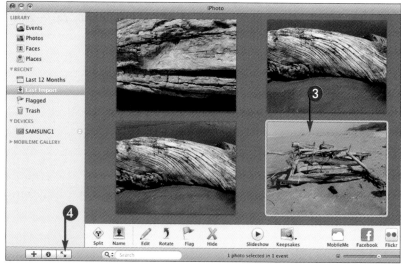

iPhoto displays the photo you clicked full screen.

⑤ Press ⬅ to display the next photo or ➡ to display the previous photo.

⑥ To jump to another photo, move the mouse pointer to the top of the screen.

The thumbnail bar appears.

⑦ Click the thumbnail for the photo you want to see.

iPhoto displays that photo.

Note: *Move the mouse pointer down toward the middle of the screen to hide the thumbnail bar again.*

⑧ Move the mouse to the bottom of the screen.

iPhoto displays the full-screen control bar, which contains tools for editing photos.

⑨ Click **Exit full screen** (⊗).

iPhoto exits full screen and displays its window again.

What are Events, Photos, Faces, and Places in the iPhoto sidebar?

Click **Events** to browse photos by the time-related Events iPhoto creates when you import photos. Double-click an Event to display its photos. Click **Photos** to see all the photos in your iPhoto library. Click ▶ to expand a collapsed group of photos or ▼ to collapse an expanded group. Click **Faces** to open the Faces feature for using facial recognition to identify the people in photos. Click **Places** to use the Places feature for sorting photos by their GPS location or locations you add manually.

Crop a Photo to the Right Size

To improve a photo's composition and emphasize its subject, you can crop off the parts you do not want to keep. iPhoto enables you to crop to any rectangular area within a photo, so you can choose exactly the part of the photo that you need.

① Click the photo you want to crop.

② Click **Edit** (✐).

iPhoto opens the photo for editing and displays the editing tools.

③ Click **Crop** (▣).

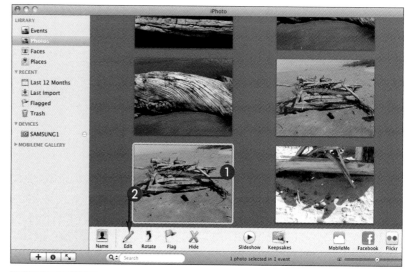

iPhoto displays the cropping tools.

④ If you want to crop to specific proportions or dimensions, click **Constrain** (☐ changes to ☑).

⑤ Click ⬆ and choose the size or proportions — for example, **Square** or **4 × 3**.

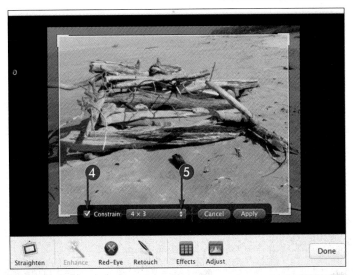

⑥ Click in the cropping rectangle and drag it so that the center square covers the middle of the area you want.

⑦ Click and drag a corner handle to crop to the area you want.

⑧ Click **Apply**.

iPhoto crops the picture to the area you chose.

⑨ Click **Done**.

iPhoto hides the editing tools again.

 TIP

I cropped off the wrong part of the photo. How can I get back the missing part?

You can undo an edit by choosing **Edit** and **Undo** or pressing ⌘+Z, but you can also return to a photo's previous state. To do so, choose **Photos** and **Revert to Previous**. You can use this command multiple times to undo a sequence of changes. When only one change remains, the command becomes **Revert to Original**.
You can click this command to go back to the original version of the photo.
A dialog opens to make sure that you want to revert to the original. Click **OK** (●).

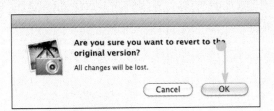

Rotate or Straighten a Photo

If you take a photo with the camera sideways or the wrong way up, you can easily rotate the photo by 90 or 180 degrees in iPhoto to fix the problem. iPhoto also enables you to straighten a photo by rotating it up to 10 degrees, automatically cropping off the parts that no longer fit.

Rotate a Photo

① Click the photo you want to rotate.

② Click **Rotate** (🔄) on the toolbar.

   iPhoto rotates the photo 90 degrees counterclockwise.

③ If you need to rotate the photo further, click **Rotate** (🔄) again.

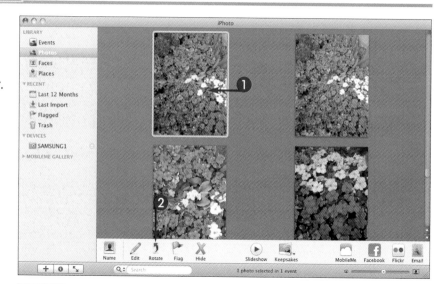

Straighten a Photo

① Click the photo you want to straighten.

② Click **Edit** (✏️).

- iPhoto opens the photo for editing and displays the editing tools.

3 Click **Straighten** ().

- iPhoto displays the straightening tools.

4 Click and drag the **Change angle of photo** slider to straighten the photo.

Note: *Use the major and minor gridlines in the straightening grid to judge when lines in the picture have reached the horizontal or the vertical.*

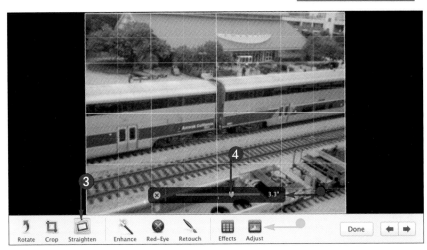

5 Click **Done**.

iPhoto hides the editing tools again.

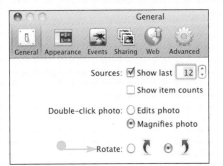

TIP

How can I rotate a photo clockwise instead of counterclockwise?

To quickly rotate a photo clockwise, Option-click the **Rotate** button (↺) on the toolbar or in the editing tools. If you usually need to rotate clockwise rather than counterclockwise, choose **iPhoto** and **Preferences**. The Preferences window opens. Click **General** on the toolbar. The General preferences pane opens. Select the clockwise **Rotate** option (●), and then click 🔲.

Remove Red-Eye from a Photo

A camera's flash can make all the difference when taking photos in dark or dull conditions, but flash often gives people *red-eye* — glaring red spots in the eyes. iPhoto's Red-Eye tool enables you to remove red-eye from your photos, making your subjects look normal again.

Remove Red-Eye from a Photo

① Click the photo that contains the red-eye.

② Click **Edit** (✏️).

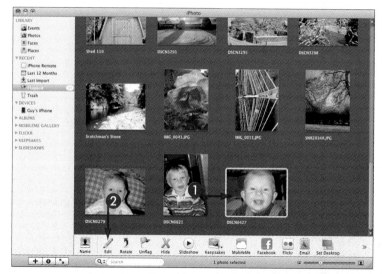

iPhoto opens the photo for editing and displays the editing tools.

③ Click and drag the slider to zoom in.

④ Click and drag the highlight in the Navigation window so that the red-eye is visible.

⑤ Click **Red-Eye** (👁).

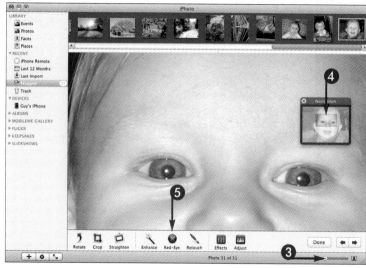

iPhoto displays the red-eye tools.

6 Drag the **Size** slider until the circle is the right size to cover the pupil of the eye in the photo.

7 Click the red-eye.

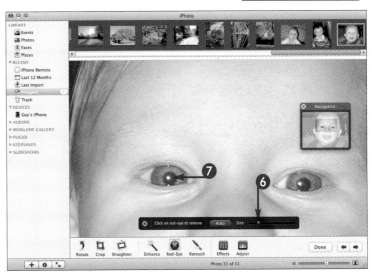

iPhoto removes the red-eye from the eye.

8 Click the other eye.

iPhoto removes the red-eye from that eye too.

9 Click **Done**.

iPhoto hides the editing tools again.

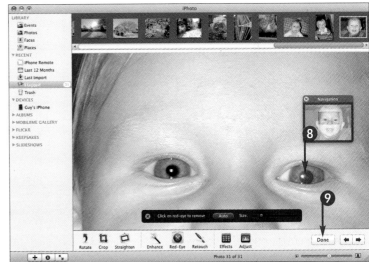

What is the Auto button in the Red-Eye tool for?

The Auto tool should be the quickest way to remove red-eye from a photo, but it generally gives less satisfactory results than removing red-eye manually. Normally, your photos look better if you click and drag the **Size** slider to the right size for the red-eye you need to remove. This takes only a moment longer than Auto, so it is usually worth doing.

Improve the Colors in a Photo

iPhoto includes powerful tools for improving the colors in your photos. If a photo is too light, too dark, or the colors look wrong, you can use these tools to make it look better. You can also use the Enhance tool to give the colors in a photo a fast and easy boost.

Improve the Colors in a Photo

Quickly Enhance the Colors in a Photo

1. Click the photo you want to enhance.

2. Click **Edit** (✐).

● iPhoto opens the photo for editing and displays the editing tools.

3. Click **Enhance** (✎).

   iPhoto adjusts the exposure and enhances the colors.

4. Click **Done**.

Improve the Colors with the Adjust Window

1. Click the photo you want to adjust.

2. Click **Edit** (✐).

● iPhoto opens the photo for editing and displays the editing tools.

3. Click **Adjust** (▦) to open the Adjust dialog.

4. To add black tones to the photo, click and drag the **Black Point** slider to the right.

5. To add white tones to the photo, click and drag the **White Point** slider to the left.

6. To adjust the gray balance, click and drag the **Midtones** slider to the left or right.

7. If white in the picture appears gray or pink, click the eyedropper (✐) and then click the color that should be white.

⑧ Click and drag **Exposure** right to make the photo lighter or left to make it darker.

⑨ Click and drag **Contrast** right to increase the contrast or left to decrease it.

⑩ Click and drag **Saturation** right to increase the color saturation or left to decrease it.

⑪ Click and drag **Definition** to increase the overall clarity of the photo.

⑫ Click and drag **Highlights** to recover lost detail in the lighter areas of the photo.

⑬ Click and drag **Shadows** to bring out detail in the darker areas of the photo.

⑭ Click **Done**.

 TIPS

What do the Sharpness and De-noise sliders in the Adjust dialog do?

Sharpness tries to make the photo look sharper by increasing the contrast between neighboring pixels that have different colors. Adjust the **Sharpness** slider gradually because big adjustments can give an unnatural look. De-noise attempts to remove incorrect colors and artifacts from the photo. Again, make changes gradually to achieve a better look.

How can I make the same change to several photos?

After making changes to one photo, click **Copy** in the Adjust dialog. Leave the Adjust dialog open while you click another photo and then click **Paste** to paste the adjustments to that photo. Repeat the paste operation as needed for other photos that need the same adjustments.

Add an Effect to a Photo

To add life and interest to a photo, you can apply one of iPhoto's effects to it. For example, you can turn a photo black and white or sepia, boost or fade the color, or turn the subject into a vignette in a blacked-out oval.

SEPIA EFFECT

Add an Effect to a Photo

① Click the photo to which you want to apply the effect.

② Click **Edit** (✐).

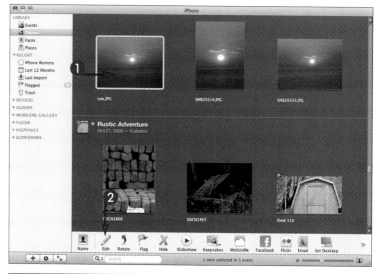

iPhoto opens the photo for editing and displays the editing tools.

③ Click **Effects** (▦).

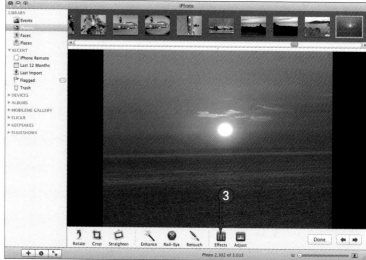

The Effects window opens.

④ Click the effect you want to apply.

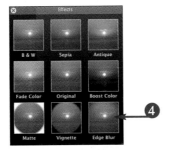

⑤ If the effect shows a number in the Effects window, click the right arrow button to increase the effect or the left arrow button to decrease it.

iPhoto adjusts the effect correspondingly.

⑥ Click ⊗.

The Effects window closes.

⑦ Click **Done**.

iPhoto hides the editing tools again.

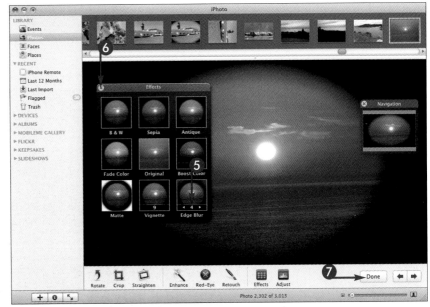

How can I remove the effects from a photo?

To remove the effects you have applied to a photo, click **Original** (●) in the middle of the Effects window.

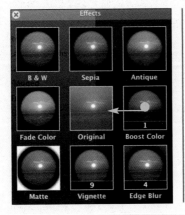

Can I apply multiple effects to a photo?

You can apply two or more effects to a photo at the same time. Some of the effects are mutually exclusive — for example, you cannot apply both B & W and Sepia to a photo at the same time. But you can apply other combinations of effects, such as applying both Sepia and Vignette to a photo.

Sort Your Photos into Events

iPhoto automatically creates Events when you import photos, but you can move photos from one Event to another as needed to keep your photos organized. You can also split one Event into two Events, or merge two existing Events into a single Event.

Move Photos from One Event to Another

1 In iPhoto, click **Events** in the sidebar.

● The list of Events appears.

Note: *Each Event appears as a stack of photos with a key photo on top. Move the mouse around over the key photo to see other photos in the Event.*

2 Click the Event that contains the photos you want to move.

3 ⌘-click the Event to which you want to move the photos.

4 Press Return.

iPhoto opens the Events.

5 In the first Event, select the photos you want to move.

6 Click and drag the photos to the other Event.

Note: *If you want to put all the photos from one Event in another Event, open the Events as described here, and then click **Merge** ( ).*

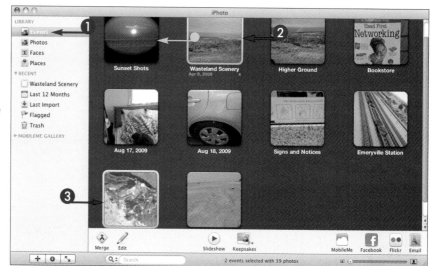

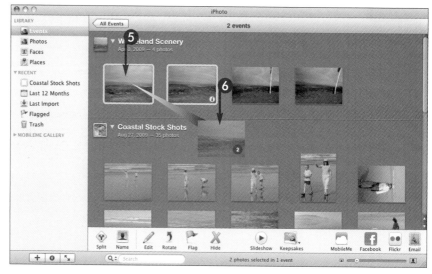

Split an Event into Two Events

1 Click **Events** in the Source list.

The list of Events appears.

2 Double-click the Event you want to open.

3 Click the photo before which you want to split the Event off to a new Event.

4 Click **Split** (🔻).

iPhoto creates a new Event named *untitled event*, starting with the photo you selected.

5 Click the Event name.

6 Type the name you want to give the Event.

7 Press Return.

The Event takes on the new name.

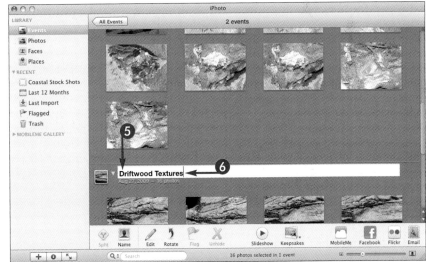

Can I change how iPhoto creates Events?

You can set iPhoto to create an Event for every two hours, every eight hours, every day, or every week. iPhoto uses the times and dates in the photos you import, not your iMac's clock. Choose **iPhoto** and **Preferences**. The Preferences window opens. Click **Events** to open the Events preferences pane. Click **Autosplit into Events** and choose **Two-hour gaps**, **Eight-hour gaps**, **One event per day**, or **One event per week**, as needed. Click 🔲 to close the Preferences window.

Create Albums of Your Photos

When you want to assemble a custom collection of photos, create a new album. You can then add to it exactly the photos you want and arrange them into your preferred order.

iPhoto can also create *smart albums* that automatically include all photos that meet the criteria you choose.

---

① Click **New** (⊞).

The New dialog opens.

② Type the name for the album.

③ Click **Create**.

Note: *You can also create an album quickly by selecting photos, clicking **New** (⊞), and making sure **Use selected items in new album** is selected (☑) before you click **Create**.*

● The new album appears in the Albums list in the sidebar.

④ Click **Photos** in the sidebar.

Note: *You can also add photos to the album from Events, from Last Import, or from any of the other items in the sidebar.*

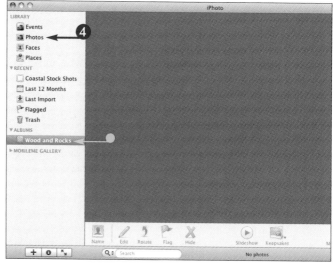

The list of photos appears.

⑤ Select the photos you want to add to the album.

⑥ Click in the selection and drag the photos to the new album.

iPhoto adds the photos to the album.

⑦ Click the album in the sidebar.

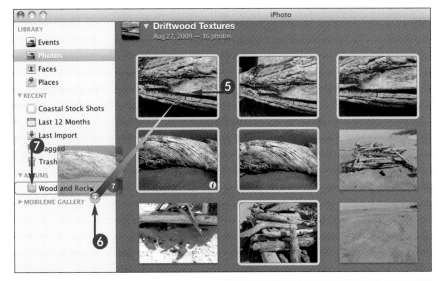

The photos in the album appear.

⑧ To change the order of the photos, click a photo and drag it to where you want it.

iPhoto arranges the photos.

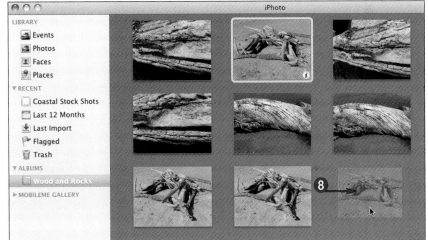

 TIP

What is a smart album, and how do I create one?

A smart album is an album based on criteria you choose. For example, you can create a smart album of photos with the keyword "family" and a rating of four stars or better. iPhoto then automatically adds each photo that matches those criteria to the smart album. To create a new smart album, choose **File** and **New Smart Album**, and then set your criteria in the New dialog. Click ⊞ (●) to add another row of criteria to the smart album.

Create a Slideshow of Your Photos

One of the best ways to enjoy your photos and share them with others is to create a slideshow. You can either create a simple, silent slideshow or one that includes effects and transitions and is accompanied by music.

Create a Slideshow

① Click **New** (➕).

The New dialog opens.

② Click **Slideshow** (▣).

③ Type the name for the slideshow.

④ Click **Create**.

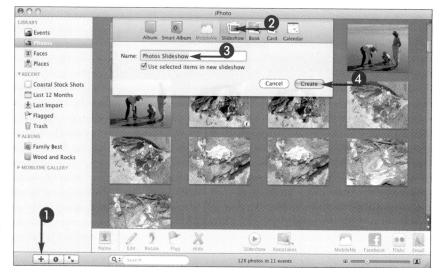

The new slideshow appears in the Slideshows list in the sidebar.

⑤ Click **Photos** in the sidebar.

Note: You can also add photos to the slideshow from Events, from Last Import, or from any of the other items in the sidebar.

The list of photos appears.

⑥ Select the photos you want to use in the slideshow.

⑦ Click in the selection and drag the photos to the new slideshow.

iPhoto adds the photos to the slideshow.

⑧ Click the slideshow in the sidebar.

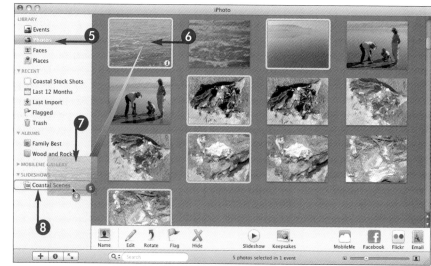

The photos in the slideshow appear.

9 Click and drag the photos into order.

10 Click **Music** ().

11 In the Music Settings dialog, choose the music to play with the slideshow.

Note: *For a silent slideshow, click **Play music during slideshow** (☑ changes to ☐).*

12 Click **Apply**.

13 Click **Settings** ().

14 In the Slideshow Settings dialog, choose how long to play each slide (○ changes to ◉).

15 Choose whether to play transitions between slides (☐ changes to ☑).

16 Click .

17 Click **Play** ().

The slideshow starts playing.

18 Use the controls on the control bar to move from slide to slide or stop the slideshow.

 TIPS

What is the Themes button on the iPhoto toolbar for?

Click **Themes** () to open a dialog for controlling the slideshow's overall look. Classic gives a regular slideshow. Ken Burns pans and zooms over each photo to add interest. Scrapbook presents each photo on a scrapbook page. Shatter adds vigorous animation. Sliding Panels gradually uncovers each new slide. Snapshots piles each slide on top of the previous slide like a stack of photos.

What does the Slideshow button on the main iPhoto toolbar do?

The Slideshow button on the toolbar enables you to run an instant slideshow without saving a group of slides in the slideshow. In the Photos library, an Event, an album, or other item, select the photos you want to view. Click **Slideshow** () on the toolbar. The Slideshow dialog opens, and you can choose slideshow settings as discussed on these pages before starting the slideshow.

Publish Photos to a MobileMe Gallery

If you subscribe to Apple's MobileMe service, you can publish photo albums from iPhoto to your MobileMe Gallery. You can choose who can view each album and decide whether to let others download photo files or upload their own photos.

Publish Photos to a MobileMe Gallery

1 Click an album in the sidebar.

2 Click **MobileMe** ( ).

*Note: If you are not currently signed in to MobileMe, a MobileMe dialog opens. Click **Sign In**.*

The Would You Like to Publish *Album* to Your MobileMe Gallery? dialog opens.

3 Choose who can view your album. Click **Everyone** for the gallery to be viewable by everyone. Click **Only me** to keep it private.

4 Click **Downloading of photos or entire album** (changes to) if you want visitors to be able to download high-quality versions of the photos.

5 Click **Uploading of photos via web browser** (changes to) if you want visitors to be able to upload photos.

6 Click **Adding of photos via email** (changes to) if you want to e-mail photos to the gallery.

7 Click **Show Advanced**.

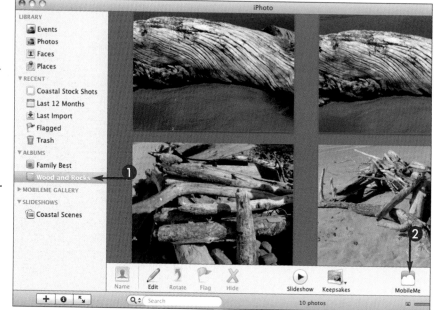

An extra section appears at the bottom of the dialog.

8 Click **Hide album on my Gallery page** (☐ changes to ☑) if you want to hide the album.

9 If you selected **Downloading of photos or entire album**, click 🔽 next to Download Quality and choose **Optimized** or **Actual Size**.

10 Click **Publish**.

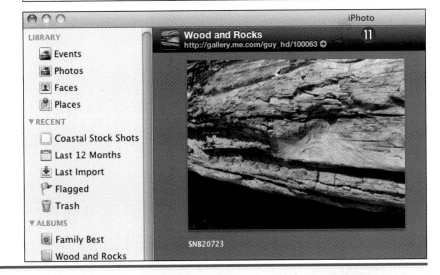

Would you like to publish "Wood and Rocks" to your MobileMe Gallery?

This will create an album in Guy Hart-Davis's MobileMe Gallery. The album can be viewed with Safari or any modern web browser. The title of this album will be visible to everyone viewing your Gallery.

Album Viewable by: Everyone

Allow: ☑ Downloading of photos or entire album
☐ Uploading of photos via web browser
☐ Adding of photos via email

Show: ☑ Photo titles
☐ Email address for uploading photos

Advanced: ☐ Hide album on my Gallery page
Download quality: Actual Size

Hide Advanced   Cancel   Publish

iPhoto adds the album to the MobileMe Gallery in the sidebar and publishes the album to your MobileMe Gallery.

11 Click the link to open the gallery in a Web browser.

TIPS

Why would I hide an album on my Gallery page?

Hiding an album is useful when you want to share it only with some people. You can e-mail the album's Web address to the people who need to see the album. Other people do not see the album on your Gallery page and so cannot access it without guessing the address. Alternatively, you can password-protect the album but not hide it.

Should I choose Optimized or Actual Size for downloadable photos?

Choose **Actual Size** if you want visitors to download full-quality versions of the photos so that they can edit them. Choose **Optimized** to provide visitors with high-quality versions of photos for viewing on their computers. Full-size photos take longer for you to upload and for visitors to download than optimized photos.

Send a Photo via E-mail

From iPhoto, you can quickly start an e-mail message containing one or more photos. You can then add text to the message in Mail and send it to any of your contacts.

You can either include the full version of the photo or create a smaller version of it that will transfer more quickly.

Send a Photo via E-mail

① In iPhoto, click the photo you want to send via e-mail.

② Click **Email** (🖼).

The Mail Photo dialog opens.

③ Choose a size for the photo. See the tip for recommendations.

④ Click **Titles** (☑ changes to ☐) if you do not want to include a title with each photo.

⑤ Click **Descriptions** (☑ changes to ☐) if you do not want to include a description with each photo.

⑥ Click **Location information** (☐ changes to ☑) if you want to include the photo's location.

⑦ Click **Compose Message**.

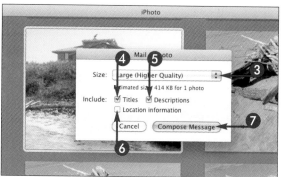

A new message in Mail opens, including the photo.

8 Type the recipient's address.

9 Edit the subject for the message as needed.

10 Type any message text you want to include.

11 Click **Send** ( ).

Mail sends the message.

TIP

Which size should I use for sending a photo?
In the Mail Photo dialog, choose **Small (Faster Downloading)** if the recipient needs only to view the photos at a small size in the message. Choose **Medium** to let the recipient view more detail in the photos in the message. Choose **Large (Higher Quality)** to send versions of the photos that the recipient can save and use in albums or Web pages. Choose **Actual Size (Full Quality)** to send the photos unchanged, so that the recipient can enjoy, edit, and use them at full resolution.

Take Photos or Videos of Yourself

Your iMac includes a built-in iSight camera that is great not only for video chats with iChat but also for taking photos and videos of yourself using the Photo Booth application. You can use Photo Booth's special effects to enliven the photos or videos.

① Click **Finder** (🖥️) on the Dock.

A Finder window opens to your default folder.

② Click **Applications**.

The Applications folder opens.

③ Press and hold ⟨Option⟩ while you double-click **Photo Booth**.

The Finder window closes, and the Photo Booth window opens.

④ If your face appears off center, tilt your iMac's screen or move yourself so that it is correctly positioned.

⑤ Choose the type of picture to take:

● For a single still, click **Take a still picture** (□).

● For four pictures, click **Take four quick pictures** (⊞).

● For a video, click **Take a movie clip** (▣).

⑥ To add effects to the photo or video, click **Effects**.

The Photo Booth window shows eight effects applied to the preview.

Note: *To see more effects, click*  *. The center effect on each screen is Normal. Use this effect to remove any other effect.*

7 Click the effect you want to use.

8 Click **Take Photo** (⊙) or **Take Movie** (⊙).

Photo Booth counts down from three and then takes the photo or photos, or starts recording the movie.

If you are taking a movie, click ⊡ when you are ready to stop.

● Photo Booth adds the photo or movie to the photo well.

TIP

How can I use the photos and video I take in Photo Booth?

After taking a photo or video, click it in the photo well. Photo Booth displays buttons for using the photo or video. Click **Email** (●) to send it in a message. Click **iPhoto** (●) to add it to iPhoto. Click **Account Picture** (●) to use it as your account picture. Click **Buddy Picture** (●) to make it your buddy picture in iChat.

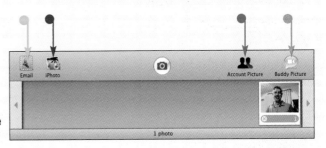

Creating Your Own Movies

Your iMac includes all the software you need to make professional-quality movies from your own video footage. You can import video from either a tape camcorder or a digital camcorder, edit the footage, add titles and credits, and give the movie a soundtrack. You can then share the movie with other applications, export the movie to a file, or post it on YouTube.

Open and Close iMovie 240

Import Video from a Tape Camcorder 242

Import Video from a Digital Camcorder 244

Import Video from a Digital Camera 246

Import Video Files from Your iMac 248

Create a Movie Project 250

**Select the Video Footage You
    Want to Use** 252

Build the Movie Project from Clips 254

Add Transitions between Video Clips 256

Add a Still Photo to the Movie Project 258

Create a Soundtrack for the Movie 260

Add Titles and Credits 262

Share the Movie on YouTube 264

Open and Close iMovie

iMovie is a powerful but easy-to-use application for importing video from camcorders, editing the video, and creating movies from it.

To work with iMovie, you must first open the application, either from the Dock or from the Applications folder. After you have finished using iMovie, close the application to free up your Mac's hardware resources again.

Open and Close iMovie

Open iMovie

1 Click **iMovie** () on the Dock.

*Note: If iMovie does not appear on the Dock, click the desktop, and then choose **Go** and **Applications**. In the Finder window that opens, double-click **iMovie**.*

The iMovie window opens.

If this is the first time you have run iMovie, the application creates a new movie project named My First Project.

If you have already run iMovie and created other projects, iMovie displays your most recent project.

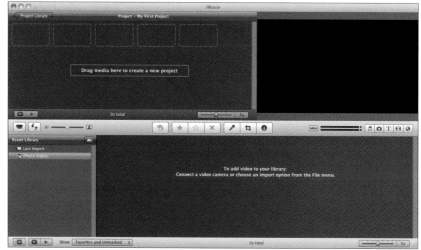

Close iMovie

1 Click **iMovie**.

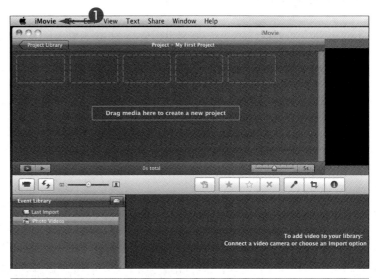

The iMovie menu opens.

2 Click **Quit iMovie**.

iMovie closes.

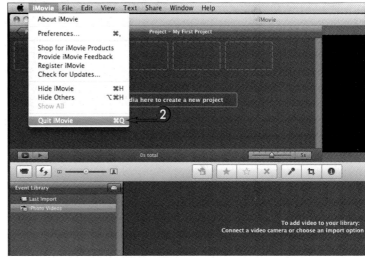

Where do I create my movies in iMovie?

To enable you to make movies as easily as possible, the iMovie window has the Project Library and the Project pane share the same space. From the Project Library, double-click a project to open it in the Project pane so that you can work in it. From the Project pane, click the **Project Library** button to close the project and display the Project Library again.

How do I save changes to a movie project in iMovie?

After you create a movie project, iMovie automatically saves changes to the project for you. This means that you do not need to save changes manually as you have to do in many applications.

Import Video from a Tape Camcorder

If you have video footage on a camcorder that records on to video tape, you can connect the camcorder to your iMac with a FireWire cable and import the video. You can either import all of the footage at once or select the parts of it to import, using your iMac to control the camera's playback.

Import Video from a Tape Camcorder

Import All Footage

① Connect the camcorder to your iMac using a FireWire cable.

② Switch the camcorder to play mode or VCR mode. iMovie recognizes the camcorder and opens if it is not already running.

③ In the Import From window, click **Import**.

④ In the import options dialog, click 🔼 and choose the hard disk to save the video on.

⑤ Click **Create new Event** (⦿ changes to ⦿).

⑥ Type the name for the Event.

⑦ Click **Split days into new Events** (☑ changes to ☐) if you do not want to make each day a separate Event.

⑧ Click **Analyze for stabilization after import** (☐ changes to ☑) to apply stabilization automatically.

⑨ Click **Import**, and iMovie winds the tape back to the beginning and imports the video footage.

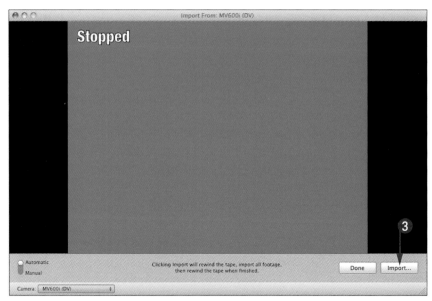

Import Chosen Footage

1 Repeat steps **1** and **2**.

2 In the Import From window, click **Manual**; iMovie displays playback controls.

3 Wind the tape to where you want to start importing:

● Click ▶ to start playback.

● Click ▶▶ to speed up playback forward.

● Click ◀◀ to reverse playback at speed.

4 Click **Import**.

5 In the import options dialog, click **Create new Event** (○ changes to ◉).

6 Type the name for the Event.

7 Click **Split days into new Events** (☑ changes to ☐) if you do not want to make each day a separate Event.

8 Click **Analyze for stabilization after import** (☐ changes to ☑) to apply stabilization automatically.

9 Click **Import**.

10 Click **Stop** (■) at the end of the video you want to import.

11 Click **Done**.

Which hard disk should I save the video footage on?

When you are starting to use iMovie, save the video to your iMac's hard disk, which is normally called Macintosh HD unless you have renamed it. But if you have connected a high-speed external hard disk that you can devote to iMovie files, choose that disk instead.

What is an Event, and how do I use Events?

An Event is a way of dividing up your video clips by the date and time you took them or by their theme. When you import video, you can choose between putting it in an existing Event or creating a new Event. You can create further Events later as needed and move video clips to them.

Import Video from a Digital Camcorder

If you have video footage on a camcorder that records on to a memory card, a hard disk, or a DVD, you can connect the camcorder to your iMac with a USB cable and import the video. Because the video clips are stored as separate files, you can choose which clips to import, or simply import all of them at once.

Import Video from a Digital Camcorder

① Connect the camcorder to your iMac with a USB cable.

Note: *Connect the USB cable to a USB port on the iMac, not to a port on the keyboard (if your iMac has a wired keyboard).*

② Switch the camcorder on and put it in Play mode or VCR mode.

iMovie recognizes the camcorder and opens if it is not already running.

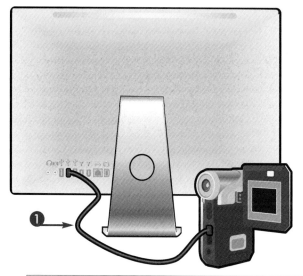

The Import From window opens.

Note: *If you want to import all the clips, go to step 5.*

③ Click **Manual**.

④ Click ☑ for each clip you do not want to import (☑ changes to ☐).

Note: Click **Uncheck All** *if you need to uncheck all the boxes quickly.*

⑤ Click **Import All**.

A dialog of import options opens.

⑥ Click **Create new Event** (○ changes to ◉).

⑦ Type the name for the Event.

⑧ Click **Split days into new Events** (☑ changes to ☐) if you do not want to make each day a separate Event.

⑨ Click **Analyze for stabilization after import** (☐ changes to ☑) if you want to apply stabilization automatically.

⑩ Click **Import**.

iMovie imports the movie clips.

⑪ Click **Done**.

Should I check the Analyze for Stabilization after Import check box when importing video?

iMovie's video stabilization has two steps. First, you have iMovie analyze the video to decide which parts need stabilization; you can do this either when you import video, or later. Second, you apply the stabilization. Generally, it is better to analyze video for stabilization after importing it, for two reasons. First, the analysis makes the video importing take longer. Second, you may want to discard footage without analyzing it for stabilization, and analyze only the footage you want to use.

Import Video from a Digital Camera

If your digital camera takes videos as well as still photos, you can bring the videos into iMovie and use them in your movies.

To import videos from a digital camera, you must normally use iPhoto rather than iMovie. You can then access the videos through iMovie's iPhoto Videos collection.

Import Video from a Digital Camera

1. Connect the digital camera to your iMac with a USB cable.

2. Switch the camera on.

   iPhoto automatically launches and displays the contents of the camera.

   Note: *If the digital camera contains both photos and videos, iPhoto displays both. Each video has the* ■ *icon.*

3. Type the name you want to give the Event.

4. Optionally, type a description for the Event.

   Note: *To import just some videos, select those you want and then click* **Import Selected.**

5. Click **Import All**.

   iPhoto imports the videos.

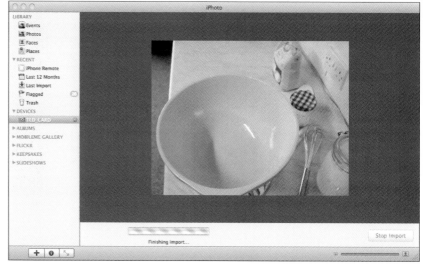

The Delete Photos on Your Camera? dialog opens.

6 Click **Keep Photos**.

Note: The Delete Photos on Your Camera? dialog always mentions photos even if you have imported videos. It is best to keep the photos or videos on the camera until you have checked what you imported.

The dialog closes, and the videos appear in the Last Import list in iPhoto.

7 In iMovie, click **iPhoto Videos** in Event Library.

● The iPhoto videos appear, and you can use them in your movies as described later in this chapter.

Can I play a video in iPhoto?
In iPhoto, double-click the video to open it in a QuickTime window. You can then control playback by using the on-screen control bar that appears (●). When the video has finished playing, choose **QuickTime** and **Quit QuickTime**.

Import Video Files from Your iMac

If you have video files stored on your iMac, you can import them into iMovie so that you can use them in your movies.

You can also use this technique to import video files from a digital camera whose memory card you can remove from the camera and connect to your iMac.

① In iMovie, click **File**.

The File menu opens.

② Click **Import**.

The Import submenu opens.

③ Click **Movies**.

④ In the Import dialog, click the folder that contains the video files.

⑤ Click the file, or select multiple files.

⑥ Click ⬘ next to Save To, and click the drive on which you want to store the files.

⑦ Click **Create new Event** (○ changes to ●).

⑧ Type the name for the Event.

Note: If you want to add the video files to an existing Event, click **Add to existing Event**, click ⬘, and then click the Event.

⑨ Make sure **Optimize video** is checked (☑).

⑩ Make sure **Full – Original Size** appears in the pop-up menu.

⑪ Click **Copy files** (○ changes to ●).

⑫ Click **Import**.

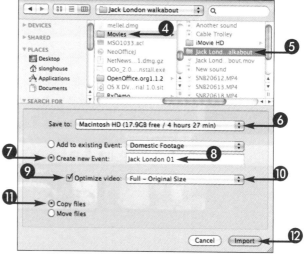

iMovie imports and optimizes the video or videos.

● The video clips appear in the Last Import area.

TIP

Why should I choose Full – Original Size when importing video?

iMovie can import high-definition video either at full quality or at reduced quality, which iMovie describes as Large. Use full quality unless your iMac is severely short of disk space. It is better to retain video quality so that your video footage is as good as possible. After making your movie, you can export it at a lower resolution if you want, while retaining a full-quality version on your iMac.

Create a Movie Project

To make a movie, you first create a *movie project*, a file that contains the details of the movie. You then add video clips to the movie project, arrange and edit them, and add transitions and titles.

iMovie automatically creates a new movie project named My First Project when you first launch the application. You can rename this project or delete it.

Create a Movie Project

① Click **New Project** ().

Note: *If the Project Library shows you two or more hard disks, first click the disk on which you want to create the project — for example, Macintosh HD. Then click* **New Project***.*

The New Project dialog opens.

② Type the name for the project.

③ Click 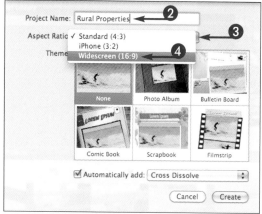 next to Aspect Ratio.

④ Choose the aspect ratio for the movie: **Widescreen (16:9)**, **Standard (4:3)**, or **iPhone (3:2)**.

⑤ If you want to apply a theme, click it in the Theme area.

Note: A theme is a predefined set of screen transitions, titles, and other effects for a movie.

⑥ If you chose a theme, make sure **Automatically add transitions and titles** is checked (☑).

*Note: If you are not using a theme, you can check **Automatically add** (☐ changes to ☑) to automatically add transitions between clips. Click ↕ and choose the transition type — for example, **Cross Dissolve**.*

⑦ Click **Create**.

● iMovie creates the project, adds it to the Project Library, and opens it in the Project pane.

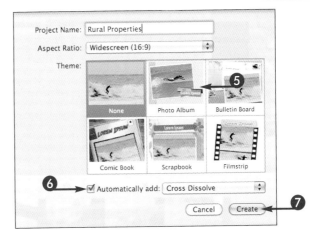

How do I rename a movie project?

To rename a movie project, double-click its name (●) in the Project Library. iMovie displays an edit box around the name. Type the new name and press Return.

How do I delete a movie project?

To delete a movie project, you move it to the Trash. Control-click or right-click the project in the Project Library, and then click **Move Project to Trash** on the shortcut menu. Deleting a movie project deletes only the details of the items it contains. The video clips remain in your Event Library, where you can use them in other projects.

Select the Video Footage You Want to Use

After importing video from your camcorder or your iMac, you have one or more Events in iMovie containing *video clips* — short sections of video.

Next, identify the video footage you want to use in your projects. To do so, you play back the clips and select the parts you want to use. You can mark a clip as a Favorite or as a reject for easy sorting.

Select the Video Footage You Want to Use

View a Clip

1. In the Event Library, click the Event that contains the clip you want to view.

2. Position the mouse pointer over a clip.

● The playhead appears as a vertical red line across the clip.

● The viewer displays the frame under the playhead.

3. Press `Spacebar`, and iMovie plays the clip in the viewer.

4. Press `Spacebar` again to stop playback.

Select Part of a Clip

1. In the Event Library, click the Event that contains the clip you want to view.

2. Position the mouse pointer over the clip.

3. Click the clip.

   iMovie selects a four-second section from where you clicked.

4. Click and drag a selection handle left or right to change the length of the selection.

Note: *To move a selection without changing its length, click the yellow line at the top of the selection and then drag.*

Mark a Selection as a Favorite or a Reject

1 Select part of a clip as explained on the previous page.

2 Click **Mark Selection as Favorite** (★).

● iMovie puts a green bar across the top of the selection, indicating that it is a favorite.

3 Select part of another clip.

4 Click **Reject Selection** (✖).

● iMovie puts a red bar across the top of the selection, indicating it is a reject.

5 Click **Unmark Selection** (☆), and iMovie removes the marking from the selection.

View Only Your Favorites

1 Click ⬌ next to Show, and then click **Favorites Only**.

iMovie displays only the footage you have marked as favorites.

Note: You can choose **Favorites and Unmarked** to view favorites and footage you have not marked as rejected.

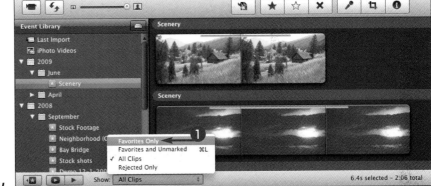

Can I change the amount of video iMovie selects when I click a clip?

Choose **iMovie** and **Preferences** to open the Preferences window, and then click the **Browser** tab (●). Click and drag the **Clicking in Events Browser selects** slider (●) to choose the number of seconds a click selects. You can also select **Clicking in Events Browser selects entire clip** (●) if you prefer. You can also set what a double-click does by selecting **Edit** or **Play** in the Double-Click To area (●). Click 🔘 to close the Preferences window.

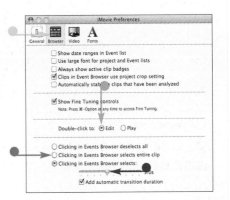

Build the Movie Project from Clips

After grading your clips, you can quickly add your favorites to the movie project to build the movie.

You can then arrange the clips into the order in which you want them to play.

Build the Movie Project from Clips

1 In the Project Library, double-click the project.

iMovie opens the project in the Project pane.

2 Select the clip or partial clip you want to add to the project.

Note: *Use the selection methods explained on the previous two pages to select part of a clip.* Option *-click to select an entire clip.*

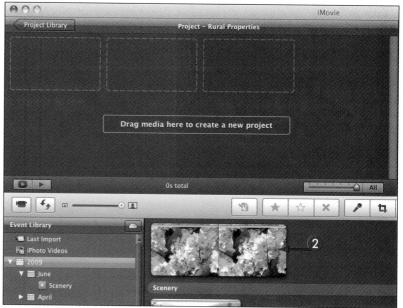

③ Click the clip and drag it to the Project pane.

iMovie adds the clip to the project.

Note: *If you chose to have iMovie add transitions to your movie automatically, a transition icon such as ▨ appears before and after each clip.*

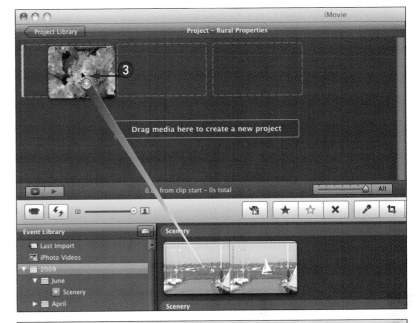

④ To rearrange the clips in the movie, click a clip and drag it to where you want it.

● The vertical green bar shows where the clip will land.

Note: *To remove a clip from a project, click the clip in the Project pane and then press* Delete *.*

 TIP

Why does iMovie break up my video footage into separate clips?

When you import video footage from a tape camcorder, iMovie automatically creates clips from different sections of the tape by using the time code stamped on the frames: Where there is a gap in the time code, iMovie creates a new clip. A camcorder that stores digital files in memory, on a hard disk, or on DVD automatically creates its own clips as you record, and iMovie preserves these clips.

Add Transitions between Video Clips

To make one clip flow better into the next, you can apply an effect called a *transition* between the clips. For example, the widely used Cross Dissolve transition gradually replaces the end of the first clip with the beginning of the second clip.

iMovie can apply transitions automatically, but you can retain greater control by applying them manually.

Add Transitions between Video Clips

① Click **Transitions** (▣).

● The Transitions browser pane opens.

② Click the transition you want to apply.

Note: *Position the mouse pointer over a transition to see a preview of its effect.*

③ Drag the transition to the Project pane and drop it between the clips.

iMovie adds an icon representing the transition.

Note: *Each transition has a different icon. With practice, you can identify transitions by their icons.*

④ Position the mouse pointer over the transition icon.

● The viewer shows a preview of the transition.

⑤ Double-click the transition icon.

An Inspector dialog opens.

⑥ Type the duration of the transition.

⑦ Make sure **Applies to all transitions** is unchecked (▢).

⑧ Click **Done**.

The Inspector dialog closes.

How can I change to a different transition?

After applying a transition between two video clips, you can switch to another transition by clicking and dragging it from the Transitions browser and dropping it on the existing transition. The replacement transition picks up the duration of the existing transition. You do not need to delete the existing transition first.

Should I add transitions to my movie automatically?

When using a theme to create a movie, set iMovie to add transitions automatically, because doing so gives you the best effect from the theme. When creating a movie without a theme, apply transitions manually, adding them only where the clips actually need them. For clips that flow easily from one to the next, leave a *straight cut* with no transition.

Add a Still Photo to the Movie Project

As well as video clips, you can use still photos in your movie projects. This capability lets you enrich your movies with your iPhoto library.

You can crop a photo to show exactly the right part, and you can bring life and movement to it by adding a Ken Burns effect, panning and zooming across the photo.

Add a Still Photo to the Movie Project

① Click **Photos** (📷).

● The Photo browser pane opens.

② Click a photo, drag it to the Project pane, and drop it where you want it to appear.

③ Double-click the photo in the Project pane.

An Inspector dialog opens.

④ Set the number of seconds you want the photo to play for.

⑤ Make sure that **Applies to all stills** is unchecked (☐).

⑥ Click **Done**.

The Inspector dialog closes.

⑦ Click the photo.

Control buttons appear on the photo.

⑧ Click **Action** (⚙▾).

The Action menu opens.

⑨ Click **Cropping, Ken Burns & Rotation**.

The viewer displays the cropping tools.

⑩ Click **Ken Burns**.

The Ken Burns tools appear.

⑪ Click and drag the green rectangle to cover the area where you want the Ken Burns effect to start.

⑫ Click and drag the red rectangle to cover the area where you want the effect to end.

● To switch the green and red rectangles, click .

⑬ Click **Play Clip** (▶).

iMovie plays a preview of the effect.

⑭ Click **Done**.

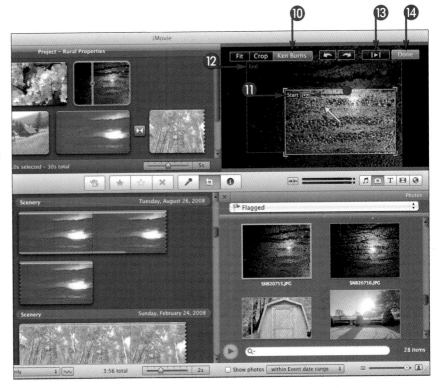

TIP

How do I crop or rotate a photo?

Click the photo in the Project pane, click **Action** (⚙▾), and then click **Cropping, Ken Burns & Rotation**. Click **Crop** (●) to display the cropping tools. Click and drag a corner handle (●) to specify the cropping. Click ◀ (●) to rotate 90 degrees counterclockwise, or click ▶ (●) to rotate 90 degrees clockwise. Click **Done** (●) when you have finished cropping and rotating.

Create a Soundtrack for the Movie

Your movie includes any audio you recorded along with your video clips, but you can also create a soundtrack for a movie by adding a song or playlist that plays in the background.

You can also add a sound effect at a particular point in a movie, or add narration to any footage that needs it.

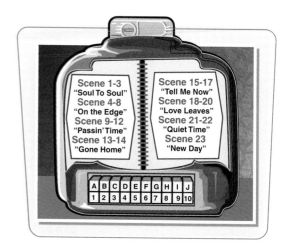

Create a Soundtrack for the Movie

Add a Background Track

1 Click **Music and Sound Effects** (🎵).

● The Music and Sound Effects browser pane opens.

2 Click ⬍ and choose the source of music — for example, **iTunes**.

3 Click a song and drag it to the Project pane.

Note: *Make sure the Project pane shows a green background when you drop the song. This means the song becomes a background track for the first part of the movie.*

4 Click **Play Project from Beginning** (▶).

iMovie plays the movie with the soundtrack.

Add a Sound Effect to a Video Clip

1 Click **Music and Sound Effects** (♫).

● The Music and Sound Effects browser pane opens.

2 Click ⬍ and choose the source of sound effects — for example, **iLife Sound Effects**.

3 Click a sound effect and drag it to the Project pane.

4 Move the mouse pointer across a clip to the frame at which you want the sound effect to start playing.

5 Drop the sound effect.

● iMovie attaches the sound effect to the clip.

Set the Sound Level

1 Double-click the audio clip or background in the Project pane.

An Inspector dialog opens.

2 Click **Audio**.

The audio controls appear.

3 Click and drag the **Volume** slider.

4 Click **Done**.

The Inspector dialog closes.

How do I add narration to a movie?

Click **Voiceover** (🎤) to open the Voiceover dialog. Click ⬍ (●) next to Record From and choose the microphone. Speak sample text and click and drag the **Input Volume** slider (●) to set the input volume. Position the mouse pointer over a clip to position the playhead where you want narration to start, then click to start recording. When you have finished recording, click again. Click ⊗ or 🎤 to close the Voiceover dialog.

Add Titles and Credits

To give your movie an identity and a professional look, add a title, subtitle, and credits. iMovie provides a wide variety of title types suitable for different kinds of movies.

You can also add title screens to other parts of the movie that need them — for example, to make a change of scene explicit to the audience.

Add Titles and Credits

Add a Title

1 Click **Titles** ($\boxed{\text{T}}$).

● The Titles browser pane opens.

2 Click a title and drag it to the beginning of the movie. Drop the title before the first clip.

iMovie adds the title and displays the Choose Background dialog.

3 Click the background you want.

iMovie closes the Choose Background dialog and applies the background.

4 Click each placeholder and type your text in its place.

Note: *If you do not need one of the placeholders, select it, and then press* Delete *to delete it.*

5 Click **Done**.

iMovie applies the text to the title.

Add Credits

1 Click **Titles** (⊤).

● The Titles browser pane opens.

2 Click the Scrolling Credits title and drag it to the end of the movie. Drop the title after the last clip.

iMovie adds the title to the movie and displays the Choose Background dialog.

3 Click the background you want.

iMovie applies the background.

4 Click each placeholder and type your text in its place.

Note: *If you do not need one of the placeholders, select it, and then press* Delete *to delete it.*

5 Click **Done**.

iMovie applies the text to the title.

6 Click **Titles** (⊤).

The Titles browser pane closes.

Can I superimpose a title or credits on a screen?

Yes. Click the title in the Titles browser and drag it to the Project pane. Position the mouse pointer over a clip until the playhead is at the frame where you want the title to start playing and then drop the title. You can then edit the title text in the viewer (●). When you superimpose a title like this, iMovie does not display the Choose Background dialog because the title uses the clip as its background.

Share the Movie on YouTube

To share a movie with everybody on the Internet, you can post it to the YouTube video-sharing site. iMovie includes a built-in command for creating movies in the format that YouTube requires and for posting movies to the site.

Movies you post on YouTube must be less than 10 minutes long and less than 100 MB in size.

① In the Project Library, **Control**-click or right-click the project.

② Click **Publish to YouTube**.

*Note: The first time you open the Publish Your Project to YouTube dialog, click **Add**. The Add Account dialog opens. Type your YouTube account name, and then click **Done**.*

③ Make sure the Account pop-up menu is showing the right account.

④ Type your YouTube password.

⑤ Click ▲ and choose the category to assign to the movie.

⑥ Type a title.

⑦ Type a description.

⑧ Type tags for the movie. See the second tip.

⑨ Click the size you want to publish (○ changes to ●). Usually, **Medium** is the best choice.

⑩ Click **Make this movie personal** (☑ changes to ☐) if you want the movie to be available to everyone on YouTube.

⑪ Click **Next**.

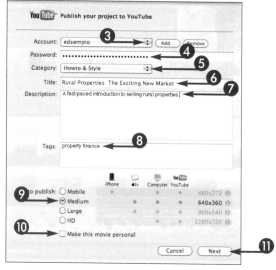

The YouTube Terms of Service
screen opens.

⑫ Read the terms.

⑬ Click **Publish**.

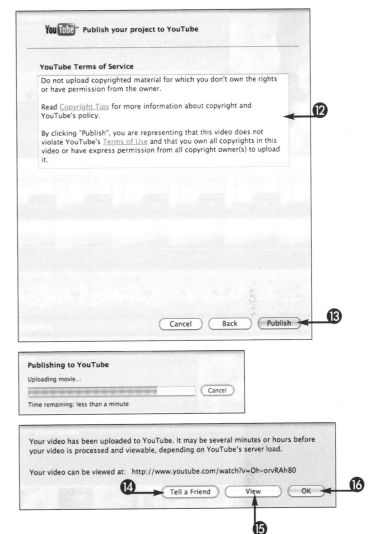

iMovie publishes the project to
YouTube.

A dialog opens.

⑭ Click **Tell a Friend** if you want to
start an e-mail message to friends
telling them the movie is available.

⑮ Click **View** if you want to check
that the movie has transferred
properly.

⑯ Click **OK** to close the dialog.

How do I get an account on YouTube?

Click **Safari** (🧭) on the Dock to open a
browser window. Triple-click in the Address
field, type **youtube.com**, and press
(Return). Safari displays the YouTube home
page. Click the **Create Account** link, and
then follow the instructions on the Web
page that appears. Be sure to review the
Google Terms of Service and YouTube
Terms of Service before accepting the
agreement.

What are tags and why should I use them?

A *tag* is a text term that helps
explain concisely what a movie
is about. YouTube uses tag
information in searches, so the
tags help people find movies
they are interested in. By adding
suitable tags to your movie, you
can make your movie easier to
find and increase its audience.

Customizing Your iMac to Suit You

Mac OS X looks great and is easy to use straight out of the box, but you can customize it further to suit your needs. You can change many aspects of Mac OS X. For example, you can change the desktop background, apply a screen saver, change the icons on the Dock, give yourself more screen space, and make the keyboard and mouse easier to use. You can also give your iMac commands with your voice, run applications each time you log in, or put your iMac to sleep when you are not using it.

Change Your Desktop Background 268

Set Up a Screen Saver.................................270

**Make the Dock Show the Icons
   You Need** 272

Create Hot Corners to Run Exposé Easily ...274

Give Yourself More Desktop Space.............276

**Add a Second Monitor So You Can
   See More**...278

**Make the Keyboard and Mouse Easier
   to Use** 280

Make the Screen Easier to See 282

Tell Spotlight Which Folders to Search......284

Control Your iMac with Your Voice.............286

**Save Time by Running Applications
   Each Time You Log In**...................................288

**Save Power by Putting Your iMac to
   Sleep** 290

**Choose When to Check for Software
   Updates**..292

Change Your Desktop Background

The easiest way to make your iMac look different is to change the desktop background. Mac OS X includes a wide variety of backgrounds, but you can also use your own photos.

You can choose between displaying a single picture on the desktop and displaying a series of images that change automatically.

1 **Control**-click or right-click the desktop.

   The shortcut menu opens.

2 Click **Change Desktop Background**.

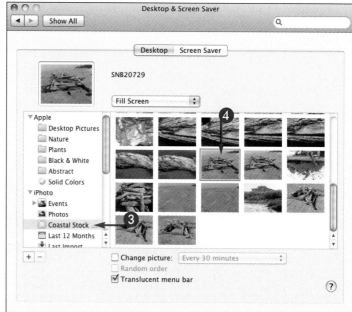

   The Desktop tab of Desktop & Screen Saver preferences opens.

3 Click the category of image you want to see.

Note: *The Apple section of the categories list contains the built-in desktop backgrounds. The iPhoto section contains your iPhoto albums. If you add folders, as described in the tip, they appear in the Folders section.*

   The images in the category appear in the right-hand pane.

4 Click the image you want to apply to the desktop.

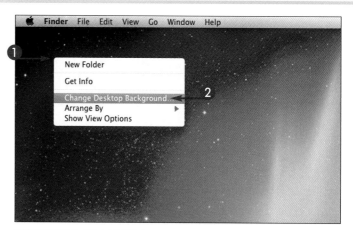

The image appears on the desktop.

5 If you chose a photo or picture of your own, click and choose how to fit the image to the screen. See the tip for details.

6 If you want to set a series of background images, click the category.

7 Click **Change picture** (☐ changes to ☑).

8 Click ▲ next to Change Picture and choose the interval — for example, **When logging in** or **Every 30 minutes**.

9 Click **Random order** (☐ changes to ☑) if you want the images to appear in random order.

10 Click **Translucent menu bar** (☑ changes to ☐) if you want the menu bar to appear solid gray rather than translucent.

11 Click the **System Preferences** menu and click **Quit System Preferences** to close System Preferences.

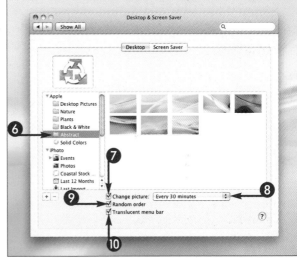

TIPS

Which option should I choose for fitting the image to the screen?

In the Desktop & Screen Saver preferences, choose **Fit to Screen** to match the image's height or width (whichever is nearest) to the screen. Choose **Fill Screen** to make an image fill the screen without distortion but cropping off parts that do not fit. Choose **Stretch to Fill Screen** to stretch the image to fit the screen exactly, distorting it as needed. Choose **Tile** to cover the desktop with multiple copies of the image. Choose **Center** to display the image at full size in the middle of the desktop.

I have a folder of pictures I want to use as desktop backgrounds. Can I add them to the Desktop tab?

Click **Add** (⊞) below the categories box. A dialog opens. Click the folder, and then click **Choose**. The folder appears in the Folders section of the categories list. Click the folder, and then click the picture you want.

Set Up a Screen Saver

A *screen saver* is an image, a sequence of images, or a moving pattern that Mac OS X displays to hide what your screen is showing when you leave your iMac idle. You can choose what screen saver to use and how soon to start it. If you prefer, you can use no screen saver at all.

① **Control** -click or right-click the desktop.

The shortcut menu opens.

② Click **Change Desktop Background**.

● The Desktop pane of Desktop & Screen Saver preferences opens.

③ Click **Screen Saver**.

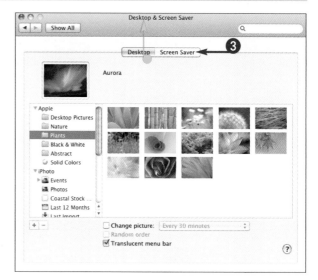

The Screen Saver pane appears.

④ Click a screen saver in the list on the left.

Note: The Apple category of screen savers contains the screen savers supplied with Mac OS X. The Pictures category enables you to create screen savers from your photos or from pictures included with Mac OS X.

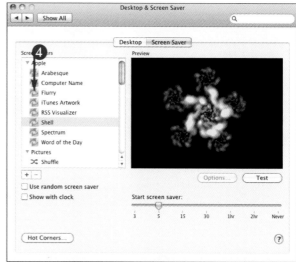

The screen saver you clicked starts playing in the Preview area.

5 Click and drag **Start screen saver** to set the length of time before the screen saver starts.

*Note: To turn the screen saver off, click and drag **Start screen saver** to Never, all the way to the right.*

6 Click **Test** if you want to see the full screen saver.

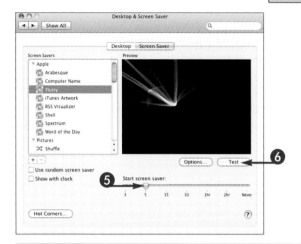

The screen saver plays full screen.

7 Click anywhere on the screen saver when you want to stop the preview.

The Screen Saver pane of the Desktop & Screen Saver pane appears again.

8 Click the **System Preferences** menu and click **Quit System Preferences** to close System Preferences.

TIPS

Must I use a screen saver to protect my iMac's screen from damage?

Screen savers originally protected cathode ray tube (CRT) monitors from having static images "burned in" to their screens. LCD screens, such as that on your iMac, do not suffer from this problem, so you need not use a screen saver. Nowadays you can use a screen saver to protect the information on-screen or to provide visual entertainment.

What are the Display Style buttons that appear when I click a screen saver in the Pictures category?

After selecting a Pictures screen saver, you can click **Slideshow** (●) to make a slideshow of the pictures. Click **Collage** (●) to make each picture spiral down to form a collage on a background. Click **Mosaic** (●) to display miniature versions of the pictures tiled in a mosaic.

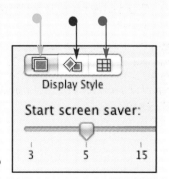

Make the Dock Show the Icons You Need

The Dock is your control center for the applications you run on your iMac, so it is well worth spending a few minutes customizing the Dock to contain the icons you need. You can add applications, files, or folders to the Dock or remove existing items.

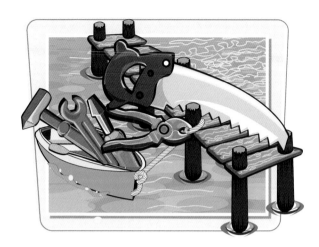

Make the Dock Show the Icons You Need

Add an Application to the Dock

1 Click **Finder** (🖥) on the Dock.

2 In the Finder window, click **Applications** in the sidebar.

3 In the list of applications, click and drag the application you want to the left side of the Dock.

An icon for the application appears on the Dock.

Note: After you open an application from the Applications folder, you can Control-click or right-click its icon on the Dock, highlight or click **Options**, and then click **Keep in Dock**.

Add a File or Folder to the Dock

1 Click **Finder** (🖥) on the Dock.

2 In the Finder window, navigate to the file or folder you want to add to the Dock.

3 Click and drag the file or folder to the right side of the Dock.

An icon for the file or folder appears on the Dock.

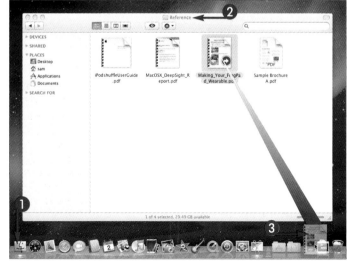

Remove an Item from the Dock

1 Click and drag the icon from the Dock to the desktop.

The icon vanishes in a puff of smoke.

Resize the Dock

1 Click the Dock divider bar and drag it up to make the Dock bigger or down to make the Dock smaller.

The Dock icons grow or shrink so that they occupy all the space on the Dock.

 TIP

Can I customize the Dock further?

You can position the Dock on the left or right side of the screen instead of at the bottom. You can hide the Dock so that it appears only when you move the mouse pointer to the bottom or side of the screen. You can also turn on magnification, which makes the Dock icons grow for easy identification when you position the mouse pointer over them. To reach these options, Control-click or right-click the Dock divider bar (●) and use the shortcut menu. You can also find all these options in the Dock preference pane in System Preferences.

Create Hot Corners to Run Exposé Easily

As discussed in Chapter 3, Exposé lets you see all your open windows and pick the one you need.

To run Exposé with the mouse, set up a *hot corner*, a screen corner that automatically triggers Exposé when you position the mouse pointer there. You can also set up hot corners for starting and stopping the screen saver or putting the display to sleep.

Create Hot Corners to Run Exposé Easily

Set Up a Hot Corner

1 Click .

The Apple menu opens.

2 Click **System Preferences**.

● The System Preferences window opens.

3 Click **Exposé & Spaces**.

The Exposé & Spaces preference pane opens.

4 Click **Exposé**.

The Exposé pane opens.

Note: *If the Exposé & Spaces pane opens with the Exposé pane already at the front, you do not need to click **Exposé**.*

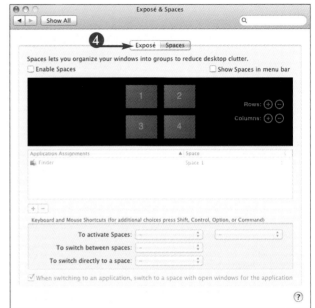

5 Click ⬍ for the hot corner you want to set.

The pop-up menu opens.

6 Click the action you want. For example, click **All Windows** to make the hot corner show all open windows.

7 Choose other hot corner actions as needed.

Note: You can set up two or more hot corners for the same action if you want.

8 Click the **System Preferences** menu and click **Quit System Preferences** to close System Preferences.

Use a Hot Corner to Run Exposé

1 Move the mouse pointer to the hot corner you allocated to Exposé.

Exposé resizes and moves the windows. For example, Exposé shows all the windows.

2 Click the window you want to use.

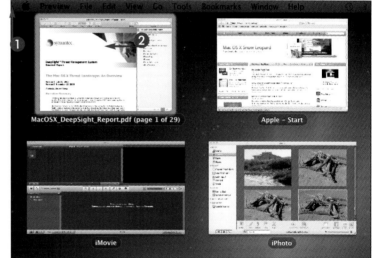

Are there other ways I can run Exposé using the mouse?

As well as using a hot corner, you can use the mouse's secondary button or middle button to run Exposé. In the Exposé section on the Exposé pane, click the ⬍ next to All Windows (●) and choose the keystroke. Press and hold ⌘, Alt, Control, Shift, or a combination of the four keys to add them to the keystroke. Use the same technique for the Application Windows pop-up menu and the Show Desktop pop-up menu.

Give Yourself More Desktop Space

No matter how large your iMac's screen is, it is often useful to have more space to spread out your projects. The Spaces feature lets you create from 2 to 16 *virtual desktops*, separate desktop areas that you can switch among as needed. You can tether an application to a particular space or allow it to appear in any space.

Give Yourself More Desktop Space

Set Up Spaces

1. Click , **System Preferences**, and then **Exposé & Spaces**.

● The Exposé & Spaces preference pane opens.

2. Click **Spaces**.

3. In the Spaces pane, click **Enable Spaces** (☐ changes to ☑).

4. Click **Show Spaces in menu bar** (☐ changes to ☑) if you want to add the Spaces menu to the menu bar.

5. Click the **Rows** ⊕ one or more times to set the number of rows.

6. Click the **Columns** ⊕ one or more times to set the number of columns.

7. Click ⊞, and then click **Other**.

Note: If the application appears on the pop-up menu, click it to add it.

8. In the dialog that opens, click the first application you want to add.

9. ⌘-click each other application to add.

10. Click **Add**.

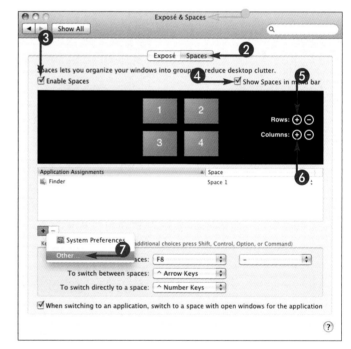

The applications you added appear in the Application Assignments list box.

⑪ Click ⚬ next to an application.

The pop-up menu opens.

⑫ Click the space you want to assign the application to.

⑬ Repeat steps **11** and **12** for each application you want to assign to a space.

⑭ Click the **System Preferences** menu and click **Quit System Preferences** to close System Preferences.

Going to a Space

① Press [F8].

Spaces displays each Space on a grid.

② Click the Space you want to display.

Spaces displays that space full screen.

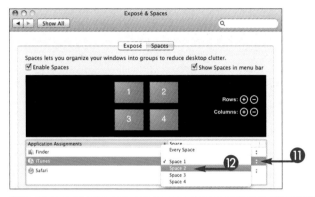

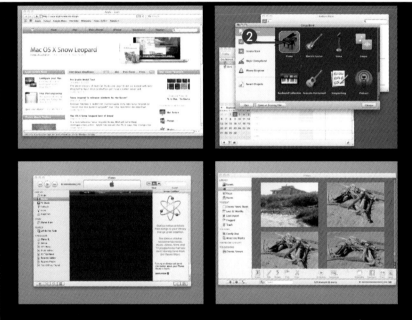

Can I use other ways of switching among spaces?

If you added the Spaces menu to the menu bar in step **6**, click the menu (⚬), and then click the space (●). Alternatively, drag the Spaces application from the Applications folder to the Dock, and then click it; or use the Keyboard and mouse shortcuts area under the Exposé tab of the Exposé & Spaces preference pane to set up your preferred shortcuts for running Spaces. The default keyboard shortcuts are ⌘ and an arrow key to move up, down, left, or right, and ⌘ and a number key to move to a space by number.

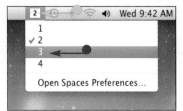

Your iMac has a bright and beautiful screen built in, but you can also add an external monitor to give yourself more space for your work. For a digital LCD screen, you need a mini DisplayPort–to-DVI connector cable. For a CRT monitor or analog LCD screen, you need a mini DisplayPort–to-VGA connector.

Add a Second Monitor So You Can See More

1. Plug the mini DisplayPort connector at the end of the connector cable into the mini DisplayPort on the back of the iMac.

2. Plug the monitor's cable into the DVI port or VGA port on the other end of the connector cable.

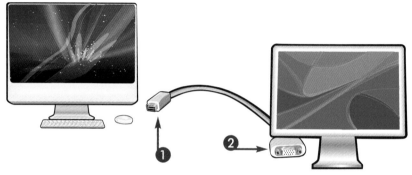

3. Connect the monitor's power supply.

4. Turn the monitor on.

5. Click .

   The Apple menu opens.

6. Click **System Preferences**.

 ● The System Preferences window opens.

7. Click **Displays**.

Note: *Your iMac may automatically open the Displays pane of System Preferences after you connect the monitor and turn it on.*

⑧ In the external monitor's Displays pane, click **Display** if it is not already highlighted.

⑨ Click the resolution you want.

⑩ If the Brightness slider is available, drag it to adjust the display's brightness.

⑪ If the Colors pop-up menu appears, make sure it shows Millions.

⑫ For a CRT, click ⬍ next to Refresh Rate, and then click the highest refresh rate available.

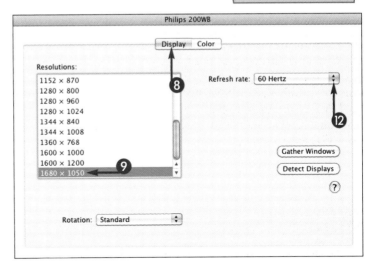

⑬ In the iMac's Displays pane, click **Arrangement**.

⑭ In the Arrangement pane, click and drag either monitor icon to match the monitors' physical locations.

⑮ To move the menu bar and Dock, click and drag the menu bar from the iMac's icon to the external display's icon.

⑯ Click the **System Preferences** menu and click **Quit System Preferences** to close System Preferences.

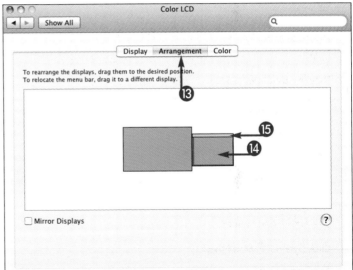

How big of an external monitor can I connect to my iMac?

Recent iMacs can drive an external LCD as large as Apple's 30-inch Cinema display, which has a resolution of 2560 x 1600 pixels. For this, you need a Mini DisplayPort to Dual-Link DVI Adapter cable. Older iMacs can drive external LCDs at resolutions of up to 1920 x 1200 pixels. Check your iMac's documentation for details of its capabilities.

Is there any way to add a third monitor?

Your iMac is built to use only its own screen and one external monitor, but you can add further external monitors by using a USB device such as the ViBook from Village Tronic (villagetronic.com). Such a device adds an extra graphics port via USB, enabling you to connect an extra monitor. You can use two or more ViBooks at once.

Make the Keyboard and Mouse Easier to Use

Your iMac's keyboard and mouse come with default settings that work well for many people, but you may need to change the settings to make the keyboard and mouse easier and more comfortable for you to use.

Control the Keyboard's Repeat Rate

1 Click , **System Preferences**, and then **Keyboard**.

2 In the Keyboard pane, click **Keyboard** if it is not already highlighted.

3 Click and drag the **Key Repeat Rate** slider to control how quickly a key repeats when you hold it down.

4 Click and drag the **Delay Until Repeat** slider to set the length of time Mac OS X waits before repeating a key you hold down.

5 Click **Show All** to see the full set of System Preferences.

Make the Mouse Easier to Use

6 Click **Mouse**.

7 In the Mouse preference pane, click and drag the **Tracking Speed** slider to control how fast the mouse pointer moves.

8 Click and drag the **Scrolling Speed** slider to control how fast the mouse scrolls.

9 Click and drag the **Double-Click Speed** slider if you want to make double-clicks faster or slower.

10 Click **Show All**.

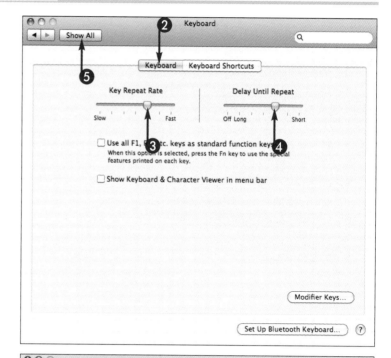

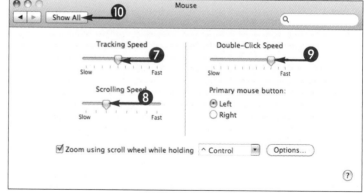

The full set of System Preferences appears.

⑪ Click **Universal Access**.

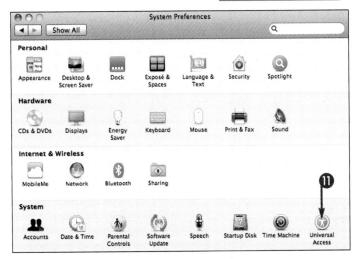

The Universal Access pane opens.

⑫ Click **Mouse**.

The Mouse options appear.

⑬ To make the mouse pointer respond more slowly, drag the **Initial Delay** slider to the right.

⑭ To slow down the mouse pointer's movements, drag the **Maximum Speed** slider to the left.

⑮ To make the mouse pointer easier to see, drag the **Cursor Size** slider to the right.

⑯ Click the **System Preferences** menu and click **Quit System Preferences** to close System Preferences.

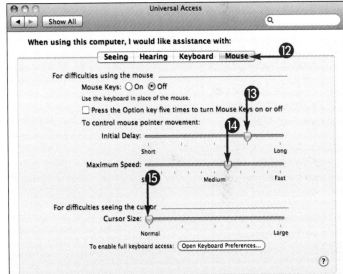

What are the options on the Keyboard tab in Universal Access?

The Keyboard tab in Universal Access contains options for making the keyboard easier to use if you have trouble pressing multiple keys at once. The Sticky Keys feature (⬤) lets you press a modifier key, such as ⌘ or Option, and then the key it modifies, instead of pressing both keys at once. The Slow Keys feature (⬤) helps you cut out unintentional repeated keystrokes if the controls in the Keyboard & Mouse pane are not sufficient.

Sticky Keys: ○ On ⊙ Off
Treats a sequence of modifier keys as a key combination.
☑ Press the Shift key five times to turn Sticky Keys on or off
☑ Beep when a modifier key is set
☑ Display pressed keys on screen

Slow Keys: ○ On ⊙ Off
Puts a delay between when a key is pressed and when it is accepted.
☑ Use click key sounds
Acceptance Delay: Long —————— Short

Make the Screen Easier to See

If you have trouble seeing the screen on your iMac, you can use the Universal Access preferences to make it easier to see.

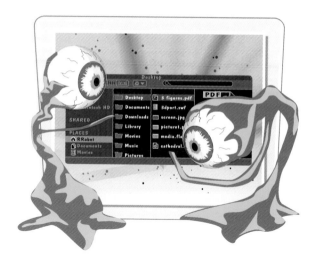

① Click .

The Apple menu opens.

② Click **System Preferences**.

● The System Preferences window opens.

③ Click **Universal Access**.

The Universal Access pane opens.

④ Click **Seeing** if it is not already highlighted.

⑤ To make items on-screen larger, click **On** (○ changes to ◉) under Zoom.

⑥ Click **Options**.

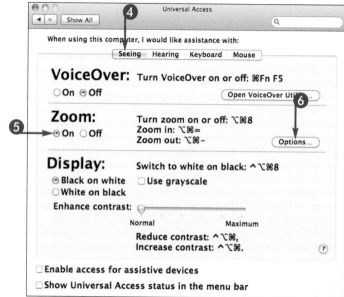

The Options dialog for zooming opens.

7 Click and drag the **Maximum Zoom** slider to set the maximum zoom.

8 Click and drag the **Minimum Zoom** slider to set the minimum zoom.

9 Click **Done**.

The Options dialog for zooming closes.

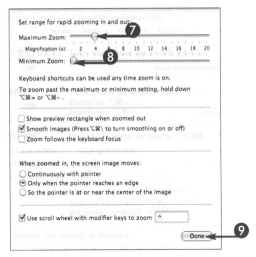

10 Click **White on black** (○ changes to ●) if you want to reverse the video to make the screen easier to see. The effect is like viewing a photographic negative, with each color inverted.

11 Click and drag the **Enhance contrast** slider if you want to increase the contrast.

12 Click the **System Preferences** menu and click **Quit System Preferences** to close System Preferences.

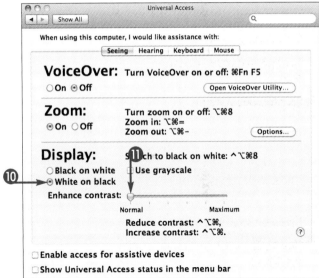

What is the quickest way to turn on the Universal Access features for seeing the screen?

To turn on the Universal Access features for seeing the screen, use keyboard shortcuts. Press ⌘ + Option + 8 to toggle zoom on or off. Press ⌘ + Option + = to zoom in or ⌘ + Option + − to zoom out. Press ⌘ + Option + Control + 8 to toggle White on Black on or off.

Tell Spotlight Which Folders to Search

Mac OS X's Spotlight feature is great for locating the files and folders you need. But if Spotlight finds irrelevant results, or if it does not find the results you are looking for, you can change the folders that Spotlight searches. This is easy to do, but it makes a huge difference to the search results you get.

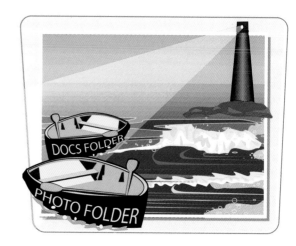

DOCS FOLDER

PHOTO FOLDER

Tell Spotlight Which Folders to Search

1 Click 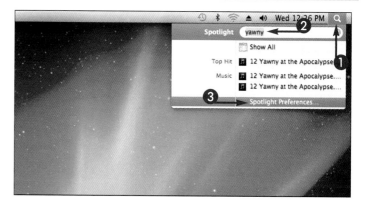.

The Spotlight search field opens.

2 Type a few letters in the search field.

The list of search results appears.

3 Click **Spotlight Preferences**.

The System Preferences window opens with the Spotlight pane at the front.

4 Click **Search Results** if it is not already highlighted.

5 Click ☑ next to any item for which you do not want to see search results (☑ changes to ☐).

6 If you want to change the order of search result categories, click and drag a category up or down the list. The horizontal blue line (●) shows where it will land.

7 Click **Privacy**.

The Privacy pane of Spotlight preferences opens.

8 Click ⊞.

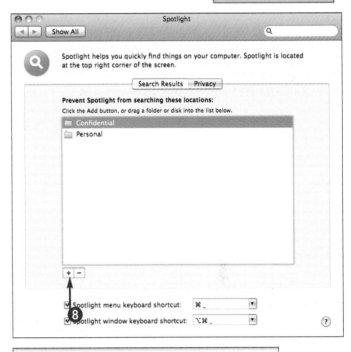

A dialog opens.

9 Click the folder you want to add.

Note: You can select two or more folders by clicking the first and then ⌘ -clicking each of the others.

10 Click **Choose**.

The dialog closes, and the folder appears in the list.

11 Click the **System Preferences** menu and click **Quit System Preferences** to close System Preferences.

Is there another way to add folders to the Privacy list?

Instead of using the dialog to build the list of folders you do not want Spotlight to search, you can work from a Finder window instead. Click **Finder** (⬜) on the Dock to open a Finder window, and position it so that you can see both it and the Spotlight preference pane. Click and drag the folders you want to protect from the Finder window to the Spotlight preference pane to add them to the list. You can select multiple folders at once to save time.

Control Your iMac with Your Voice

To save wear and tear on your fingers and wrists, Mac OS X enables you to control your iMac by speaking commands into a microphone.

For best results, you will need to connect an external microphone to your iMac rather than use the built-in microphone. The best kind is a headset microphone that keeps the microphone positioned near to your mouth.

Control Your iMac with Your Voice

① Click 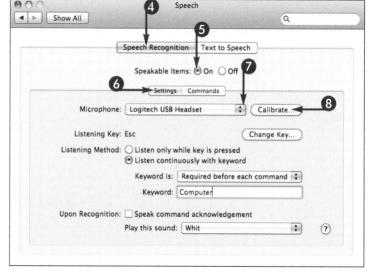.

The Apple menu opens.

② Click **System Preferences**.

● The System Preferences window opens.

③ Click **Speech**.

The Speech preference pane opens.

④ Click **Speech Recognition** if it is not already highlighted.

⑤ Next to Speakable Items, click **On** (○ changes to ⊙).

⑥ Click **Settings** if it is not already highlighted.

⑦ Click ⊕ next to Microphone and choose the microphone you want to use.

⑧ Click **Calibrate**.

The Microphone Calibration dialog opens.

⑨ Speak into the microphone, and click and drag the **input volume** slider until the volume meter registers up to the right end of the green bars but not into the red bars.

⑩ Click **Done** to close the Microphone Calibration dialog.

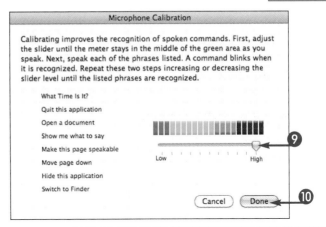

⑪ Click **Commands**.

The Commands sub-tab opens.

⑫ Select the check box for each set of commands you want to use.

⑬ To choose settings for a command set, click the set and click **Configure**.

A configuration dialog opens.

⑭ Choose settings for the commands.

Note: *Different sets of commands have different options. Some sets have no options.*

⑮ Click **OK**.

⑯ Click the **System Preferences** menu and click **Quit System Preferences** to close System Preferences.

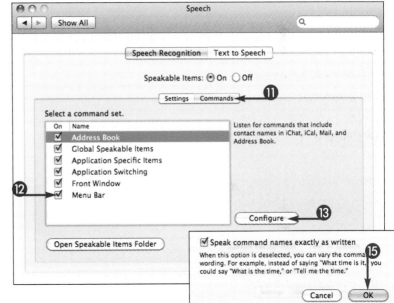

Should I choose Listen Only While Key Is Pressed or Listen Continuously with Keyword?

This depends on how much you will use spoken commands. Click **Listen only while key is pressed** (○ changes to ◉) if you will use speech recognition only seldom and you do not want to waste the iMac's computing power listening to commands that do not come. Click **Listen continuously with keyword** if you will use speech recognition frequently and you are prepared to say the keyword each time you need the computer's attention. Type the word you want to use in the Keyword field.

Save Time by Running Applications Each Time You Log In

Of the many applications installed on your iMac, you most likely run some every day, others less frequently, and the rest hardly ever. You can save time by setting Mac OS X to open your most-used applications automatically each time you log in to your iMac. You can set this up either from the Dock or from System Preferences.

Save Time by Running Applications Each Time You Log In

Use the Dock to Set an Application to Run at Login

① If the application does not have an icon on the Dock, open the application as usual.

② Control -click or right-click the application's icon.

The shortcut menu opens.

③ Click or highlight **Options**.

The Options submenu opens.

④ Click **Open at Login**.

Mac OS X places a check mark next to Open at Login.

Use System Preferences to Set an Application to Run at Login

① Click .

The Apple menu opens.

② Click **System Preferences**.

The System Preferences window opens.

③ Click **Accounts**.

● The Accounts preference pane opens showing your user account.

④ Click **Login Items**.

The list of login items appears.

Note: You can click *in the Hide column (changes to) for an application to hide the application when it launches. This setting is useful for applications that run in the background but not for applications you need to see.*

5 Click ⊞.

A dialog opens showing a list of the applications in the Applications folder.

6 Click the application you want to run automatically at login.

Note: To select multiple applications, click the first, and then ⌘ *-click each of the others.*

7 Click **Add**.

The dialog closes, and the application appears in the list on the Login Items pane.

8 Click the **System Preferences** menu and click **Quit System Preferences** to close System Preferences.

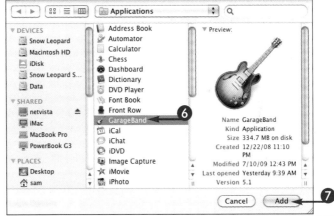

TIPS

Is there another way to add an application to the Login Items pane of Accounts preferences?

Instead of clicking ⊞ and using the dialog to pick the applications, you can click and drag the applications from a Finder window. Click **Finder** ( ) on the Dock to open a Finder window, and then click **Applications** in the sidebar. Click the application you want, and then drag it across to the Login Items pane of Account preferences.

Is there a disadvantage to running applications at login?

The more applications you run at login, the longer the login process takes. Normally, it is best to run only a handful of applications at login — those you use in every computing session. Run other applications from the Dock when you need them instead of launching them at login in case you need them later.

Save Power by Putting Your iMac to Sleep

When you are not using your iMac, you can put it to sleep to save electricity. When you know you will be away from your iMac for a while, you can put it to sleep manually, but you can also set the Energy Saver feature to put your iMac to sleep after a period of inactivity.

① Click .

The Apple menu opens.

② Click **System Preferences**.

● The System Preferences window opens.

③ Click **Energy Saver**.

The Energy Saver pane appears.

④ Click and drag the **Computer sleep** slider to set the length of time to wait before putting the iMac to sleep.

⑤ Click and drag the **Display sleep** slider to set the amount of time to wait before blanking the display.

Note: Set Display Sleep to a shorter time than Computer Sleep.

⑥ If you want to have your iMac go to sleep or wake up on a schedule, click **Schedule**.

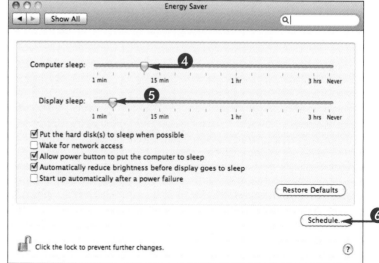

The Schedule dialog opens.

7 To set a wake-up time, click **Start up or wake** (☐ changes to ☑).

8 Click ⬍ and choose the frequency: Weekends, Weekdays, Every Day, or a particular day of the week.

9 Click ⬍ to set the wake-up time.

10 To set a sleep or shutdown time, click ☐ on the second row.

11 Click ⬍ and choose **Sleep** or **Shut Down**.

Note: *You can also set the iMac to restart on schedule. Generally, this setting is less useful than sleep or shutdown.*

12 Click ⬍ and choose the frequency.

13 Click ⬍ to set the time.

14 Click **OK**.

15 Click the **System Preferences** menu and click **Quit System Preferences** to close System Preferences.

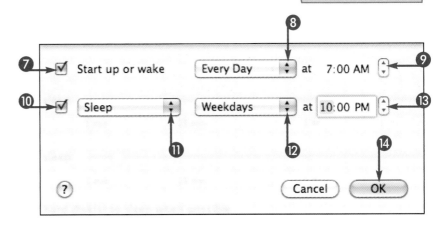

TIPS

Which button do I press to wake my iMac from sleep?

You can press any key on the keyboard to wake the iMac. If you are not certain whether the iMac is asleep or preparing to run a screen saver, press Shift or ⌘. These keys do not type a character if the iMac turns out to be awake rather than asleep.

Is it a good idea to select the Automatically Dim the Display Brightness Before Display Sleep check box?

Dimming the screen saves some power, but having the screen dim when you are taking a moment to compose your thoughts can be distracting. You may find it more helpful to set a shorter Display sleep time and clear the Automatically Dim the Display Brightness Before Display Sleep check box.

Choose When to Check for Software Updates

To keep your iMac running smoothly and protect it from both online and offline threats, you should apply the software updates that Apple releases for Mac OS X and for Apple applications. Usually, it is easiest to have the Software Update utility check for updates automatically, but you can check manually instead if you prefer.

① Click .

The Apple menu opens.

② Click **System Preferences**.

The System Preferences window opens.

③ Click **Software Update**.

The Software Update pane opens.

④ Click the **Scheduled Check** tab.

⑤ Make sure **Check for updates** is selected (☑).

⑥ Click ⬍.

The Check for Updates pop-up menu opens.

⑦ Click **Daily**, **Weekly**, or **Monthly**, as appropriate. See the first tip for advice.

⑧ Make sure **Download updates automatically** is selected (☑).

⑨ Click **System Preferences**.

The System Preferences menu opens.

⑩ Click **Quit System Preferences**.

The System Preferences window closes.

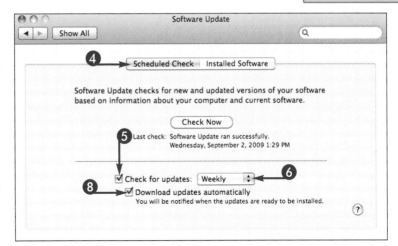

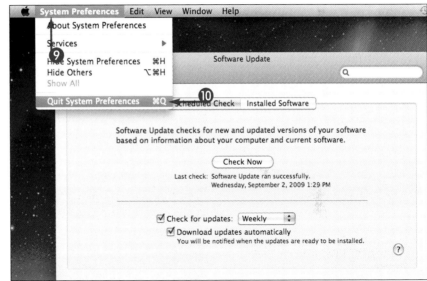

TIPS

How frequently should I check for software updates?

If you have an always-on Internet connection, set Software Update to check for updates daily. This ensures you receive the updates as soon as possible, so that your iMac remains up to date and protected against the latest threats. Use the Weekly setting if you find the updates frequent enough to interrupt your work. Avoid the Monthly setting because it may leave your iMac unprotected for several weeks.

Will I need to restart my iMac after installing updates?

Some updates to Mac OS X require you to restart your iMac, whereas most updates to Apple applications do not need a restart. Software Update always warns you when an update requires a restart, so you can delay applying the update if the timing is not convenient.

CHAPTER
13

Using Your iMac on a Network

When you have connected your iMac to a network, as explained in Chapter 1, you can share your folders and printers with other computers on the network and use the folders and printers they are sharing. You can even share your iMac's screen or view your iMac from another Mac on the same network or across the Internet.

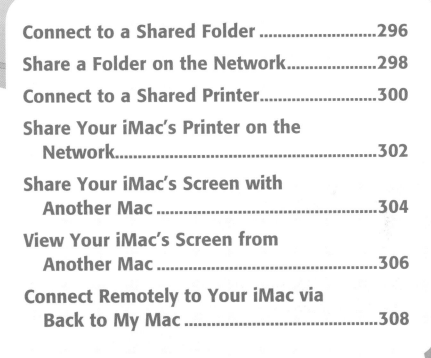

Connect to a Shared Folder 296

Share a Folder on the Network....................298

Connect to a Shared Printer..........................300

Share Your iMac's Printer on the
    Network...302

Share Your iMac's Screen with
    Another Mac 304

View Your iMac's Screen from
    Another Mac 306

Connect Remotely to Your iMac via
    Back to My Mac 308

Connect to a Shared Folder

After sharing an Internet connection, sharing files is one of the most popular uses of a network. To access files that someone else is sharing, you need to connect to the shared folder.

Connect to a Shared Folder

1 Click **Finder** (🖥️) on the Dock.

A Finder window opens.

2 If the Shared category is collapsed, click ▶ (▶ changes to ▼) to expand it.

3 Click the computer that is sharing the folder.

4 Click **Connect As**.

Note: *If you do not have a user account on the computer sharing the folder, use Guest access to the shared folder. Do not click Connect As; instead, go to step* **8**.

The Connect As dialog opens.

5 Type your user name for the computer you are accessing.

6 Type your password for that computer.

Note: *Click Remember this password in my keychain (☐ changes to ☑) if you want to store your password for future use.*

7 Click **Connect**.

● The full list of shared folders appears.

Note: The shared folders you see are the folders you have permission to access. Different folders may be shared with other users than are shared with you.

⑧ Click the folder whose contents you want to see.

⑨ Work with files as usual. For example, open a file to work on it, or copy it to your iMac.

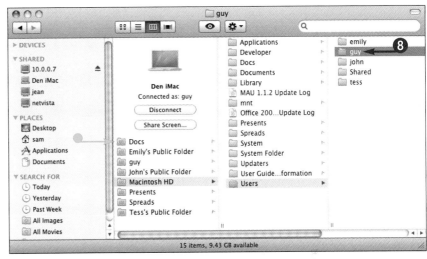

⑩ When you finish using the shared folder, click ⏏ next to the computer's name in the Shared list.

Your iMac disconnects the shared folder.

*Note: If the Finder window is in Column view, you can click **Disconnect** in the first column to disconnect the shared drive.*

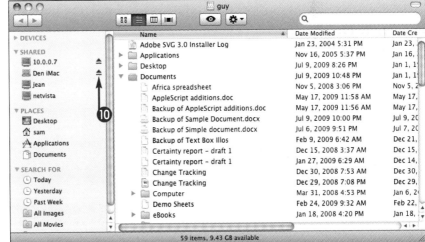

TIP

How can I connect to a shared folder that does not appear in the Shared list in the Finder window?
If the shared folder does not appear in the Shared list, find out the name or IP address of the computer sharing the folder. Open the **Go** menu and choose **Connect to Server**. The Connect to Server dialog opens. In the Server Address field (●), type or paste the computer's name or IP address, and then click **Connect**. To reconnect to a server you have used before, click **Choose a Recent Server** (⎯) in the Connect to Server dialog.

Share a Folder on the Network

Just as you can connect to folders that other people are sharing on the network, you can share one or more of your iMac's folders on the network. To share them, you need to set up the File Sharing service and decide who you will allow to access the folder.

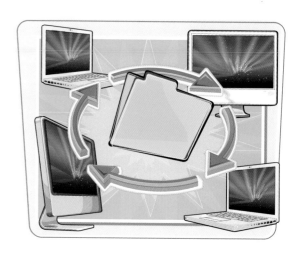

Share a Folder on the Network

① Click 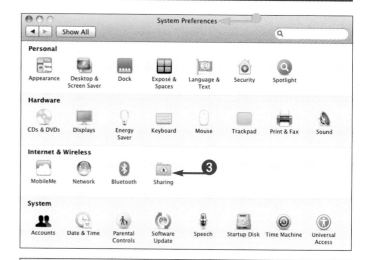.

The Apple menu opens.

② Click **System Preferences**.

● The System Preferences window opens.

③ Click **Sharing**.

The Sharing preferences pane opens.

④ Click ☐ next to **File Sharing** (☐ changes to ☑).

Mac OS X turns on file sharing.

⑤ Click **Add** (⊞) under the Shared Folders box.

A dialog for choosing a folder opens.

⑥ Click the folder you want to share.

⑦ Click **Add**.

The dialog closes, and the folder appears in the Shared Folders list.

⑧ Click **Everyone**.

⑨ Click the Permissions pop-up menu and choose **Read & Write** if you want all users to be able to create and change files in the folder.

Note: If you want other people to be able only to open or copy the files, choose **Read Only**.

⑩ Click the **System Preferences** menu and click **Quit System Preferences** to close System Preferences.

How do I share files with Windows users?

To share files with Windows users, click **Options** in Sharing preferences. In the dialog that opens, click **Share files and folders using SMB (Windows)** (☐ turns to ☑). In the list box, click the user name (●), enter the user's password, and then click **Done**.

Can I share files without setting up the File Sharing service?

Yes, you can. Place the files you want to share in the Public folder in your user account. Other Macs on the network can then view the files and copy them; they cannot change the files on your iMac. They can copy files to the Drop Box folder in your Public folder, but they cannot see its contents.

Connect to a Shared Printer

Sharing one or more printers on a network is a great way of keeping costs down while enabling each computer to print different types of documents as needed.

This section shows you how to connect to a shared printer. The following pages show you how to share your iMac's printer.

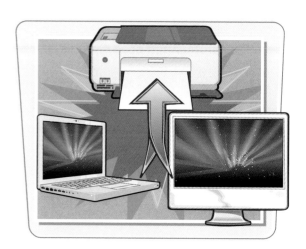

Open Print & Fax Preferences

① Click and then **System Preferences**.

The System Preferences window opens.

② Click **Print & Fax**.

⬤ The Print & Fax preferences pane opens.

Add a Printer Shared by a Mac

① Click **Add** (⊞).

The Add Printer dialog opens.

② Click **Default** to open the Default pane.

③ In the Printer Name list box, click the printer.

⬤ You can change the printer's name and location.

④ Click **Add**.

Mac OS X adds the printer. The printer appears in the Print & Fax preferences pane.

⑤ Click the **System Preferences** menu and click **Quit System Preferences** to close System Preferences.

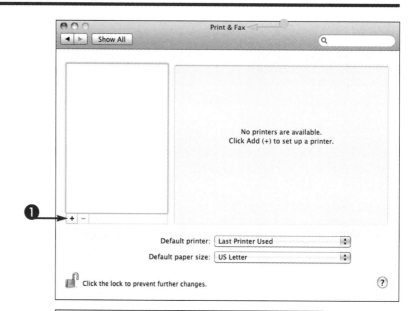

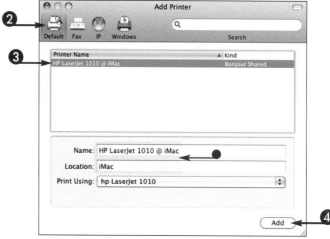

Add a Printer Shared by a Windows PC

① In the Print & Fax preferences pane, click **Add** (+).

● The Add Printer dialog opens.

② Click **Windows** to open the Window pane.

③ Click the name of the network or workgroup that contains the printer.

A list appears of the computers sharing printers.

④ Click the computer sharing the printer you want to add.

⑤ If you have a user name and password for the computer, type them. Otherwise, click **Guest** (○ changes to ⦿).

⑥ Click **Connect**.

The list of printers appears in the Add Printer dialog.

⑦ Click the printer.

● You can change the printer's name and location.

⑧ Click **Add**.

The printer appears in the Print & Fax preferences pane.

⑨ Close System Preferences.

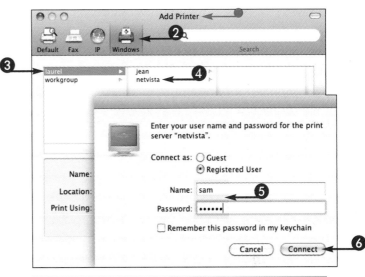

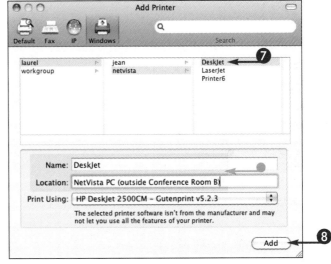

TIP

What shall I do when the Print Using pop-up menu says "Choose a Driver or Printer Model"?

This message appears when Mac OS X cannot identify the driver software needed for the printer. Click the Print Using pop-up menu and then click **Select Printer Software**. The Printer Software dialog opens. Type a distinctive part of the name in the search box to see a list of matching items, and then click the driver for the printer model (●). Click **OK**.

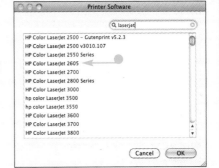

Share Your iMac's Printer on the Network

If you have a printer connected to your iMac, you can share it with other computers on the network. To do so, you turn on the Printer Sharing feature, and then choose which printer or printers to share.

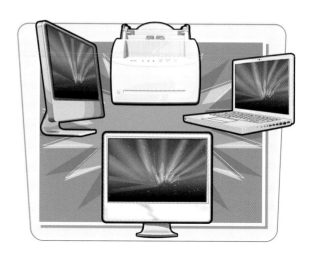

Share Your iMac's Printer on the Network

① Click 🍎.

The Apple menu opens.

② Click **System Preferences**.

● The System Preferences window opens.

③ Click **Sharing**.

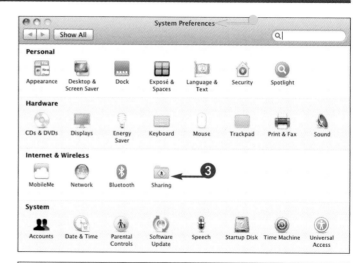

The Sharing preferences pane opens.

④ Click 🔲 next to Printer Sharing (🔲 changes to ☑).

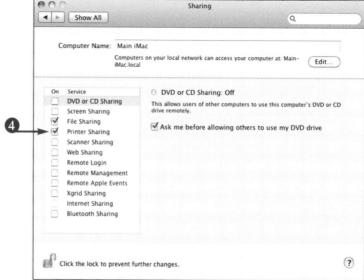

Mac OS X turns on Printer Sharing and displays the Printer Sharing preferences.

⑤ Click ☐ next to each printer you want to share (☐ changes to ☑).

⑥ If you want to control who can use the printer, click **Add** (⊕).

● A dialog for selecting users opens.

⑦ Click the user you want to add.

Note: To select multiple users, click the first, and then ⌘-click each of the others.

⑧ Click **Select**.

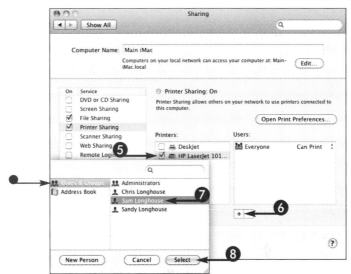

● The user appears in the Users list.

⑨ For each user, choose **Can Print** or **No Access**, as needed.

⑩ Click the **System Preferences** menu and click **Quit System Preferences** to close System Preferences.

Can Windows users share my iMac's printer?

Users of PCs running Windows need to install Apple's Bonjour for Windows to access shared printers. Bonjour for Windows is available free from http://support.apple.com/downloads/Bonjour_for_Windows. After installing Bonjour for Windows, the user runs the Bonjour Printer Wizard and chooses the printer she wants to install (●).

Share Your iMac's Screen with Another Mac

When you need to collaborate on a project, you can share your iMac's screen with another Mac. Your colleague or friend can then see everything that happens on your iMac's screen and can control your iMac.

Share Your iMac's Screen with Another Mac

Turn On Screen Sharing

1 Click and then **System Preferences**.

● The System Preferences window opens.

2 Click **Sharing**.

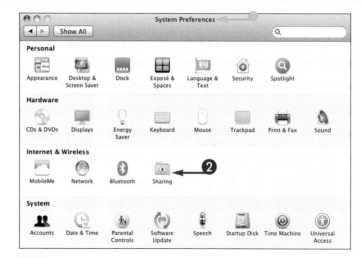

The Sharing preferences pane opens.

3 Click ☐ next to **Screen Sharing** (☐ changes to ☑).

4 Change the name in the Computer Name field if necessary.

Note: *The name in the Computer Name field is the name other people will see for your iMac on the network. Make the name explicit — for example, Jill's iMac or iMac in Den.*

5 In the Allow access for area, click **All users** (○ changes to ●) if you want any user to be able to share the screen.

Note: *The users you choose here can control your iMac via Screen Sharing. Limit the users to those you trust.*

6 Click **Computer Settings**.

⑦ In the Computer Settings dialog, click **Anyone may request permission to control screen** (☑ changes to ☐) if you want to prevent people other than the users you have chosen in the Allow access for area requesting control of your iMac.

⑧ Click **OK**.

⑨ Close System Preferences.

Accept a Request for Screen Sharing

A Control Request dialog opens when someone asks to share your screen.

① Click **Share Screen**.

● A Screen Sharing icon (🖳) appears on the right side of the menu bar.

Note: *When one of the people you have permitted to take control of your iMac connects via Screen Sharing, the Control Request dialog does not appear. The person simply takes control. Your only indication is the Screen Sharing icon on the menu bar.*

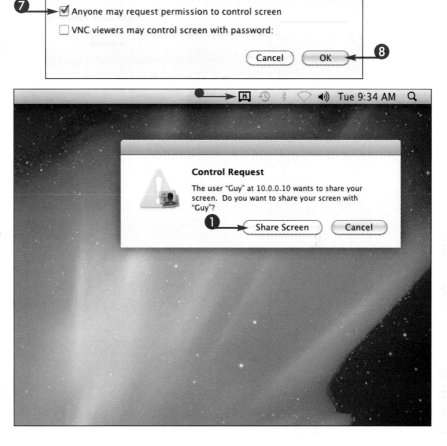

⑦ ☑ Anyone may request permission to control screen
☐ VNC viewers may control screen with password:
Cancel   OK ← ⑧

Control Request
The user "Guy" at 10.0.0.10 wants to share your screen. Do you want to share your screen with "Guy"?
① → Share Screen   Cancel

How do I end a Screen Sharing session?
To end a Screen Sharing session, click **the Screen Sharing** icon (🖳) on the menu bar, and then click **Disconnect** (●) on the menu that opens. If you want to prevent further connections, open Sharing preferences and click **Screen Sharing** (☑ changes to ☐).

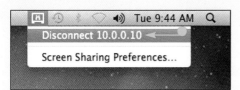

Can I share my iMac's screen with Windows users?
To share your iMac's screen with Windows users, click **Computer Settings** in the Sharing preferences pane, click **VNC viewers may control screen with password** (☐ changes to ☑), type a password, and click **OK**. Windows users can then connect with a VNC client program such as RealVNC (www.realvnc.com).

View Your iMac's Screen from Another Mac

After setting up Screen Sharing as described on the previous pages, you can view your iMac's screen from another Mac on the same network. You can also use Screen Sharing to view the screen of another Mac that has Screen Sharing turned on.

Connect to Your iMac from Another Mac

1. Click **Finder** (▣) on the Dock to open a Finder window.

2. If the Shared category is collapsed, click ▶ (▶ changes to ▼) to expand it.

3. Click your iMac.

4. Click **Share Screen**.

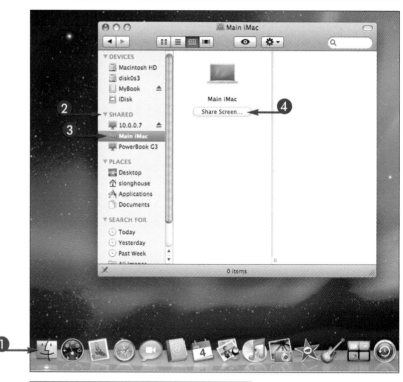

5. In the Screen Sharing dialog, type your account name for the iMac to which you are connecting.

Note: When connecting to a Mac on which you do not have an account, click By asking for permission (○ changes to ●). Skip step 6.

6. Type your password.

Note: Click Remember this password in my keychain (□ changes to ☑) if you want to store your password for future use.

7. Click **Connect**.

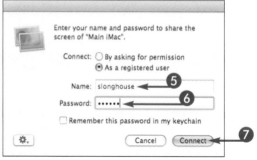

Note: *If you connect to a Mac on which you do not have an account, the person using the Mac can deny your request to connect.*

The Screen Sharing window opens.

Work on the iMac as you would work on the Mac you are using.

● Click **Fit screen in window** () if the remote screen is too big for the window you are using.

● Click **Get the remote clipboard contents** (🔳) to copy the iMac's clipboard contents to the clipboard on the Mac you are using.

● Click **Send clipboard contents to remote clipboard** (🔳) to put this Mac's clipboard contents on the iMac's clipboard.

End the Screen Sharing Session

① Click **Screen Sharing**.

② Click **Quit Screen Sharing**.

The Screen Sharing window closes.

TIPS

Why does the By Asking for Permission option not appear?

The By Asking for Permission option appears only if the administrator of the Mac to which you are connecting has turned on the Anyone May Request Permission to Control Screen option in Sharing preferences.

What if my iMac has two screens and the Mac I am using has only one?

If your iMac has two screens, Screen Sharing displays them both in the same window. Click the **Select which remote display to view** pop-up menu (●) and choose the display you want.

307

Connect Remotely to Your iMac via Back to My Mac

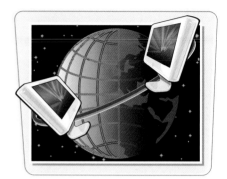

To connect remotely to your iMac across the Internet, use the Back to My Mac feature. This feature lets you share files or view your iMac's screen and control the iMac via an Internet connection. You must first turn on Screen Sharing or File Sharing, or both, as described earlier.

Back to My Mac works through Apple's MobileMe service, so you must have a MobileMe subscription to use Back To My Mac.

Connect Remotely to Your iMac via Back to My Mac

Turn on Back to My Mac

1. Click , **System Preferences**, and then **MobileMe**.

● The MobileMe preferences pane opens.

2. Click **Back to My Mac** to open the Back to My Mac pane.

3. Click **Start**.

4. On the Mac from which you will connect, repeat steps **1** to **3**.

Use File Sharing via Back to My Mac

1. Click **Finder** ( ) on the Dock.

2. If the Shared category is collapsed, click (changes to).

3. Click your iMac.

4. Click **Connect As**.

5. In the Connect As dialog, type your user name and password.

6. Click **Connect**.

Your Mac's files appear, and you can copy them to the Mac you are using.

7. When you have finished working with files, click **Disconnect**.

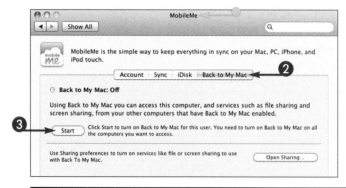

Use Screen Sharing via Back to My Mac

1 Click **Finder** () on the Dock to open a Finder window.

2 If the Shared category is collapsed, click ▶ (▶ changes to ▼) to expand it.

3 Click your iMac.

4 Click **Share Screen**.

5 In the Screen Sharing dialog, type your account name and password for the iMac to which you are connecting.

6 Click **Connect**.

7 Work as described on the previous section.

End the Screen Sharing Session

1 Click **Screen Sharing**.

2 Click **Quit Screen Sharing**.

The Screen Sharing window closes.

 **TIPS**

Why does Back to My Mac fail to connect and give a message about NAT-PMP?

Back to My Mac establishes a two-way path through your Internet router to the MobileMe servers using either the Network Address Translation Port Mapping Protocol, NAT-PMP, or Universal Plug and Play, UPnP. If Back to My Mac cannot connect, turn on NAT-PMP or UPnP on your router.

What else may be preventing Back to My Mac from connecting to the MobileMe servers?

If you use the Mac OS X firewall to protect your iMac from dangerous Internet traffic, you must allow File Sharing connections and Screen Sharing connections for Back to My Mac to work. If you use the Block all incoming connections feature of the firewall, Back to My Mac cannot work.

14

Keeping Your iMac and Your Data Safe

When you share files with others or connect your iMac to the Internet or a network, you expose it to threats. To keep your iMac and your data safe, you must understand these threats, install and use antivirus software, turn off automatic login, and set up the Mac OS X firewall.

**Understanding Threats to Your iMac
and Your Data** 312

Install Antivirus Software 314

Scan Your iMac for Viruses 316

Turn Off Automatic Login 318

**Increase the Security of the Mac OS X
Firewall**...320

Recognize and Avoid Phishing Attacks 322

Understanding Threats to Your iMac and Your Data

To keep your iMac and your data safe, understand the main threats they face. These threats range from malevolent software to people accessing your iMac without permission, from deliberate attacks to accidental data corruption or hard-disk failure.

Viruses and Malevolent Software

Just as you expose yourself to viruses and bacteria in public, so you expose your iMac to computer viruses and malevolent software when you use the Internet or share files. Viruses and malevolent software can delete your data or corrupt your iMac's operating system or applications, so you must protect the iMac with antivirus software.

Unauthorized People Accessing Your iMac

Anyone who can log in to your iMac in person or across the Internet can attack your data. For example, an intruder can copy your files, steal them, or simply delete them. To ensure that each user must log in to the iMac, always log out when you have finished using the computer, and turn off automatic login.

Internet Attacks

When your iMac is connected to a network or the Internet, it needs protection from possible attacks from other computers. Mac OS X includes a powerful firewall that can protect your iMac against many threats, but you may need to turn it on and change its configuration to enjoy full protection.

Phishing Attacks

Be on your guard against phishing attacks, attacks in which a phisher attempts to make you divulge valuable information such as bank account login names, passwords, or credit card numbers. Most phishing takes place via e-mail, but phishers also use instant messaging and telephones to persuade people to give up information against their interests.

Power Outages and Hardware Failures

To protect your iMac from power outages or electric surges, give it power through an uninterruptible power supply (UPS) or a surge suppressor instead of directly from a socket. A UPS uses a battery to provide steady, conditioned power to your iMac and enable you to save files and shut down when a power outage occurs. To protect your data against hardware failure, back up your data as explained in Chapter 15.

Install Antivirus Software

Malevolent hackers on the Internet target Macs as well as Windows PCs, so you must protect your iMac by installing and running antivirus software. This section shows you how to install VirusBarrier, a widely used antivirus package, and keep it updated.

1 Buy the antivirus software on CD or download it.

Note: If you have an Internet connection, buy your antivirus software online and download it. That way, you get the latest version.

2 Insert the CD in your iMac's optical drive, or open the file you downloaded.

3 Double-click Installer to start the installation.

4 Click the **Install** button.

5 Follow the steps of the Installer.

6 When Installer prompts you to restart your iMac, click **Restart**.

After the restart, the antivirus software runs automatically to protect your iMac.

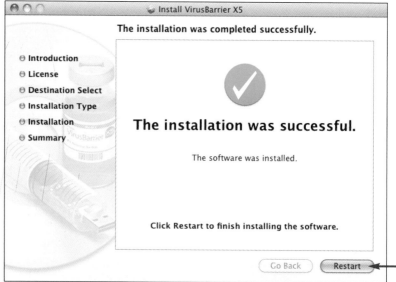

Keep Your Antivirus Software Up-to-Date

1 Click the application's menu on the menu bar.

2 Click **NetUpdate**.

A dialog opens telling you whether updates are available.

3 Click **OK**.

The dialog closes.

If updates are available, the NetUpdate window shows the updates in boldface.

4 Click each available update you want to install (☐ changes to ☑).

5 Click **Update**.

NetUpdate downloads and installs the updates.

6 If NetUpdate prompts you to restart your iMac, click **Restart**.

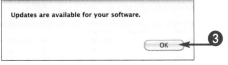

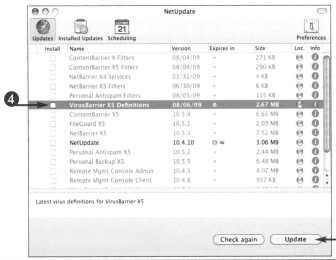

 TIPS

Which antivirus software shall I get for my iMac?

Widely used antivirus software includes VirusBarrier from Intego and Norton Antivirus for Mac or Norton Internet Security for Mac from Symantec. Intego offers a 30-day trial version of VirusBarrier, so you can evaluate the software before you buy it. If you prefer not to pay and are prepared to put a little more effort into setup, look at ClamXav (www.clamxav.com).

What features should I look for in antivirus software?

The main feature to look for is protection against malevolent software. This includes viruses, Trojan-horse programs that hide harm in a program that seems helpful, and rootkits, which try to build secret entry points into your computer. Protection against spyware programs, phishing messages, and infected Web sites are useful too.

Scan Your iMac for Viruses

After installing antivirus software as described on the previous two pages, you should run a full scan of your Mac. This section shows you how to run a scan using VirusBarrier from Intego.

Scan Your iMac for Viruses

① Click the software's menu on the menu bar.

② Highlight **VirusBarrier X5**.

The submenu opens.

③ Click **Open VirusBarrier X5**.

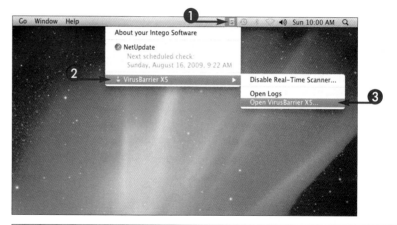

The VirusBarrier X5 window opens.

④ Click **Scan**.

VirusBarrier counts the files and then scans them.

The green light indicates all is well.

The light turns red when VirusBarrier finds an infected file.

A VirusBarrier dialog opens showing a list of infected files.

5 Click the file.

6 Click the button for the action you want to take:

● Click **Reveal in Finder** to open a Finder window showing the folder that contains the file.

● Click **Ignore** to ignore the infected file.

● Click **Put in Quarantine** to place the file in VirusBarrier's quarantine zone.

● Click **Repair** (if the button is available) to repair the file, removing the infection so that you can use the file.

After you click a button, VirusBarrier removes the file from the list.

When you have dealt with all the infected files, the dialog closes.

7 Click the **VirusBarrier X5** menu and then click **Quit VirusBarrier X5**.

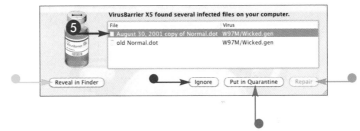

TIP

What happens when I place an infected file in quarantine?

Placing a file in quarantine puts it in a secure area so that you can review it later. Quarantine prevents the infected file from damaging your iMac but does not remove the infection. Click **Malware Quarantine** to open the quarantine area. Click the file you want to deal with and click the appropriate action button: **Repair**, **Scan**, **Consider Safe**, or **Delete from Disk**.

Turn Off Automatic Login

When you install Mac OS X from scratch, Installer sets up your iMac with automatic login for the administrator account you first create. Automatic login is convenient when you are the only person who uses your iMac, but you can make your iMac more secure by turning off automatic login so each user must log in.

Turn Off Automatic Login

1 Click .

The Apple menu opens.

2 Click **System Preferences**.

The System Preferences window opens.

3 Click **Security**.

● The Security preferences pane opens.

4 Click **General**.

The General pane appears.

5 Click .

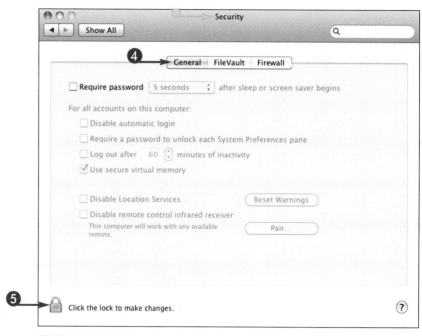

The Authenticate dialog opens.

6 Type your password.

7 Click **OK**.

The Authenticate dialog closes.

Mac OS X enables the preferences
(🔒 changes to 🔓).

⑧ Click **Disable automatic login**
(☐ changes to ☑).

⑨ For greater security, click **Require
password *N* seconds after
sleep or screen saver begins**
(☐ changes to ☑).

⑩ Click 🔼 and choose
Immediately or a short time: **5
seconds**, **1 minute**, or **5
minutes**.

⑪ Click **Log out after *N* minutes
of inactivity** (☐ changes to ☑).

⑫ Click 🔼 to choose a short time,
such as 5 minutes.

⑬ Click 🔓 (🔓 changes to 🔒).

⑭ Click the **System Preferences**
menu and click **Quit System
Preferences** to close System
Preferences.

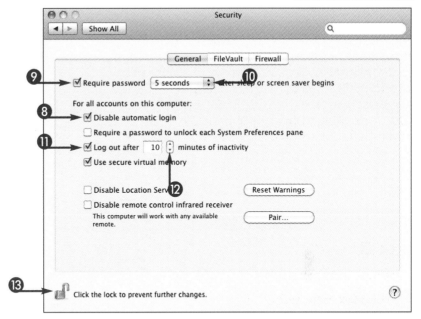

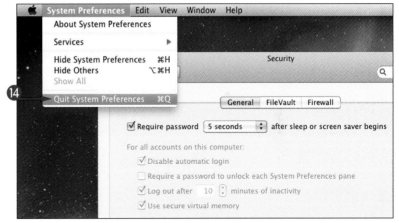

**Are there other options for tightening my iMac's
security?**

In Accounts preferences, click **Login Options**. You can then click
Name and password (○ changes to ⦿) to hide the list of user
names so that anyone logging on must type a user name as well
as a password. Click **Show the Restart, Sleep, and Shut Down
buttons** (☑ changes to ☐) to remove these buttons from the
login screen, so that nobody can shut down or restart the iMac
without logging in (●) unless he turns off the Mac's power. Click
Show password hints (☑ changes to ☐) if you want to prevent
password hints from appearing.

Increase the Security of the Mac OS X Firewall

A firewall protects your iMac from unauthorized access by other computers on your network or on the Internet. Your Internet router likely has its own firewall to keep Internet threats out of your network, but Mac OS X also includes a built-in firewall to give your iMac even greater protection.

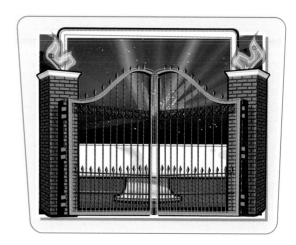

① Click .

The Apple menu opens.

② Click **System Preferences**.

The System Preferences window opens.

③ Click **Security**.

● The Security preferences pane opens.

④ Click **Firewall**.

The Firewall pane appears.

⑤ Click 🔒.

The Authenticate dialog opens.

⑥ Type your password.

⑦ Click **OK**.

The Authenticate dialog closes.

● 🔒 changes to 🔓.

⑧ If "Firewall: Off" appears, click **Start**.

The firewall starts, and "Firewall: On" appears.

⑨ Click **Advanced**.

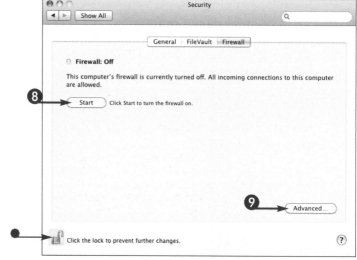

10 In the Advanced dialog, click **Automatically allow signed software to receive incoming connections** (☑ changes to ☐) if you want to prevent your iMac accepting connections automatically across the network.

11 Click **Enable stealth mode** (☐ changes to ☑) if you want to prevent your iMac from responding to network test applications.

12 To allow incoming connections to a particular application, click **Add** (⊞).

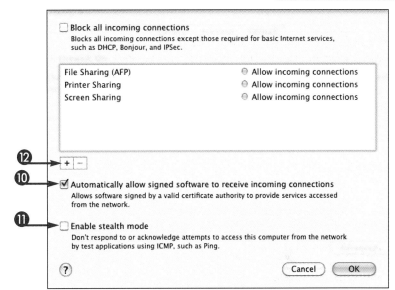

13 In the Add dialog, click the application.

14 Click **Add**.

Mac OS X adds the application to the list.

15 Click **OK** to close the Advanced dialog.

16 In the Security preferences pane, click 🔓 (🔓 changes to 🔒).

17 Click the **System Preferences** menu.

18 Click **Quit System Preferences**.

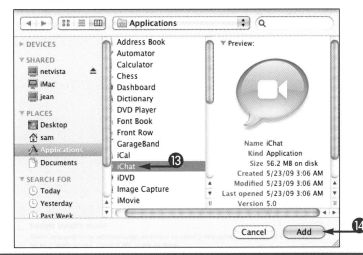

TIPS

When should I use the Block all incoming connections option?

Click **Block all incoming connections** when you need to tighten security as much as possible. The usual reason for blocking all connections is connecting your iMac to a network that you cannot trust, such as a public wireless network. This option is more widely used with MacBooks than with desktop Macs.

Can I block incoming connections only to a specific application?

To block incoming connections only to a specific application, add that application to the list in the Advanced dialog as described on this page. Then click the application's **Allow incoming connections** button in the list and click **Block incoming connections** (●).

Recognize and Avoid Phishing Attacks

Phishing is an attack in which someone tries to make you provide valuable information such as bank account login names, passwords, or credit card numbers. After acquiring this information, the phisher either uses it directly — for example, withdrawing money from your bank account — or sells it to criminals.

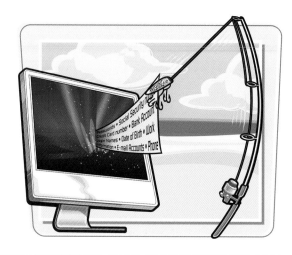

Recognize a Phishing E-mail Message

1. In Mail, open the message.

2. Look for signs of phishing:

- Mail has detected suspicious signs in the message.

- The message does not show your name as the recipient.

- The message has a generic greeting, such as Dear Customer, or no greeting at all.

- The message claims you need to take action, such as clearing a security lockout or reenabling your account.

- The message contains links it encourages you to click.

Note: *Phishers frequently target eBay customers. Genuine eBay messages always address you by your member name and include the actual name you have given eBay.*

3. Position the mouse pointer over a link but do not click.

- A ScreenTip appears showing the address to which the link leads.

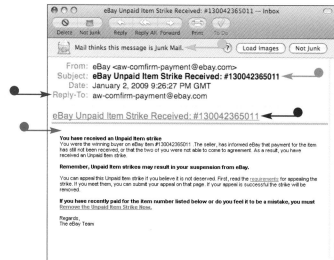

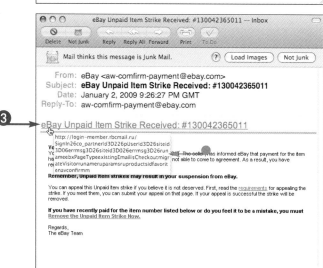

Connect Securely to a Web Site

① Click **Safari** () on the Dock.

A Safari window opens.

② Click the address box.

③ Type the address of the Web site and press **Return**.

Safari opens the Web site.

④ Click the padlock icon (🔒).

Note: *Safari displays the padlock icon when you have connected securely to a Web site. The address of a secure connections starts with https:// rather than http://.*

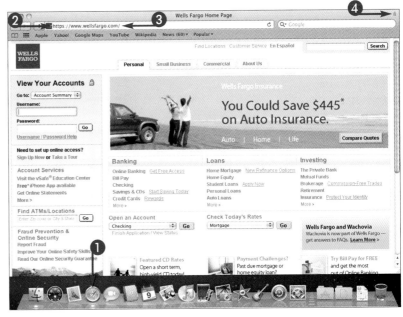

A dialog opens showing the details of the digital certificate that identifies the Web site.

⑤ Click ▶ (▶ changes to ▼) to expand the dialog.

⑥ Verify that the certificate is valid.

⑦ Click **OK** to close the dialog.

⑧ If you are convinced that the Web site is genuine, log in to it.

TIPS

Is it possible to make a secure connection to a dangerous Web site?

Yes. The padlock icon means only that the connection between your iMac and the Web site server is secure and cannot be read in transmission. The Web site may be safe or it may be dangerous; it is up to you to establish which.

Is a message definitely genuine if it includes my name?

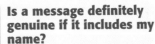

Even if a message includes your name, be alert for other signs of phishing. Some phishers send customized phishing messages in the hope of ensnaring particular high-value victims. This technique is called spear-phishing. Evaluate the message's content for sense and likelihood, and remember that anything too good to be true is usually not true.

15

Maintaining and Troubleshooting Your iMac

Apple has built your iMac and Mac OS X to keep running as smoothly as possible, but even so, you will need to perform basic maintenance, such as emptying the Trash, updating your iMac with the latest fixes, and backing up your files. If things go wrong, you will also need to troubleshoot your iMac.

Reclaim Space by Emptying the Trash 326

Keep Your iMac Current with the Latest Updates.................................328

Back Up Your Files with Time Machine 330

Recover Your Files from a Time Machine Backup 332

Remove Applications You No Longer Need...334

See Which Application Is Causing Your iMac Problems.................................336

Force a Crashed Application to Quit...........338

Recover When Mac OS X Crashes.................340

Solve Problems with Corrupt Preference Files...342

Troubleshoot Disk Permission Errors.........344

Repair Your iMac's Hard Disk.......................346

Reinstall Mac OS X to Solve Severe Problems...347

Reclaim Space by Emptying the Trash

When you throw a file in the Trash, it remains there in case you change your mind and decide to recover it. But when you need to reclaim space on your iMac's hard disk, you can empty the Trash and get rid of all the files and folders in it permanently.

Reclaim Space by Emptying the Trash

Empty the Trash

1 Click **Trash** (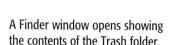) on the Dock.

A Finder window opens showing the contents of the Trash folder.

2 Double-check the files and folders in the Trash to make sure there is nothing you want to keep.

● To quickly view the contents of a file, use Quick View. Click the file, and then click **Quick View** (👁) on the toolbar or press
Spacebar.

③ Click **Empty**.

A dialog opens to confirm the action.

④ Click **Empty Trash**.

Mac OS X empties the Trash and then closes the Finder window.

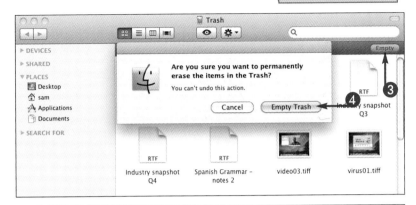

Restore a File or Folder to Its Previous Location

① In the Trash folder, click a file or folder.

② Click **Action** (⚙▾).

③ Click **Put Back**.

Mac OS X restores the file or folder to its previous location.

Is there a quicker way to empty the Trash?

If you are sure that the Trash contains no files or folders you need, Control -click or right-click **Trash** (🗑) on the Dock. The Dock menu opens. Click **Empty Trash**. A confirmation dialog opens. Click **Empty Trash**. To turn off this warning, click **Finder** and **Preferences**, click **Advanced**, and click **Show warning before emptying the Trash** (☑ changes to ☐).

What does the Secure Empty Trash command do, and when should I use it?

When you need to get rid of files and folders and make sure no one can recover them, use the Secure Empty Trash command. Click the desktop, and then choose **Finder** and **Secure Empty Trash**. A confirmation dialog opens. Click **Secure Empty Trash** (●). Mac OS X overwrites the files and folders beyond recovery.

Keep Your iMac Current with the Latest Updates

To keep your iMac running smoothly, use the Software Update feature to install the latest updates and fixes that Apple provides for Mac OS X and Apple's applications.

Your iMac must be connected to the Internet in order to check for and download the updates. You can install the updates when your iMac is either online or offline.

Keep Your iMac Current with the Latest Updates

① Click .

The Apple menu opens.

② Click **Software Update**.

The Software Update window opens, and Software Update automatically checks for updates.

If updates are available, the New Software Is Available for Your Computer dialog opens.

Note: If Software Update displays the message "Your software is up to date," click **Quit**. Software Update then quits.

③ If you do not want to install any of the updates, click ☑ next to them (☑ changes to ☐).

Note: Normally, it is best to install all available updates unless you have heard that a specific update may cause problems with your iMac.

④ Click **Install N Items**, where N is the number of items.

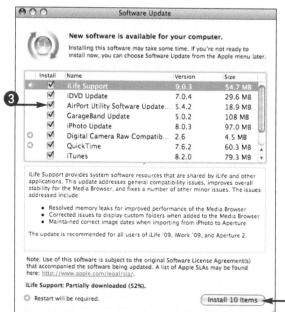

Note: *If one or more License Agreement dialogs open, read each license, and then click **Install** if you accept the agreement.*

Software Update downloads the updates and then installs those that do not require restarting the iMac.

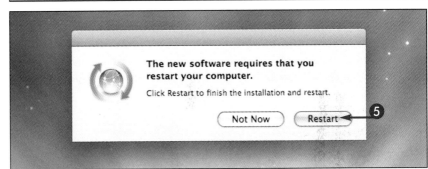

⑤ If Software Update prompts you to restart your iMac, save any unsaved work, and then click **Restart**.

Mac OS X logs you out, installs the updates that require the restart, and then restarts.

Note: *If you are too busy to restart your iMac when Software Update prompts you, click **Not Now**. You can then restart your iMac whenever it suits you.*

TIPS

Why does Software Update sometimes prompt me to install updates?

In Mac OS X, Software Update comes set to check for updates automatically; when it finds updates, it prompts you to install them.
You can change the frequency of these checks, choose whether to download important updates automatically, or turn off automatic checks. See Chapter 12 for instructions.

Why does Software Update check the boxes for some updates but not for all of them?

Normally, Software Update checks the boxes for all available updates, but sometimes updates do not apply to your iMac — for example, updates built for other Mac models. Software Update does not check the boxes for such updates because your iMac does not need them.

Back Up Your Files with Time Machine

To help keep your valuable files safe, Mac OS X includes an automatic backup application called Time Machine. Time Machine automatically saves copies of your files to an external hard disk connected to your iMac. You can choose which drive to use, how frequently to back up your files, and which folders to include.

① Connect an external hard disk to your iMac.

Note: When you connect an external hard disk to your iMac for the first time, a dialog may open asking if you want to use the disk for Time Machine. If you do, click **Use as Backup Disk**; if not, click **Cancel**.

② Click ■ and then **System Preferences**.

● The System Preferences window opens.

③ Click **Time Machine**.

The Time Machine preference pane opens.

④ Click **Select Backup Disk**.

Note: If you have already selected your backup disk, go to step **8**.

The Select Backup Disk dialog opens.

⑤ Click the disk you want to use.

⑥ Click **Use for Backup**.

The Select Backup Disk dialog closes.

The disk appears in the Time Machine pane, with the Time Machine switch turned on.

⑦ Make sure Show Time Machine Status in the Menu Bar is checked. If not, click it (☐ changes to ☑).

⑧ Click **Options**.

The Exclude These Items from Backups dialog opens.

⑨ Click ⊞.

A dialog opens.

⑩ Select each drive or folder you want to exclude from backup.

⑪ Click **Exclude**.

The dialog closes, and Time Machine adds the items to the Exclude These Items from Backups dialog.

⑫ Click **Done**.

The Exclude These Items from Backups dialog closes.

⑬ Click the **System Preferences** menu and click **Quit System Preferences** to close System Preferences.

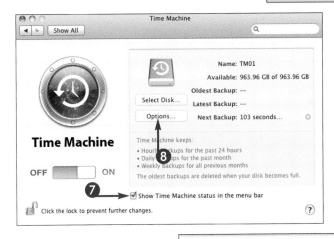

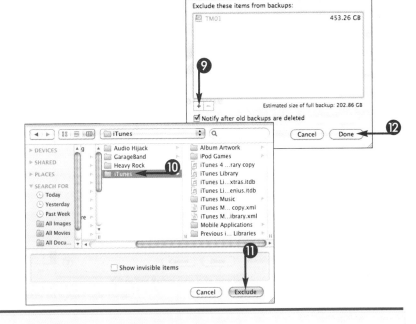

TIPS

What kind of disk should I use for Time Machine?

You can connect an external hard disk to your iMac by using USB, FireWire 400 on an older iMac that has a FireWire 400 port, or FireWire 800. A FireWire 800 disk gives the best performance. It is best to buy a high-capacity disk — for example, one or two terabytes (TB) so that you have plenty of space for backups.

How often does Time Machine back up my files?

Time Machine backs up all your files two minutes after you set it up. After that, it creates an hourly backup of files that have changed since the last backup. Time Machine also creates a daily backup for each day in the past month, plus weekly backups for the months before that.

Recover Your Files from a Time Machine Backup

When you find that you have deleted, damaged, or lost a vital file, you can recover it from a Time Machine backup. Normally, you will want to recover the most recent undamaged version of the file because this contains the latest changes, but you can also recover older versions if you need to.

Jan. 2, 2010
10:00 A.M.

Jan. 18, 2010
3:00 P.M.

Recover Your Files from a Time Machine Backup

① Click **Finder** (📁) on the Dock.

A Finder window opens to your default folder.

② Navigate to the folder that contains the file you want to recover.

③ Click **Time Machine** (🕐) on the Dock.

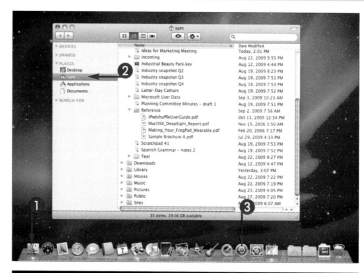

Time Machine launches and takes over the entire desktop, including the Dock area.

● The Finder window you opened appears at the front.

● Backups of the folder appear behind it, from newest to oldest.

● The timeline on the right shows how far back in time the available backups go.

④ In the timeline, click the date or time to which you want to go back.

Note: *You can also click one of the Finder windows behind the front Finder window to display its contents.*

Time Machine brings the backup you chose to the front.

⑤ Select the item or items you want to restore.

⑥ Click **Restore**.

Time Machine disappears, and you see your desktop and the Dock again.

If restoring a file will overwrite a file in the current version of the folder, the Copy dialog opens.

⑦ Choose how to handle the file conflict:

● Click **Replace** if you want to replace the current file with the older file.

● Click **Keep Original** if you want to keep the current file and not restore the file from Time Machine.

● Click **Keep Both** if you want to keep both versions of the file. Time Machine adds "(Original)" to the name of the current version of the file so that you can distinguish the two.

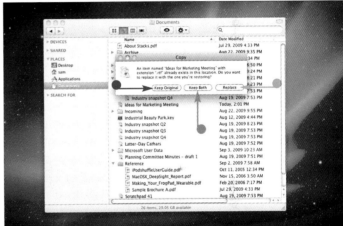

 TIPS

What are the arrow buttons above the Restore button for?

The two arrow buttons are for navigating among the available backups. Click the upward arrow to move to the previous backup, further in the past. Click the downward arrow to move to the next backup, nearer to the present.

Can I create Time Machine backups manually?

You can create a Time Machine backup any time you want. Click the **Time Machine status** icon (⏱) on the menu bar, and then click **Back Up Now** (●). The menu also enables you to quickly access Time Machine and Time Machine preferences.

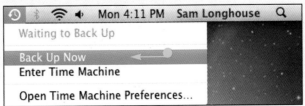

Remove Applications You No Longer Need

If you install applications frequently, you will probably end up with many applications that you no longer need. These useless applications take up disk space and may cause your iMac to run more slowly, so it is a good idea to remove them.

You can remove some applications by placing them in the Trash. Other applications include uninstall utilities.

Remove Applications You No Longer Need

Remove an Application by Moving It to the Trash

① Click open space on the desktop.

The Finder becomes active.

② Click **Go**.

The Go menu opens.

③ Click **Applications**.

A Finder window opens showing your Applications folder.

④ Click the application you want to remove.

⑤ Click **Action** (⚙️▾).

The Action pop-up menu opens.

⑥ Click **Move to Trash**.

Mac OS X moves the application to the Trash.

⑦ Click 🔘.

The Finder window closes.

Remove an Application by Using an Uninstall Utility

1 Click open space on the desktop.

The Finder becomes active.

2 Click **Go**.

The Go menu opens.

3 Click **Applications**.

A Finder window opens showing your Applications folder.

4 Double-click the uninstall utility. See the tip for instructions on where to find the utility.

The uninstall utility opens.

5 Follow through the steps of the uninstall utility. For example, click **Continue**.

6 When the uninstall utility has finished running, close it.

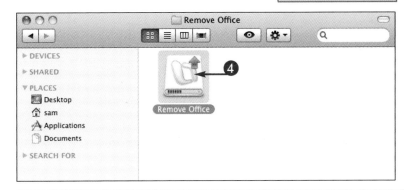

TIP

Where do I find the uninstall utility for an application?

If the application has a folder within the Applications folder, look inside that folder for an uninstall utility. If there is no folder, open the CD, DVD, or disk image file from which you installed the application, and look for an uninstall utility there. Some applications use an installer for both installing the application and uninstalling it, so if you do not find an uninstall utility, try running the installer and see if it contains an uninstall option.

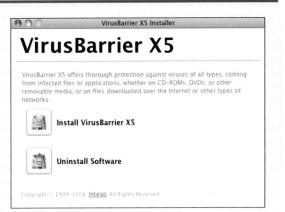

See Which Application Is Causing Your iMac Problems

Sometimes you may find that your iMac starts to respond slowly to your commands, even though no application has stopped working. When this occurs, you can use the Activity Monitor utility to see which application is consuming more of the processors' cycles than it should. To resolve the problem, you can quit that application, and then restart it.

See Which Application Is Causing Your iMac Problems

① Click **Finder** ( ) on the Dock.

A Finder window opens to your default folder.

② Click **Go**.

The Go menu opens.

③ Click **Utilities**.

The Finder window shows the items in the Utilities folder.

④ Press and hold Option and double-click **Activity Monitor**.

The Activity Monitor window opens, listing all running applications and system items.

5 Click **CPU**.

The details of your iMac's central processing units, or CPUs, appear.

Note: *Most iMacs have dual-core processors that appear in Activity Monitor as two separate CPUs. If your iMac has a quad-core processor, you will see four separate CPUs in Activity Monitor.*

6 Click **% CPU** once or twice to display ▶.

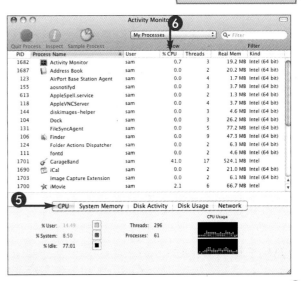

Activity Monitor sorts the applications and items by CPU activity so that you see which is using most processor cycles.

7 Identify the application that is using most processor cycles.

8 Click that application's Dock icon.

9 Save your work in the application, and then quit it.

10 Click the Activity Monitor window.

11 Click the **Activity Monitor** menu and click **Quit Activity Monitor** to close Activity Monitor.

What should I do if I cannot quit or force quit the problem application?

If you cannot force quit the application from the Dock or the Force Quit Applications dialog, try force quitting from Activity Monitor. In Activity Monitor, click the application's process name, and then click **Quit Process** on the toolbar. A confirmation dialog opens. Click **Force Quit**.

How do I see whether my iMac is running short of memory?

In Activity Monitor, click **System Memory** (●). The details of memory usage appear. Free shows unused RAM. Wired shows used RAM that cannot currently be released. Active shows RAM currently using information actively. Inactive shows RAM holding data but not using it actively. The four totals add up to your iMac's amount of RAM.

Force a Crashed Application to Quit

Sometimes an application may stop responding to the keyboard or mouse, so that you cannot quit it as usual. The application may freeze, so that the window does not change, or it may display the spinning beach ball that indicates that the application is busy. When this happens, you usually need to *force quit* the application — force it to quit — so that you can resume work.

Force a Crashed Application to Quit

Force Quit an Application from the Dock

① Holding down **Option**, click the application's icon on the Dock. Keep holding down the mouse button until the Dock menu appears.

② Click **Force Quit**.

Mac OS X forces the application to quit.

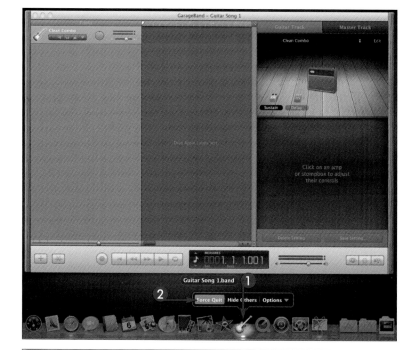

Force Quit an Application from the Force Quit Applications Dialog

① Click .

The Apple menu opens.

② Click **Force Quit**.

Note: *You can open the Force Quit Applications dialog from the keyboard by pressing* **⌘** + **Option** + **Esc**.

The Force Quit Applications dialog opens.

③ Click the application you want to force quit.

④ Click **Force Quit**.

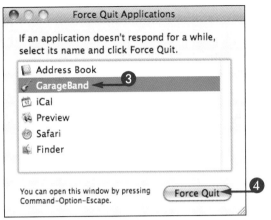

A dialog opens to confirm that you want to force quit the application.

⑤ Click **Force Quit**.

Mac OS X forces the application to quit.

⑥ Click .

The Force Quit Applications dialog closes.

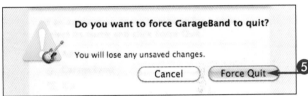

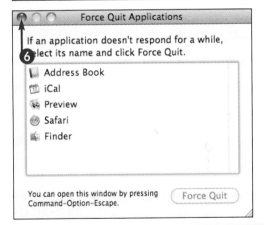

TIP

How do I recover the unsaved changes in a document after force quitting the application?

When you force quit an application, you normally lose all unsaved changes in the documents you were using in the application. However, some applications automatically store unsaved changes in special files called *recovery files*. Such applications then open any recovery files when you relaunch them after force quitting. For other applications, if the unsaved changes are visible on-screen, press ⌘ + Shift + 3 to capture a picture of your desktop to a file on the desktop so that you can see the changes you will need to make again.

Recover When Mac OS X Crashes

Normally, Mac OS X runs stably and smoothly for days or weeks on end, but sometimes the operating system may suffer a crash.

Your iMac may detect that the crash has occurred and display an informational message, but in other cases the iMac's screen may simply freeze and continue displaying the same information.

Recover from the Screen Freezing

① If the mouse pointer is showing the "wait" cursor that looks like a spinning beach ball, wait a couple of minutes to see if Mac OS X can recover from the problem. If the mouse pointer has disappeared, go straight to step **2**.

② To verify that your iMac is not responding, press keys on the keyboard or move the mouse.

③ Press and hold ⌘ + Control and press the iMac's power button.

④ If the iMac does not respond to that key combination, press and hold the iMac's power button for about four seconds.

The iMac turns off.

⑤ Wait eight seconds, and then press the power button once to restart the iMac.

Recover from a Detected Crash

When your iMac detects a Mac OS X crash, it dims the screen and displays a message in the center.

1 Read the message for information.

2 Press and hold the iMac's power button for about four seconds.

The iMac turns off.

3 Wait eight seconds, and then press the power button once to restart the iMac.

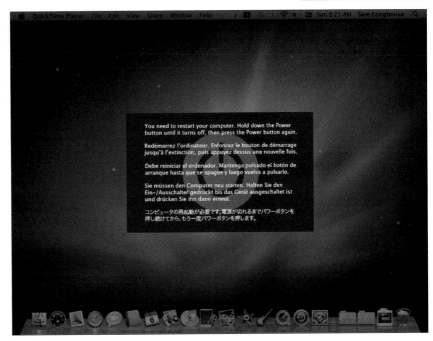

What causes Mac OS X to crash, and how can I avoid crashes?

Crashes can occur because of power fluctuations or bad memory chips, because your iMac is running too many applications, because an application is corrupted, or because of problems with disk permissions.

- Limit the number of applications you run at once. When you have finished using an application, close it.

- Make sure your iMac has hard disk space free. Click **Finder** ( ) on the Dock to open a Finder window, click your iMac's hard disk in the Devices area, and then look at the status bar readout of space available. Try to keep at least 20GB free.

- If you notice that running a particular application causes your iMac to crash, uninstall that application, and then reinstall it.

- You may also need to repair disk permissions, as discussed later in this chapter.

Solve Problems with Corrupt Preference Files

Each application stores details of its configuration in a special file called a *preference file*. Sometimes a preference file becomes corrupted, leading to the application not running properly or even crashing.

To fix the problem, you delete the preference file. This forces the application to create a new preference file from scratch.

Solve Problems with Corrupt Preference Files

① Quit the problem application if it is running.

Note: If you cannot quit the application by using its Quit command, force quit it as described earlier in this chapter.

② Click open space on the desktop.

The Finder becomes active.

③ Click **Go**.

The Go menu opens.

④ Click **Home**.

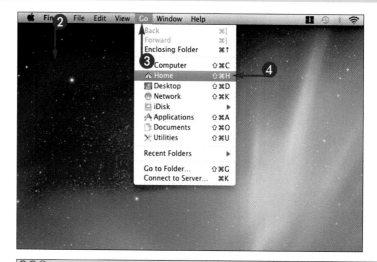

A Finder window opens showing the contents of your Home folder.

⑤ Double-click the Library folder.

The contents of the Library folder appear.

⑥ Double-click the Preferences folder.

The contents of the Preferences folder appear.

⑦ Click the preference file for the problem application. See the tip for help on identifying the file.

Note: *If the application has two or more preference files, move them all to the Trash.*

⑧ Click **Action** (⚙▾).

The Action menu opens.

⑨ Click **Move to Trash**.

Mac OS X moves the file to the Trash.

⑩ Start the application.

⑪ Set preferences in the application. In most applications, click the application's menu and click **Preferences** to open the Preferences dialog.

The application automatically creates a new preference file.

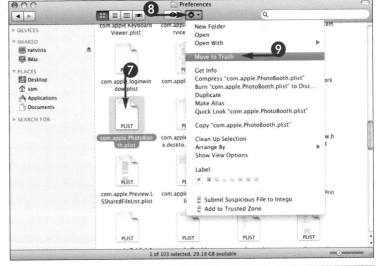

How do I find the right preference file to delete?

The names of most preference files use the format com.*company.application*.plist, where *company* is the manufacturer's name, *application* is the application's name, and .plist is the file extension for a property list file. For example, com.apple.TextEdit.plist is the TextEdit preference file, and com.microsoft.Excel.plist is the Excel preference file.

Preferences

Name
com.apple.iChat.AIM.plist
com.apple.iChat.Jabber.plist
com.apple.iChat.plist
com.apple.iChat.StatusMessages.plist
com.apple.iChat.SubNet.plist
com.apple.iMovie8.plist
com.apple.installer.plist
com.apple.internetconfig.plist

Troubleshoot Disk Permission Errors

To control what your iMac's users, applications, and different parts of the operating system itself can do, Mac OS X uses a complex system of permissions. Sometimes the permissions on some files become corrupted, which prevents Mac OS X or the applications from running as normal. When this happens, you can often fix the problem by repairing the disk permissions.

Permissions Need Repair

① Click the desktop.

② Click **Go**.

The Go menu opens.

③ Click **Utilities**.

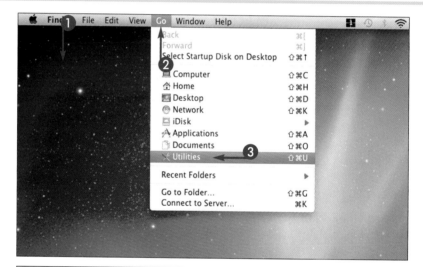

The Utilities folder opens.

④ Press and hold Option and double-click **Disk Utility**.

The Finder window closes, and the Disk Utility window opens.

⑤ Click your iMac's hard disk.

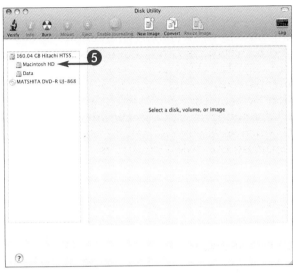

The controls for manipulating the hard disk appear.

⑥ Click **First Aid** if the First Aid tab is not already highlighted.

⑦ Click **Repair Disk Permissions**.

Mac OS X repairs the disk permissions. The process may take several minutes.

⑧ Click the **Disk Utility** menu and click **Quit Disk Utility** to close Disk Utility.

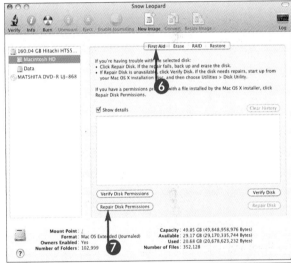

What are the symptoms of problems with permissions?

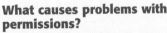

If your iMac has problems with permissions, it may run more slowly than usual. You may also find that applications quit unexpectedly or freeze so that you have to force quit them.

What causes problems with permissions?

The two main causes of problems with permissions are installing software and power outages. A badly written installation script can set permissions incorrectly on not only its own folder but also other folders. Power outages can leave files or folders with permissions temporarily changed to enable certain operations but not changed back as they would normally be.

Repair Your iMac's Hard Disk

If your iMac does not start properly or if it crashes frequently, and repairing permissions does not fix the problem, you may need to repair the iMac's hard disk. To do so, you need to start your iMac using the Mac OS X installation DVD, and then run Disk Utility.

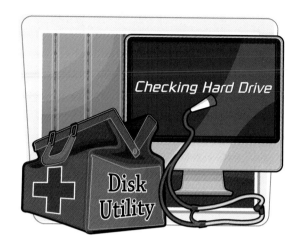

① Insert the Mac OS X installation DVD.

② Restart the iMac.

③ At the startup chime, press and hold C until the Apple logo appears.

④ On the first screen that appears, click the language you want to use, and then click ⬤.

⑤ In the Install Mac OS X dialog, click the **Utilities** menu and click **Disk Utility**.

The Disk Utility window opens.

⑥ Click your iMac's hard drive.

⑦ Click **First Aid**.

⑧ Click **Repair Disk**.

● Disk Utility repairs the disk, displaying its progress.

⑨ Click the **Disk Utility** menu and click **Quit Disk Utility**.

Disk Utility closes, and the Install Mac OS X dialog opens.

⑩ Click the **Installer** menu and click **Quit Installer**.

⑪ In the confirmation dialog, click **Restart**.

Your iMac restarts into Mac OS X from the hard disk.

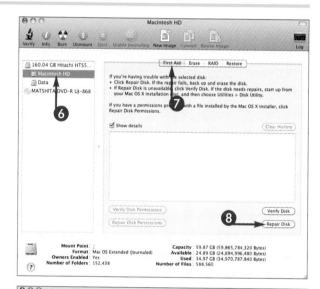

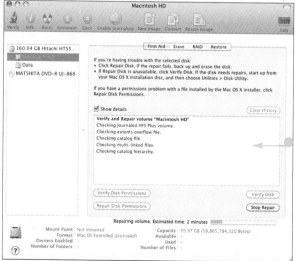

After a power outage or severe software damage, you may not be able to restart your iMac at all. When this happens, you need to reinstall Mac OS X from the original installation DVD to fix the problem.

You can also reinstall Mac OS X if your iMac crashes frequently and you find that repairing the permissions and the disk does not help.

Reinstall Mac OS X to Solve Severe Problems

① Insert the Mac OS X installation DVD in your iMac's optical drive.

② Restart the iMac.

③ At the startup chime, press and hold C until the Apple logo appears.

④ On the first screen that appears, click the language you want to use, and then click ⊙.

The Install Mac OS X dialog opens.

⑤ Click **Continue**.

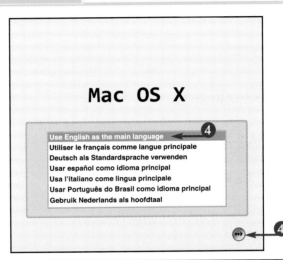

The Software License Agreement dialog opens.

⑥ Click **Continue**.

A dialog opens telling you that you must agree to the terms of the software license agreement to proceed.

⑦ Click **Agree**.

The Installer then installs Mac OS X.

⑧ After your iMac restarts, log in. You can then access your files as before.

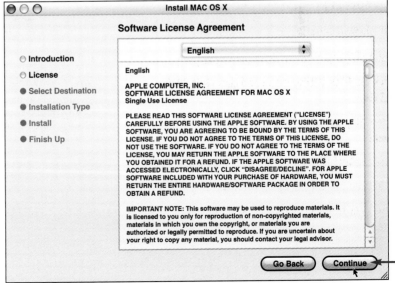

Index

Numerics

802.11n (Wireless N) standard, 13

A

AAC files (Advanced Audio Coding), 189
accounts. *See also* user accounts
    Administrator, 4, 30–31
    MobileMe, 5
Activity Monitor, 336–337
Address Book
    closing, 165
    contacts
        adding, 166–167
        editing, 168–169
        organizing into groups, 170–171
    opening, 164
Adjust window (iPhoto), 222–223
Administrator account, 4, 30–31
Advanced Audio Coding (AAC) files, 189
AirPort, 12–13
Analyze for Stabilization after Import (iMovie), 245
antivirus software, 314–315
Application Switcher feature, 55
applications
    adding to Dock, 51, 272
    choosing user account, 38–39
    closing, 51, 55
    documents
        closing, 60
        creating, 58
        editing, 62–63
        opening, 61
        saving, 59
    help, 64–65
    hiding, 55
    installing, 52–53
    opening, 50–51
    removing, 334–335
    running, 288–289
    switching between, 54–55
    troubleshooting, 336–337
    viewing open, 56–57
Applications folder, 51
appointments (iCal), 154–157
Archive Utility, 89
attachments, 134–137
Auto button (iPhoto), 221
automatic login
    disabling, 318–319
    Fast User Switching, 33
    iMac, 7

B

Back to My Mac feature, 308–309
back up, 330–331
Block All Incoming Connections option, 321
bookmarks, 110–111
Bounce command (Mail), 131
buddies
    adding, 176–177
    blocking, 179
    removing, 177
    renaming in iChat, 177
    sending videos to, 181
    texting, 178–179

C

cable connections, 9
cable routers, 8
cables
    digital camera, 213
    mini DisplayPort-to-DVI connector, 278
    parallel-to-USB adapter, 15
calendars. *See* iCal
Camino, 99
CDs. *See also* DVDs
    adding to iTunes library, 188–189
    burning files to, 90–91
    capacity of, 91
    creating custom, 200–201
    erasing, 92–93
    types, 91
chatting. *See* iChat
color enhancement in photos, 222–223
Column view (Finder), 71
connections
    external drives, 18–19
    Internet, 8–9
    iPhone/iPod, 16–17
    printer, 14–15, 300–301
    remote, 308–309
    shared folders, 296–297
    wired networks, 10–11
    wireless networks, 12–13
contacts (Address Book)
    adding, 166–167
    deleting, 167
    editing, 168–169
    groups, 170–171
cookies, 119
Copy and Paste command, 63, 81
corrupt preference files, 342–343
Cover Flow view (Finder), 71
Cover Flow view (iTunes), 193
cropping photos, 216–217, 259
Cut command, 63

D

De-noise slider (iPhoto), 223
desktop
    customizing background, 268–269
    searching files and folders from, 74
    virtual, 276–277
DHCP (Dynamic Host Configuration Protocol), 11
digital camcorders, 244–245
digital cameras, 211–213, 246–247
disk permission errors, 344–345
Disk Utility, 92–93
Dock, 50–51, 272–273
documents
    closing, 60
    copying text, 63

creating, 58
deselecting text, 62
editing, 62–63
moving text, 63
opening, 61
saving, 27, 59
selecting text, 62
Documents folder, 68
drivers, printer, 14, 301
drives
    external, 18–19
    moving files between, 82–83
DSL connections, 8–9
DVD Player, 206–207
DVDs. *See also* CDs
    burning to, 90–91, 201
    capacity, 91
    erasing, 92–93
    rewriteable, 93
    viewing, 206–207
Dynamic Host Configuration Protocol (DHCP), 11

E

Easy Transfer, 88–89
effects, photo, 224–225
802.11n (Wireless N) standard, 13
E-mail. *See also* Mail (Apple)
    controlling, 52–53
    sending photos via, 234–235
events
    iCal
        creating all-day, 155
        ending repeating, 157
    iMovie, 243
    iPhoto
        creating, 227
        overview, 213, 215
        sorting photos into, 226–227
Exposé feature, 56–57, 274–275
external drives, 18–19
external monitors, 278–279

F

Faces feature (iPhoto), 215
Fast User Switching, 32–35
files and folders
    AAC (Advanced Audio Coding), 189
    adding
        to Dock, 272
        to privacy list, 285
    burning to CD/DVD, 90–91
    compressing, 88–89
    connecting to shared folders, 296–297
    copying files between folders, 80–81
    corrupt preferences, 342–343
    creating folders, 78–79
    downloading, 114–115, 183
    erasing CDs and DVDs, 92–93
    Home folder, 69
    Mac OS X, 51, 68–69

moving files between folders, 82–83
MP3, 189
naming folders, 78–79
Quick Look feature, 72–73
receiving
    as attachments, 136–137
    in iChat, 183
recovering from Time Machine backup, 332–333
renaming files, 84–85
restoring, 95, 327
searching, 74–75, 284–285
sending
    as E-mail attachments, 134–135
    in iChat, 182
sharing on networks, 298–299
smart folders, 76–77
Spotlight feature, 74–75
storing files, 68–69
trashing files, 94–95
viewing information, 86–87
Finder
    activating, 22
    files and folders
        burning files to CDs/DVDs, 90–91
        compressing files, 88–89
        copying files between folders, 80–81
        creating folders, 78–79
        erasing CDs/DVDs, 92–93
        moving files between folders, 82–83
        naming folders, 78–79
        Quick Look feature, 72–73
        renaming, 84–85
        searching for, 74–75
        smart folder, 76–77
        storing, 68–69
        throwing files in trash, 94–95
        viewing information about, 86–87
    searching files and folders from, 74–75
    views, 70–71
Firefox (Mozilla), 99
firewall, 320–321
FireWire, 18–19
Forward as Attachment command, 133

G

General preferences, 108–109
Genius sidebar, 187
Google Search feature, 112
Grid view (iTunes), 192
groups, 171

H

hard disk, 243, 346
hardware, 4, 313
help, 64–65
History list, 106–107
Home folder, 68–69
home page, 108–109
Hot Corners, 274–275

Index

I

iCal
  closing, 149
  creating
    appointments, 154–157
    calendars, 152–153
    to-do items, 158–159
  keyboard shortcuts, 151
  navigating, 150–151
  opening, 148
  sharing calendars, 160–161
  subscribing to calendars, 162–163
iChat
  adding buddies, 176–177
  blocking buddies, 179
  controlling, 42–43
  displaying buddy names, 177
  downloading files, 183
  opening, 174–175
  receiving files, 183
  sending files, 182
  texting with buddies, 178–179
  video chats with buddies, 180–181
Icon view (Finder), 70
icons
  Dock, 272–273
  resizing, 71
  Trash, 95
IMAP (Internet Mail Access Protocol), 125
iMovie
  adding
    credits, 253
    narration, 261
    still photos, 258–259
    titles, 262
    transitions between clips, 256–257
  Analyze for Stabilization after Import, 245
  closing, 241
  creating
    movie projects, 241, 250–251, 254–255
    soundtracks, 260–261
  cropping photos, 259
  deleting movie projects, 251
  events, 243
  importing video, 242–249
  opening, 240
  quality, 249
  renaming movie projects, 251
  rotating photos, 259
  selecting video footage, 252–253
  sharing movies on YouTube, 264–265
  superimposing, 263
inappropriate content, 40–41
Info window, 87–88
Internet
  attacks, 313
  bookmarks, 110–111
  browsing Web pages, 104–105
  changing home page, 108–109

  closing Safari, 99
  connections, 8–9
  downloading files, 114–115
  following links, 101
  news feeds, 116–117
  opening
    Safari, 98
    Web pages, 100, 102–103
  radio, 202–203
  returning to Web pages, 106–107
  searching, 112–113
  security settings, 118–119
Internet Mail Access Protocol (IMAP), 125
IP (Internet protocol) address, 11
iPhone connection, 16–17
iPhoto
  adding effects, 224–225
  Adjust window, 222–223
  Auto button, 221
  browsing photos, 214–215
  creating
    albums, 228–229
    events, 227
    slideshows, 230–231
  cropping photos, 216–217
  De-noise slider, 223
  download size, 233
  enhancing colors, 222–223
  events, 213
  Faces feature, 215
  hiding albums, 233
  importing from digital camera, 212–213
  iSight camera, 236–237
  Photo Booth, 236–237
  photo size, 235
  playing videos, 247
  publishing to MobileMe Gallery, 232–233
  removing
    effects from photos, 225
    red-eye, 220–221
  rotating photos, 218–219
  sending photos via E-mail, 234–235
  Sharpness slider, 223
  sidebar, 215
  Slideshow button, 231
  smart album, 229
  sorting into events, 226–227
  straightening photos, 218–219
  Themes button, 231
iPod connection, 16–17
iSight Web Cam, 180–181, 236–237
iTunes
  adding CDs to library, 188–189
  closing, 187
  Cover Flow view, 193
  creating
    custom CDs, 200–201
    playlists, 196–197
  Genius sidebar, 187
  Grid view, 192

Internet radio, 202–203
Match Only Checked Items option, 199
opening, 186
overview, 16–17
playing
    songs, 192–193
    videos, 194–195
podcasts, 204–205
smart playlists, 198–199
Store, 190–191

J

junk mail, 144–145

K

keyboard
    giving commands from, 21
    iCal shortcuts, 151
    navigating Web pages with, 105
    organization, 280
    switching applications with, 55
Keyboard tab (Universal Access), 281

L

Library folder, 69
links, 101
List view (Finder), 70
List view (iTunes), 193
Locked setting, 87

M

Mac OS X
    help system, 64–65
    recovering, 340–341
    reinstalling, 347
    renaming files and folders in, 85
Mail (Apple)
    account set-up, 124–125
    blocking, 42–43
    Bounce command, 131
    closing, 123
    creating
        notes, 140–141
        to-do items, 142–143
    files
        receiving as attachments, 136–137
        sending as attachments, 134–135
    messages
        forwarding, 132–133
        reading, 129
        receiving, 128
        replying to, 130–131
        sending, 126–127
    MobileMe, 138–139
    opening, 122
    spam, 144–145
mail servers, 125
maintenance
    backing up, 330–331
    emptying trash, 326–327

recovering files, 332–333
removing applications, 334–335
updates, 328–329
malevolent software, 137, 312
Match Only Checked Items option (iTunes), 199
memory checking, 337
menus
    choosing feature groups on, 20
    compared with toolbars, 21
    giving commands from, 20
    moving files with commands, 83
mini DisplayPort-to-DVI connector cable, 278
MobileMe
    creating
        accounts, 5
        calendars, 153
    instant messaging account, 175
    overview, 138–139
    publishing photos to gallery, 232–233
    sharing calendars with, 160
monitors, 278–279
More Info section, 87
mouse
    organization, 280–281
    running Exposé with, 57, 275
    switching applications with, 54–55
movie projects. *See also* iMovie
    adding
        from clips, 254–255
        credits, 263
        narration, 261
        still photos, 258–259
        titles, 262
    creating
        overview, 241, 250–251
        soundtracks, 260–261
    deleting, 251
    renaming, 251
    sharing on YouTube, 264–265
    superimposing, 263
    tags, 265
Movies folder, 69
Mozilla Firefox, 99
MP3 files, 189
music
    iTunes
        adding CDs to library, 188–189
        burning to DVD, 201
        closing, 187
        creating custom CDs, 200–201
        creating playlists, 196–197
        Genius sidebar, 187
        Internet radio, 202–203
        opening, 186
        playing songs, 192–193
        recording from iTunes radio, 203
        smart playlists, 198–199
        Store, 190–191
    Sound Check, 200–201
Music folder, 69

Index

N

narration, 261
NAT-MPM, 309
network
    connecting
        remotely, 308–309
        to shared folders, 296–297
        to shared printers, 300–301
    overview, 11
    sharing
        folders on, 296–299
        printers on, 300–303
        screens, 304–305
    troubleshooting, 309
    viewing screen remotely, 306–307
    wired, 10–11
    wireless, 12–13
news feeds, 116–117
notes, 140–141

O

organization
    Address Book
        adding contacts, 166–167
        closing, 165
        editing contacts, 168–169
        opening, 164
        organizing contacts into groups, 170–171
    bookmarks, 110–111
    iCal
        appointments, 154–157
        calendars, 152–153
        closing, 149
        navigating, 150–151
        opening, 148
        sharing calendars, 160–161
        subscribing to calendars, 162–163
        to-do items, 158–159
    keyboard, 280
    mouse, 280–281
    playlists, 197
    running applications, 288–289
    saving power, 290–291
    screen, 282–283
    software updates, 292–293
    Spotlight feature, 284–285
    voice control, 286–287

P

parallel-to-USB adapter cable, 15
parental controls
    activating, 36–37
    E-mail and Chat, 42–43
    inappropriate content, 40–41
    time limits, 44–45
    tracking actions, 46–47
passwords, 9, 31
Paste. *See* Copy and Paste command
phishing attacks, 313, 322–323
Photo Booth, 236–237

photos
    adding
        effects, 224–225
        to movie projects, 258–259
    albums, 233
    browsing, 214–215
    closing iPhoto, 211
    cropping, 216–217, 259
    enhancing color, 222–223
    iPhoto overview, 168–169
    opening iPhoto, 210
    publishing to MobileMe Gallery, 232–233
    removing effects from, 225
    rotating, 218–219, 259
    sending via E-mail, 234–235
    sorting into Events, 226–227
    straightening, 218–219
    using as desktop background, 269
Photos feature (iPhoto), 215
Pictures folder, 69
Places feature (iPhoto), 215
playlists
    creating, 196–197
    smart, 198–199
podcasts, 204–205
POP (Post Office Protocol), 125
pop-ups, 119
ports
    FireWire, 18–19
    USB, 17
power
    outages, 25, 313
    saving, 290–291
Print and Fax Preferences, 300
printers
    connections, 14–15
    drivers, 301
    help topics, 65
    sharing, 300–303
privacy list, 285
Public folder, 69

Q

Quick Look feature, 72–73

R

radio (Internet), 202–203
Really Simple Syndication (RSS), 116–117
red-eye, 220–221
Redirect command (Mail), 131
routers, 8–9
RSS (Really Simple Syndication), 116–117

S

Safari
    bookmarks, 110–111
    browsing Web pages, 104–105
    changing home page, 108–109
    choosing security settings, 118–119
    closing, 99

downloading files, 114–115
following links, 101
news feeds, 116–117
opening
overview, 98, 99
Web pages, 100, 102–103
returning to Web pages, 106–107
searching, 112–113
tabs and windows, 103
screen saver, 270–271
screens
dimming, 291
organization, 282–283
sharing, 304–305
viewing remotely, 306–307
Secure Empty Trash command, 327
security
choosing settings, 118–119
disabling automatic login, 318–319
downloading, 115
firewall, 320–321
installing antivirus software, 314–315
phishing attacks, 322–323
scanning for viruses, 316–317
threats to, 312–313
Send Again command (Mail), 131
servers (mail), 125
set up
E-mail account, 124–125
hardware, 4
overview, 4–5
setting(s)
applications to run, 288–289
choosing security, 118–119
Locked, 87
synchronization, 17
time limits, 44–45
Sharpness slider (iPhoto), 223
Show All History command, 107
shut down
compared with sleep, 25
logging users out, 35
using, 26–27
sidebar
adding smart folders, 77
Genius, 187
iPhoto, 215
Simple Finder, 39
Sites folder, 69
sleep mode, 24–25, 290–291
Slideshow button (iPhoto), 230–231
smart albums, 229
smart folders, 76–77
smart playlists, 198–199
software
antivirus, 314–315
malevolent, 137, 312
updates, 292–293
Software Update feature, 328–329
songs. See music
Sound Check, 200–201

soundtracks, 260–261
Spaces feature, 276–277
spam, 144–145
Spotlight feature, 74–75, 284–285
subnet mask, 8
synchronization settings (iPhone/iPod), 17
System Preferences window, 32, 38

T

tabs (Safari), 103
tags (movie), 265
tape camcorders, 242–243
text, 62–63
Themes button (iPhoto), 231
time limits, 44–45
Time Machine, 330–333
titles (movie projects), 262
to-do items, 142–143, 158–159
toolbars, 21
transitions (iMovie), 256–257
Trash, 94–95, 326–327
troubleshooting
applications, 53, 336–337
compressed files, 89
corrupt preference files, 342–343
disk permission errors, 344–345
force quitting, 338–339
iPhoto, 217
networks, 309
printers, 15
recovering Mac OS X, 340–341
reinstalling Mac OS X, 347
repairing hard disk, 346
user name display, 7

U

unauthorized users, 312
uniform resource locator (URL), 100
uninstall utility, 335
uninterruptible power supply, 25
Universal Access, 280–283
updates (software), 292–293, 328–329
URL (uniform resource locator), 100
USB compared with FireWire, 19
USB hub, 17
user accounts
applying parental controls, 37
creating, 5, 30–31
overview, 4
password, 31
switching, 34–35
user names, 7
users, 312. See also parental controls

V

video chats, 180–181
videos
clips, 252
importing, 242–249

Index

playing
- in iPhoto, 247
- in iTunes, 194–195

quality, 249

saving, 243

selecting footage, 252–253

sending to buddies, 181

virtual desktops, 276–277

VirusBarrier, 314–317

viruses, 137, 312, 316–317

voice control, 286–287

W

Web cam (iSight), 180–181

Web pages
- blocking, 40–41
- browsing, 104–105
- following links to, 101
- History list, 106–107
- opening, 100, 102–103
- searching, 112–113

windows
- Adjust (iPhoto), 223
- closing, 23, 51
- finding, 23
- hiding, 23
- Info, 87–88
- minimizing, 23
- moving, 22
- opening, 22
- resizing, 22
- Safari, 103
- viewing open, 56–57
- zooming, 22

wired networks, 10–11

Wireless N (802.11n) standard, 13

wireless networks, 12–13

Y

YouTube, 264–265

Z

Zip files, 88–89

Zoom button, 22–23